WE'LL GET 'EM IN SEQUINS

OTHER WISDEN SPORTS WRITING TITLES

Among the Fans
by
Patrick Collins

WE'LL GET 'EM IN SEQUINS

Manliness, Yorkshire Cricket and the Century That Changed Everything

MAX DAVIDSON

WISDEN SPORTS WRITING

Published in the UK in 2012 by
John Wisden & Co
An imprint of Bloomsbury Publishing Plc
50 Bedford Square, London WC1B 3DP
www.bloomsbury.com
www.wisden.com

ISBN 978 1 4081 4595 1

A CIP catalogue record for this book is available from the British Library.

This book is produced using paper that is made from wood grown in managed,
sustainable forests. It is natural, renewable and recyclable. The logging and
manufacturing processes conform to the environmental regulations of the
country of origin.

Typeset in 10pt Haarlemmer by seagulls.net

Printed and bound in Great Britain by Clays Ltd, St Ives plc

To the immortal memory of George Hirst and Wilfred Rhodes, who got 'em in singles.

In appreciation of the generations of Yorkshire cricketers who grafted, played the game hard, never gave away 'owt and found the poetry in maiden overs; whose mams could have played Shane Warne with a stick of rhubarb; and who, for nearly a century, were the backbone of the England cricket team.

And for Darren Gough and Michael Vaughan – for daring to be different.

CONTENTS

PADDING UP

In an England cricket 11, the flesh may be
of the South, but the bone is of the North,
and the backbone is Yorkshire.

Sir Leonard Hutton

On the afternoon of 13 August 1902, at the end of a famous Test match against Australia at the Oval, all eyes were on two professional cricketers from Yorkshire: fast bowler George Hirst and left-arm spinner Wilfred Rhodes. The foundations of an England victory had been laid by a Flash Harry amateur from Gloucestershire, Gilbert Jessop, with a whirlwind century, but now it was down to the bowlers: 15 runs to make, and the last pair at the crease. The situation called for cool heads, unflinching bodies and that most elusive sporting quality – patience.

'We'll get 'em in singles,' Hirst said to Rhodes, as the two men conferred midwicket. Did he really say it? Or is it one of those apocryphal quotations one hates to let go, like a childhood friend? Hirst himself disclaimed the quote, but if he didn't say it, he *should* have said it, just as Sherlock Holmes should have said, 'Elementary, my dear Watson', but never did. The quotation has stuck because it is so true to the man to whom it is attributed: a phlegmatic, pipe-smoking Yorkshireman with a bog-standard Edwardian moustache, an air of unhurried competence and a hatred of anything that smacked of excess or ostentation.

He and Rhodes got 'em in singles or, *pace* the late Bill Frindall, got most of 'em in singles, and won a famous victory for their side.

The crowd went wild. Hats were thrown in the air. But the two Yorkshiremen in the middle were unruffled. They always were.

You did your job, you got paid a few quid, you had a beer after the match, and then you went home. But you didn't make a song and dance about it. In fact, you didn't make a song and dance about anything, certainly not if you came from Yorkshire, most sober and upright of counties.

That was the world of the professional cricketer which George Hirst inhabited, and which he graced with distinction for more than 30 years. It was a small world, a narrow world, but it was rooted in good soil, and the sporting heroes it produced were as admired by their contemporaries as any modern superstar, perhaps more so.

Just over a century later, on the same ground, in a Test match against the same opponents, another Yorkshireman took centre stage, as the England captain Michael Vaughan held the replica Ashes aloft and a nation went bananas. There were some striking similarities between the Ashes Tests of 1902 and 2005. Kevin Pietersen in 2005 might have been Gilbert Jessop brought back to life, biffing six after six in a never-to-be-forgotten century. But there were differences, too. Vaughan failed with the bat on the final day, but played a blinder in the dressing room in the lunch interval, encouraging Pietersen to go for his shots rather than play the dogged rearguard innings that the situation seemed to demand, with England needing only a draw to retain the Ashes. George Hirst would never have been so cavalier, so incautious, not in a thousand years. Cricket had changed. Yorkshire had changed. The world had changed.

Vaughan, born in Manchester but brought up in Sheffield, broke the mould, first as a free-flowing batsman, then as a captain who prized aggression above containment, self-expression above efficiency. He had no appetite for the uncompromising maiden overs that had been meat and drink to generations of Yorkshire cricket fans. He played the game with a lack of inhibition that both appalled and titillated the traditionalists.

'You don't understand this, do you?' Tony Greig asked fellow commentator Geoff Boycott, as Vaughan's England hurtled to 400 in a day at the start of the 2005 Edgbaston Test. 'You're right,' said Boycott, as proud a son of Yorkshire as ever played with his bat close to his pad. 'I don't. It's fun, though.' It was as if Yorkshire, once the gold standard of English cricket, a temple of rectitude, had suddenly become two Yorkshires: Old Yorkshire, epitomised by Boycott and the players he had grown up with – Fred Trueman, Brian Close, Ray Illingworth – and a new, less hard-bitten, generation of players. They did things differently, not because they had a different tactical appreciation of cricket, but because they were different men, in a changing world.

Relaxed, self-confident, comfortable in his own skin, Michael Vaughan was as much a man of his times as George Hirst had been. In 2004, captaining England against New Zealand, he left the ground before the end of play to attend the birth of his first child. Nobody batted an eyelid. In 2008, at the press conference when he resigned the England captaincy, he blubbed like a baby. Again, nobody batted an eyelid. Men did these things – even men's men who played cricket, took some hard knocks, then went out drinking with Freddie Flintoff.

Vaughan's period as England captain became synonymous not just with success on the field, but with the famous huddle: the circle formed by the fielding side at the start of play, with players putting their arms around each other's shoulders, geeing each other up with psychobabble, then patting each other's bottoms as they dispersed. What would Brian Close or Ray Illingworth have made of a bonding ritual with such homoerotic overtones? One shudders to think.

And if you were Old Yorkshire, and believed in Old Yorkshire ways, things were about to get ten times worse.

In the autumn of 2005, within weeks of Michael Vaughan holding the Ashes aloft at the Oval, the Yorkshire fast bowler Darren Gough – having already dismayed the traditionalists by tearing in to bowl wearing an ear-stud – went the whole fashion hog, appearing on the BBC's *Strictly Come Dancing* in lurid costumes on which it was possible, through the strobe lighting, to discern *sequins*. Was that thunder in the distance? No, it was generations of Yorkshire fast bowlers turning in their graves.

If Gough had just entered the show for a laugh, to send himself up, Old Yorkshire might have forgiven him. But the boy from Barnsley had other ideas. He threw himself into the tango and the cha-cha and the paso doble with the same zest as he had put into his bowling. He shook his booty. He swapped banter with the judges. And the nation loved it, voting for Gough in their millions until he was crowned series winner. What had gone wrong?

Or – depending whether you were Old Yorkshire or New Yorkshire – what had gone right? Wasn't there something rather exhilarating in a 90mph fast bowler and lusty tail-end batsman who could also do a nifty foxtrot in an outfit that glittered like a Christmas tree? Might we have to re-define what we meant by manliness?

We'll Get 'Em in Sequins is my attempt to grapple with that question. It is as much a social history as a cricket book, examining how attitudes to masculinity have changed in the last 100 years, sometimes at bewildering speed. The taboos of one generation became the acceptable norms of the next. Fathers bred sons who rejected many of the values they held dear. Nothing stood still. If there were rules governing how men should conduct themselves, nobody knew what they were any more. Even getting dressed in the morning, once so simple because all men dressed the same, became an obstacle course.

Impressing the opposite sex got steadily harder. Women shopped around and, if they were not satisfied, returned the goods to the store. As nine-times-married Zsa Zsa Gabor put it, 'Macho doesn't prove mucho'. A man could no longer rely on striking tough-guy postures: he had to know when to hit softer notes; when to be vulnerable; when to give ground rather than soldiering grimly on.

Historians of the 20th century have tended to focus on women rather than men. Feminism on the march made such dramatic strides that it eclipsed the subtler transformations in male attitudes and behaviour. But for men, too, it was a revolutionary century, even in a bastion of conservatism like Yorkshire County Cricket Club, fabled the world over for its unyielding toughness, a freemasonry of hard men with cold eyes, jutting chins and legs like tree trunks.

Long before Darren Gough bought his first ear-stud, the solid Edwardian certainties of George Hirst were being dismantled, brick by brick. One of the players Hirst took under his wing at Yorkshire was Herbert Sutcliffe, of whom Neville Cardus wrote that he was 'a deviation from type', wearing 'flannels of fluttering silk' on the field and Savile Row suits off it. The smell of honest sweat in the dressing room started to mingle with the smell of brilliantine and eau-de-cologne. By the 1950s, Fred Trueman was kicking over the traces like a stroppy teenager. Trueman was Old Yorkshire to his size 12 bootstraps, and on retirement, became a splendidly reactionary commentator. But there was a brashness about him in his youth that would have been alien to the pre-war generation, schooled in modesty and self-deprecation.

Some values remained constant in the Yorkshire dressing room. A man had to be physically brave, whether it was Hedley Verity facing enemy fire in Sicily in 1944 – he later died of his wounds – or tough-as-teak Brian Close letting himself be used for target practice by West Indian fast bowlers. Yorkshiremen of a certain age have tears in their eyes when they recall the exploits of Don Wilson in a match against Worcestershire in 1961, when he secured a vital victory for his side batting with his left arm in plaster from the elbow to the knuckles because of a fractured thumb. They do not actually shed the tears, being sons of Old Yorkshire, but they dab their eyes as they remember Wilson's uncomplaining fortitude. Scratch a Tyke and you find a stoic.

If courage is an eternal constant, as admired in 2012 as in 1912, many of the other attributes of manliness – how a man dresses, how he expresses his feelings, how he treats women and children – have changed with the times. It is one of the oldest clichés in sports writing to say that sport mirrors life. But in this instance, the world of Yorkshire cricket – a miniature England, but with a rich tribal folklore all of its own, with manliness at its core – has so faithfully mirrored the outside world that the cliché is unavoidable.

In these seven portraits of Yorkshire cricketers, and of the values they shared with their male contemporaries, I have tried to map the contours of a sexual earthquake whose tremors are still being felt.

CHAPTER 1
GEORGE HIRST: EDWARDIAN MAN PERSONIFIED

All women become like their mothers.
That is their tragedy. No man does. That is his.

Oscar Wilde, *The Importance of Being Earnest*

'Are you a man?' Lady Macbeth demanded of her husband. Generations of men have been subjected to the same crude virility test. In their hearts, they have resented the question. Do they ask their wives if they are women? But they have had no choice but to answer in the affirmative – then furnish the necessary proof.

Macbeth had to murder a king and look at ghosts without flinching. If he had ducked the challenge, his wife would have deemed him unmanly, a wimp, too full of the milk of human kindness. The majority of today's husbands can pass the virility test by remembering wedding anniversaries, barbecuing a few sausages and putting the bins out on Fridays. But the subtext of their lives remains the same. 'Are you a man?' That same question, reverberating down the ages, challenging men to prove themselves: in the bedroom, in the workplace, in battles of every kind.

The goalposts move from generation to generation, in subtle, incremental ways. When is it acceptable for a man to cry? Is it OK to hug another man? Should a man ever admit to feeling depressed? Are conscientious objectors just cowards by another name? Is hitting a child admissible? Boxers or Y-fronts? Mercedes or a mountain bike? Aftershave or a splash of cold water? A pint of lager or a vodka martini? And how about moustaches/sideburns/tattoos? Are they (a) naff or (b) proof positive of virility?

Men have to make up their own minds on such issues, having taken the temperature of the times. There is no reference book in which they can look up the answers, no court of last appeal. But the pressure to pass the test, or at least give a good account of oneself in comparison with one's fellow men, is an eternal constant. And the price of failure remains the same – relegation to the second rank of manhood.

Nobody ever needed to ask George Herbert Hirst, born in Kirkheaton, near Huddersfield, on 7 September 1871, if he was a man. Manliness was his birthright. He was virility made flesh. Whether it was the idealised George Hirst of the cigarette cards, with his spotless flannels and burly forearms, or the real-life cricketer, striding out to bat, pacing out his run-up or hurling himself through the air to take a catch, he epitomised the all-purpose man of action: tough, vigorous and combative, without being malicious.

To the cricket-loving Yorkshire public, who hero-worshipped him, he represented a kind of platonic ideal of what a man should be. 'Search as I might, I could find no warts whatever,' reported one of his biographers. None of his contemporaries had a bad word to say against him. 'There is something in his honest, genial, frank face that one likes,' wrote a journalist who interviewed Hirst at the start of his career. 'You feel instinctively that he will put on no side and tell you all you have any business to know.' It could be a description of the young Freddie Flintoff, before he got his own agent.

The portrait of Hirst in a 1903 edition of *Vanity Fair* is a gem of Edwardian understatement: 'He may be summed up as a really fine fellow with the heart of a lion. He has a good appetite and quite a nice smile.' That 'quite', in conjunction with the reference to his appetite, seems churlish. Had the author seen Hirst shovelling potatoes into his mouth, in no position to smile? Others were more generous. They reckoned it was a *very* nice smile, one of the sunniest in county cricket.

Hirst enjoyed the stardust of sporting celebrity in an age when professional sport was capturing the public imagination as never before. From May to September, his name was never out of the newspapers. His jovial face adorned tins of George Hirst's Yorkshire Toffee ('Unrivalled... Always Reliable'), produced by a factory in Huddersfield, his home town. Strangers stopped him in the street to ask for his autograph. But the celebrity did not go to his head. To the day he died, he kept his feet firmly on the ground. At his funeral in 1954, it was standing room only in the church, and the streets outside were so crowded that the hearse had trouble getting through. But it was a low-key service with – at his request – no music. George Hirst would have hated a fuss, a media circus. He went gently into that good night.

The adulation that he received, particularly in his home county, was not based on crass name recognition. He was admired, even revered, not just for his feats on the cricket field – where he bowled fast-medium and batted with uncomplicated gusto – but for how he conducted himself off it. He was living proof that a man of humble origins could also be a perfect gentleman. Everything that made a man a man in the early years of the 20th century could be found in that sturdy frame and modest demeanour. It was not the manliness of the bully, the show-off, the tyrant who has to dominate every situation. It was rooted in kindlier soil. Hirst could be gruff, on occasion, but never rough.

My own grandfather, Percy Horsfall, born within ten miles of Hirst, in the 1880s, might have been his younger brother. As a boy, I found him vaguely intimidating, with his walrus moustache and his aloof Edwardian manner. He was quite shy, I now realise: he could no more have started a conversation with a stranger in the street than flown to the moon. But you did not have to dig too deep to find his softer side. If I got a good school report, he would fish into his waistcoat pocket for a ten-shilling note and hand it over with a sheepish air, as if he was breaking the law. His natural reserve could not mask his benevolence.

Fate had surrounded him with women. He had four daughters and two granddaughters before I came along. His telegram to my mother after I was born was a classic: 'CONGRATULATIONS STOP AND A BOY AT THAT STOP HORSFALL'. But he didn't seem to mind. He had never been the blokeish type. The Yorkshire gruffness was leavened by affability and kindness.

It was the same with Hirst. 'Dear Willie,' he wrote to one star-struck young fan. 'You asked for my autograph. Here are two – one for yourself and one for a swap. Yours sincerely, G. H. Hirst.' Young and old alike basked in the glow of his ebullient good humour. There was nothing of machismo in his make-up. There did not have to be. He conquered by other means.

As a cricketer, he was a workhorse, not a thoroughbred. If his mastery of swing bowling, that most arcane of sciences, put people in mind of a wizard, his batting drew earthier comparisons. The poet William Kerr admired his 'crisp, Merry late cuts, and brave Chaucerian pulls' – and if Kerr had a Chaucer character in mind, it was probably the miller rather than the knight.

There was no shortage of more brilliant, more eye-catching players. Hirst's most famous achievement – the one which stands out in the record books, because it is unique – was to score 2,000 runs and take 200 wickets in a single season, 1906. Perspiration, not inspiration, was his hallmark. He soldiered on year after year, indomitable. He was hardly ever injured. The only hint of an Achilles heel was his susceptibility to seasickness. On tours to Australia, he took the train to Marseilles, and joined the rest of the team there, rather than risk the rough seas of the Bay of Biscay. But he did not make a fuss about it. That was not the George Hirst way. It was not the Yorkshire way.

In no county in England was stoicism – letting nowt get t'better of thee – more prized. Yorkshire was to London what Sparta had been to Athens: a harsher, tougher society, and proud of it. Just as a real Scotsman wore nothing under his kilt, a real Yorkshireman gritted his teeth and didn't show if he was hurting.

Like other sporting heroes of the pre-television age, George Hirst is a shadowy figure, wreathed in the inevitable sentimentality. But peer through the shadows and what you see has a reassuring solidity. Nothing has had to be sexed up. The hero is no Nietzschean superman:

he is a creature of flesh and blood, and the more impressive for it. 'When we were young, we used to nip out of Sunday school to catch a glimpse of George Herbert,' recalled one of the Yorkshire cricket fans who idolised him. 'Regular as clockwork he used to come over by bus to see his mother, and he'd come swinging along with his trilby hat and rolled umbrella, smart as a new pin. To see him smile – and he always would smile – used to set us kids up for the week.'

Every detail of this sepia-tinged vignette tugs at the heartstrings, from the neatly furled umbrella to the municipal bus – more poetic than any open-top sports car could ever be – bearing the dutiful son to visit his mother on a Sunday afternoon. Manliness can sometimes be the most humdrum of virtues, compounded of simple kindness and a neighbourly consideration for others.

Hirst was not conventionally handsome or physically imposing. He stood at just five foot seven, short for a fast bowler. He was not a dashing batsman, the sort who made spectators swoon with a flamboyant sweep or textbook cover drive. And he certainly had none of the self-confidence born of wealth, privilege or a good education. He grew up above a pub, the Brown Cow, and left school at ten. His schooling was rudimentary, Dickensian. 'Children are crowded into such a small room that it is impossible for them to move from their seats to exercise,' wrote a shocked visitor to the infant school he attended. Escaping the classroom to play cricket in the streets must have felt like a liberation.

After school, Hirst worked in mills and factories before making the grade as a professional cricketer. His rise was steady rather than meteoric, based on the hard graft that has been instilled in generations of Yorkshire cricketers. But as he blossomed into a formidable all-rounder, first for his county, then for England, he won friends wherever he went. People did not merely enjoy his company: they admired his sterling human qualities. His obituary in *The Times* in 1954 is as much a character reference as a litany of runs and wickets: 'Hirst brought to everything he did a courage, an integrity, a vigour and a tenacity that meant that no game in which he took part was decided until the last ball had been bowled.' Sir Pelham Warner, one of his England captains, declared him 'the ideal cricketer, so straight, so strong, so honest'.

There can hardly have been a sports journalist in the land who did not apply the word 'yeoman' to Hirst. Or 'salt of the earth'. Or 'unpretentious'. He invited the clichés because he could be depended on to live up to them. Perhaps the best summation of his character can be found in A. A. Thomson's double-decker biography, *Hirst and Rhodes*: 'He had the gift, normally a royal prerogative, of being able to accept adulation without being puffed up or embarrassed. His natural dignity and courtesy were proof against his ever being anything but what he was: George Herbert Hirst, a plain, honest Yorkshireman, who had the good fortune to possess high skill in a happy, vigorous game. He had, to the highest degree, the virtue that the Victorians called manliness, but without a jot of Victorian sententiousness.'

Amen to that. There was a lot of the Victorian in George Hirst. He was his own man, beholden to nobody. He had the rugged self-sufficiency admired by Sir Richard Burton, the 19th-century explorer:

Do what thy manhood bids thee do,
From none but self expect applause.
He noblest lives and noblest dies
Who makes and keeps his self-made laws.

But Hirst was far too level-headed to indulge in the airy theories of some of his contemporaries. Before Victoria came to the throne, being a man in England had been relatively simple: you just got on with doing the sort of things men did, whether it was tilling the fields or marching into battle. Now, suddenly, among what would today be called the chattering classes, there was intellectual baggage attached. What made a man a man? It was a question that exercised some of the finest minds of the day – and some of the biggest crackpots.

When the Victorians made what amounted to a cult of manliness – the word barely existed before the 19th century – they imported preconceptions that seem plain weird today. Moral and physical purity became indistinguishable. *Mens sana in corpore sano* was the anthem of the age. Men were enjoined to look after their bodies and not yield to their baser instincts. Teenage boys were viewed as accidents waiting to happen, a mass of noxious energies which needed to be stifled or, better still, channelled into harmless activities like sport, played in God's good air. A boy with a cricket bat in his hand could not get into mischief. From Ascot to Aberdeen, there was a squeamishness about bodily functions which bordered on the hysterical.

In the great public schools, where the debate about manliness raged most fiercely, masturbation was regarded as an evil to be stamped out at all costs. One headmaster of Harrow School famously insisted that the pockets of boys' trousers be sewn up. Muscular Christianity, as advocated by Thomas Hughes, author of *Tom Brown's Schooldays*, achieved the fervour of a fundamentalist creed, rooted in harsh values. A tough childhood was a good childhood. A tough childhood was character-building. Cold showers, savage beatings and a couple of hours a day running around a sports field would make a man of you.

To be judged 'manly' was one of the highest accolades to which a Victorian male could aspire. 'Lightly lie the turf upon thee, kind and manly Alfred Mynn,' wrote William Jeffrey Prowse in his obituary poem commemorating the pre-eminent English cricketer of the first half of the 19th century. A bland-seeming epithet, used very sparingly in Shakespeare, now had a far more potent ring – even if its exact meaning, because of its tautologous construction, remained rather vague.

Men were often defined as much by what they were not as by what they were. They were not women, ergo to exhibit womanly weakness was unmanly. They were not animals, ergo to surrender to their animal lusts was unbecoming. Self-denial rather than self-expression was the order of the day. 'Feelings are like chemicals,' warned Charles Kingsley, the Victorian clergyman who wrote *The Water Babies* and was one of the high priests of muscular Christianity. 'The more you analyse them, the worse they smell.' A manly man, in this new moral universe, got on with his life. He didn't indulge in introspection or wallow in depression.

It was an eccentric recipe – well summarised by E. M. Forster, who said of old-style British public schools like Eton and Rugby that they turned out boys with 'well-developed bodies, fairly developed minds and undeveloped hearts'. But it achieved a surprisingly wide currency.

And the preoccupation with manliness as a moral imperative was not confined to a few eccentric C of E pedagogues. With the Empire to defend, the suppression of *un*-manly feelings, of the type that might undermine the morale of the tribe, became a matter of public policy.

'History is strewn with the wrecks of nations which have gained a little progressiveness at the cost of a great deal of hard manliness,' wrote the constitutional historian, Walter Bagehot, one of the most influential thinkers of the age. Manliness again, reverberating like a battle cry. It was not a good time to have homosexual leanings. In fact, it was an absolutely terrible time to have homosexual leanings.

In Georgian and Regency England, social attitudes had been comparatively relaxed. While sodomy was still technically a capital offence, the crime was very hard to prove and the legislation rarely invoked. Outlandish fops like Beau Brummell – an occasional cricketer, who played for Hampshire in 1807, scoring 23 and 3 – were not just tolerated, but relished. So what if a man dressed like a dandy and wore white cravats which he had taken an hour to tie? It was a free country. Now the dandies' days were numbered.

In 1885, when Hirst was barely out of puberty, male homosexuality was designated a crime for the first time in Britain, under the Labouchere amendment to the Criminal Law Amendment Act. To the specific offence of sodomy, there was now added the much vaguer offence of 'gross indecency' between men, a coy, catch-all phrase which the judges of the day interpreted according to their own prejudices.

In May 1895, the legislation claimed its most celebrated scalp when Oscar Wilde was convicted of gross indecency and sentenced to two years' hard labour, the maximum allowable under the Act. Mr Justice Wills, presiding, declared the sentence 'totally inadequate for a case such as this'. In the Yorkshire dressing room, as newspapers were passed from hand to hand, reports of the Wilde trial must have seemed like dispatches from another planet. What was this highfalutin' nonsense about the love that dared not speak its name? By 'eck, the man had hair growing down to his shoulders! The cricket world had other things on its mind. In the very week Wilde was sentenced, all eyes were on W. G. Grace, in his *annus mirabilis*, as he closed in on the unprecedented feat of scoring 1,000 runs in May, at the age of 46. The author of *The Importance of Being Earnest* was not going to upstage *that*.

But, in the wider scheme of things, the Wilde trial cast a longer shadow than anything W. G. achieved. The new puritanism, a censoriousness that would have been unthinkable 100 years earlier, had well and truly arrived, driving homosexuality underground, where it would remain for nearly a century. 'I liked you better than suits a man to say,' wrote A. E. Housman, in a poem written to a male friend, published posthumously – it would have been unacceptable in his lifetime. There were a lot of Housmans in late Victorian England: anxious, repressed, guilty, unable to be true to themselves. The pressure to be a man – a *real* man, whatever that meant – had been ratcheted up a notch.

At this remove of time, it is tempting to view the working-class Yorkshire world of George Hirst as fundamentally distinct from the metropolitan world of Oscar Wilde and the ex-public schoolboys. But the two worlds often overlapped – and nowhere more so than on the cricket field.

The team photograph of the England XI that faced Australia at Trent Bridge in 1899 illustrates this point to perfection. Centre stage, the alpha-male, bearded like a lion, is W. G., captain of the side. Sitting beside him are K. S. Ranjitsinjhi, an Indian prince, C. B. Fry, an Oxford Blue, and F. S. Jackson, an Old Harrovian – Churchill's fag-master, no less – who would later become a member of Parliament and Governor of Bengal. The rest of the team are working-class professionals, including Hirst himself and his great Yorkshire contemporary, Wilfred Rhodes. But the men do not look ill at ease in each other's company, quite the reverse. Physically, they look extraordinarily similar – not least because every man jack of them, apart from the full-bearded Grace and the boyish Rhodes, is sporting a moustache.

Some are pencil-thin, mere smudges on the upper lip. Others are broad and bushy, like well-tended garden borders. Some droop at the edges. Others end in a playful upwards twirl. But the overall effect is as harmoniously reassuring – or as monotonous, depending on your point of view – as a school uniform.

A lot of learned ink has been expended on the moustaches that became almost compulsory facial furniture in the late 19th and early 20th century. They certainly merit a passing mention in a book about manliness because they were, for a period, *the* badge of manliness – as they still are in some parts of the world. 'The youth of 21 looks 30 with a moustache,' wrote one Edwardian commentator, pondering the rich foliage around him. 'Without it he would look 16.' If you wanted to grow up quickly – and, with only a tiny fraction of the population going on to higher education, the gap between boyhood and manhood was far more sharply defined than it is today – you skimped on shaving and kept your fingers crossed.

Winston Churchill tried to grow a moustache while a second lieutenant in the Queen's Own Hussars – and was mortified when he failed. He had to wait until he was in his sixties before a baby-faced prime minister looked the part in Downing Street. Lloyd George had a moustache. Chamberlain had a moustache. So did Hitler. So did Stalin. The fashion had a long innings. In its heyday, the moustache was such a fixture that, in china shops, you could buy specially designed cups that enabled a man to drink tea without getting his pride and joy wet.

George Hirst, naturally, grew an absolute beauty, effortlessly luxuriant, like a bed of moss on the Yorkshire moors. The moustache was his passport to manhood. And, just as significantly, it transcended class. In an age that was more egalitarian than it is sometimes presented, the moustachioed footman could look the moustachioed earl in the eye. They were both real men, albeit enjoying different stations in life.

If the moustache was a bridge between men of different classes, the same could be said of the boys' magazines which mushroomed in popularity throughout Hirst's youth and early manhood. The decade of his birth, the 1870s, saw the principle of universal education established in Britain for the first time; and with education came a new audience for unsophisticated tales of derring-do, whether in the jungles of Africa or on the school sports field. *The Boy's Own Paper*, a niche publication on its debut in 1879, acquired a nationwide readership. A boy is a boy: it does not matter how much money his parents have. Just as the Harry Potter books have been devoured by children who have never been to boarding school, so working-class children of the late Victorian and Edwardian eras gorged themselves on tales set in minor public schools, peopled by dandies, bullies, cane-wielding teachers and sporty heroes who knew how to look after themselves in the scrum.

The prototype of the genre was *The Fifth Form at St Dominic's*, published in 1881 and originally serialised in *The Boy's Own Paper*. Its author, Talbot Baines Reed, had attended the City of London School, where he was bottom of the class at maths, but on the sports field impressed with his 'strength of muscle, length of limb, boldness of attack and absolute fearlessness' – shades of George Hirst. Fearless or not, Reed understood the neuroses of adolescence, the doubts one must conquer before becoming a man. As his young hero is packed off to boarding school, and his mother reminds him to look after his flannel waistcoats or he will catch a cold, he frets that people will think him 'a milksop or mollycoddle'. You don't mind catching a cold when you are a boy of that age. You do mind being thought a sissy by your fellows.

Where Reed had led, Charles Hamilton, aka Frank Richards and umpteen other aliases, followed. Best remembered as the creator of Greyfriars School, Hamilton was one of the most prolific writers ever, in any genre, with a readership of millions. He had an uncanny understanding of what made boys tick – or not tick. His books were execrably written, but the characters were timeless and classless. Billy Bunter, the Fat Owl of the Remove, who made his bow in 1908, was a warning to schoolboys everywhere what happened if you stuffed yourself with food, told fibs to teachers or squealed on your friends. It was better to be Harry Wharton, the dashing form captain, or the cheery optimist Bob Cherry.

The world of Greyfriars was simultaneously parochial and universal. In *The Classic Slum*, Robert Roberts' memoir of growing up in Salford before the Great War, slum boys fight each other according to strict Greyfriars rules – no kicking, no striking someone when he is down, no weapons, just fists. The boys' magazines were hardly great literature. They had none of the high Christian seriousness of Thomas Arnold and other great Victorian headmasters. But, in the days before television, they shaped attitudes. They also brought a measure of social cohesion, promoting values – loyalty, courage, honesty – that were as relevant in a working-class home as in the mansions of the landed gentry.

One must tread carefully here: it is easy to fall into the trap of glib generalisation and gloss over significant differences between boys from different classes and, just as important, from different parts of the country. To treat Yorkshire County Cricket Club as a faithful microcosm of society at large would be absurd. The world of English county cricket has never, at any stage, been a simple homogenous whole. From the very inception of the County Championship in the late 1880s, a north–south divide has been clearly discernible. In the mythology of the game, players from Yorkshire or Lancashire have been made of sterner stuff than players from Kent or Sussex or Gloucestershire. They are less soft, physically. They don't don a second pullover as soon as the sun goes behind a cloud. They are less likely to get out to airy-fairy shots. They can take their drink better. To that extent, Yorkshire cricketers could be said to occupy a different position on the spectrum of manliness to those born south of the Wash.

Even away from the cricket field, Yorkshire is not England, but a sub-division of England, with its own sub-divisions – the late-lamented Ridings. The stereotypical Yorkshireman has strengths – resilience, stoicism, bluntness, common sense – and weaknesses – dourness, tight-fistedness, stubbornness – which no amount of social engineering can shift. God's own county is a law unto itself, a self-contained world, a ripe human comedy.

But, with that important caveat, I don't want to dwell unduly on the north–south divide, any more than I want to dwell on the nuances of the English class system. It is the shared attitudes of such a diverse-seeming group of men – and they *did* share attitudes, on a whole range of issues – that interest me. George Hirst's first captain at Yorkshire was an Old Etonian, Lord Hawke, a man with an even more splendid moustache than Hirst, and one of the giants of the Golden Age of cricket. As a player, his contributions were negligible, but he brought a messianic zeal to the game. Hawke is to Yorkshire cricket what Lord Reith is to the BBC: a founding father, but also a moral touchstone. What would Lord Hawke have thought of so-and-so? You still hear the question posed by men born long after Hawke was dead.

He was an amateur, with the mindset of an amateur – he was vehemently opposed to Yorkshire being captained by a professional. But his amateurism was not of the snobbish variety. Its roots lay much deeper – in the medieval age of chivalry, to which many Victorians felt an almost romantic attachment.

Married but with no children – a combination that perhaps gives rise to unspoken suspicions – Lord Hawke did not have to clamp down on homosexuality or other Wilde-like decadence at Yorkshire. His players wed and procreated, as naturally as breathing. George Hirst, who married at 25 and had three children, was wholly typical. But Hawke did have to clamp down on drinking, which had reached endemic proportions.

The team that Hawke, straight out of Cambridge, inherited as club captain in 1883 comprised 'gifted but scarcely house-trained professionals' and was dubbed 'ten drunks and a parson' – the parson being Ephraim Lockwood, a lay preacher. Hawke made the restoration of discipline his priority and, by the time Hirst cemented his place in the side in the 1890s, Yorkshire was well on its way to becoming a cricketing powerhouse, the most successful county in the land. It was no longer a drinking club, but an academy of excellence, with winning rather than entertaining being the priority. County championship after county championship was won on the back of hard-earned victories, with no quarter given, particularly to teams from Lancashire. Lord Hawke's family motto was 'Strike', and his teams played aggressively when the situation required, but their success was rooted in miserliness – not giving away cheap runs or cheap wickets.

There was the odd exception to the rule, like the batsman David Denton, nicknamed Lucky, who 'hit merrily so long as he was at the wicket', but efficiency rather than self-expression was the order of the day. The link between Yorkshire cricket and dour cricket was becoming as firmly established as the link between West Indies cricket and calypso cricket would be in the 1950s.

Douglas Moffat's mischievous 1897 poem 'As They Stood A-Blocking' might have been written after watching Yorkshire batsmen at their most uncompromising:

As they stood a-blocking, a-blocking, a-blocking.
Wearily I yawned while I sat and watched the play:
The bowling was all right,
But they did not try to smite,
Though many balls they might
Have put away:
As they stood a-blocking, I sat yawning at the play.
Yes, I sat a-yawning, a-yawning, a-yawning.
And several persons yawned who turned and looked at me:
A lady sitting nigh
Who chanced to catch my eye,
In the middle of a sigh
Yawned at me,
Sat a-yawning; it was comical to see.

Entertainment may have been at a premium at Yorkshire matches, but for spectators scouring the field for virile role models, there was no shortage of candidates. The wicketkeeper David Hunter, who had a particularly splendid moustache, was a successful amateur weightlifter, as well as a keen campanologist and concertina-player. Bobby Moorhouse, a forerunner of Brian Close, stood up so fearlessly to fast bowling that he earned the nickname The Man of Bruises. Frank Milligan volunteered for service in the Boer War and was killed in action during the relief of Mafeking. Moorhouse was a professional from Huddersfield, Milligan an Eton-educated amateur, but they shared qualities that transcended class.

No history of cricket can ignore the quaint distinction between Gentlemen and Players, which endured until 1962. But what is so fascinating about the all-conquering Yorkshire side captained by Lord Hawke, the gentleman-amateur, and spearheaded by George Hirst, the supreme county professional, is how little the waters were muddied by social frictions. The two men were on the best of terms, and would remain so for half a century. Hawke was as charmed as everyone else by Hirst's cheerful disposition. 'His smile used almost to meet at the back of his neck,' he joked. But he could also see the steel behind the bonhomie. 'It was not only what Georgie Hirst did but how he did it,' he wrote, 'coming off when an effort was most necessary and playing his best against the more formidable sides.'

When Hirst retired from the game, Hawke was instrumental in securing him the job of cricket coach at Eton, his old school, a post he held for nearly 20 years, venerated by all. There is a nice story, possibly apocryphal, about the match played to mark his retirement. The captain of the Eton XI thought it would be rather droll if the great fast bowler could bow out with a hat-trick. The scheme worked to perfection, with three batsmen surrendering their wickets to him with such artistry that the cheering spectators had no inkling it was a set-up. Hirst realised – but said nothing to show that he realised. He just entered into the spirit of the occasion.

If he had had a chip on his shoulder, the laconic cricketer, with his Huddersfield vernacular, might have been a fish out of water at Eton. His brother-in-arms at Yorkshire, Wilfred Rhodes, took up a similar coaching appointment at Harrow, but never fitted in and was replaced by Patsy Hendren of Middlesex. But Hirst's natural equanimity carried the day. He took people as he found them, the way he always had.

Like Lord Hawke, his aristocratic mentor, George Hirst the coach was a disciplinarian without being a martinet. A well-run ship did not need to involve shouting. At Eton, he insisted that pupils wore spotless flannels and clean boots, believing that, if you did not look your best, you could not play your best. But his rollickings were tempered with kindness and good humour. One boy who appeared in grass-stained flannels, explaining that his spare pair were at the cleaners, was told: 'It's a bad do, but don't fret, lad. I'll show you how to cover those stains with chalk for the afternoon. But if you come here looking like that again, by gow…'

If Hirst fitted in well at Eton, it was because of shared values, both on and off the field. How the sporting gods must have smiled when he arrived! A scion of the county that turned maiden overs into an art form teaching at the school where the 0-0 draw was regarded with equal reverence! Goals in the famously attritional Eton Wall Game are scored once every ten years or so, and in the annual St Andrew's Day fixture between the Collegers and the Oppidans – the Eton equivalent of a Roses match – no goal has been scored by either side since 1909. Hirst must have watched the boys scrabbling around in the mud, giving no quarter to their opponents, and smiled in recognition.

Whether or not the Battle of Waterloo was won on the playing fields of Eton, the school was still a tough environment for an adolescent boy – as unsentimental and unyielding, in its way, as the hard northern communities in which Hirst and his ilk were raised. Parents did not send their sons to Eton to be pampered.

Coach and pupils had a shared way of communicating. They both spoke the language of understatement. Extravagant praise was out. So were great shows of emotion, high-fives at the fall of a wicket. An unspoken code of behaviour forbade it. In the well-ordered rituals of a cricket match, there was an echo of the orderliness that characterised society at large. You went about your business. You didn't turn your life into a performance.

A horror of excess, whatever form it took, conditioned how men of Hirst's generation behaved. Self-indulgence was the ultimate betrayal, whether it took the form of drinking, wearing flash clothes or sexual shenanigans. A man had to be in control of himself and his emotions. He resisted temptation, whatever form it took.

It seems an austere code today, and it sometimes manifested itself in ridiculous ways. One of the housemasters at Eton during Hirst's time was George Lyttelton. His son was the jazz trumpeter Humphrey Lyttelton, whose account of the paternal advice he received about the facts of life belongs in a *Monty Python* sketch: 'Most of the enduring things I learnt from my father were by example rather than precept. His "serious talk" with me as I approached puberty lingers in my mind for its almost startling brevity. He was standing in the traditional position with his back to the fireplace and he uttered the injunction in a strong, resonant voice, with a stern lowering of the massive eyebrows, as if to make up in portentousness what his message lacked in length and detail. "Eschew evil," he boomed, then gave me a heavy paternal bang on the shoulder and left the room, beaming to himself.'

But if self-discipline was prized, it was prized for a reason. All around George Hirst, both at Yorkshire and Eton, there would have been examples of what happened to men who were incapable of it. Manliness might have been the ideal, but it was an ideal from which many men fall sadly short. The strong battled through. The weak went to the wall. Darwin knew what he was talking about.

Binge drinking, the *bête noire* of today's *Daily Mail*, was more prevalent in Hirst's day than the sentimentalists admit. Beneath those neatly trimmed moustaches and carefully buttoned waistcoats, chaos was lurking. Hirst himself was not a heavy drinker – 'Everything in Moderation' might have been his motto – but some of his team-mates were not so abstemious. The classic male bonding ritual of a night out at the pub often degenerated into mayhem – particularly when the players were on the road, away from home – almost as if the drinkers were using alcohol to escape the social inhibitions of the time.

One of the saddest stories of the Hawke–Hirst era at Yorkshire involves Bobby Peel, a genuinely great spin bowler whose career was blighted by chronic alcoholism. He would drink himself to sleep, then hit the bottle again in the morning. Loyal to the last, Hirst covered for his team-mate, protecting him from the wrath of his captain, but things came to a head after one epic bout of drinking during a county match. Hirst helped Peel to bed in a drunken stupor, then approached Lord Hawke before the start of play the next day. 'I'm very sorry, my lord. Peel's apologies, but he's been taken very queer in the night and won't be able to turn out this morning.' The excuse might have passed muster if Peel had not suddenly turned up in person, red-faced, his cap at an angle, three sheets to the wind.

'Leave the field at once, Peel,' ordered Lord Hawke, as his star bowler proceeded to make a spectacle of himself in the outfield, lobbing spinners towards the sightscreen. In some versions of the story, he even urinated on the wicket, the holy of holies. The bowler then added insult to injury by refusing to apologise. Hirst did his best to mediate, but it was a lost cause. Peel never played for Yorkshire again.

Another of Hirst's Yorkshire contemporaries was Ted Wainwright, the all-rounder. He had a reasonably successful career, winning five England caps, and was then appointed cricket coach at Shrewsbury School, where one of his fellow teachers was the young Neville Cardus, who remembered his drinking bouts with less than affection. 'He was a tall man who walked as if he didn't give a damn for anybody,' he wrote in his autobiography. 'There was something sinister about him. Every night he got drunk as a matter of course, quietly and masterfully.' When Cardus, on a visit to the pub, told Wainwright that he drank nothing stronger than ginger ale, Wainwright recoiled in horror: 'Christ, th'art a reight bloody cricketer.'

Many of the heaviest drinkers were also heavy smokers. Chain-smoker Jack Brown, a contemporary of Hirst at Yorkshire, was dead of heart failure by the age of 35. The life of a professional cricketer might have appeared enviable from the outside, but there were hidden strains and stresses. It was a precarious living.

Another Yorkshire player, Billy Bates, tried to commit suicide after an eye injury forced him to retire. He had been an Ashes hero in the early 1880s; his name is inscribed on the urn itself. But sporting glory could not mask the underlying sense of vulnerability. Emotional problems, whatever form they took, were swept under the carpet. It was unmanly to admit to depression or mental illness, even if one had the language to describe it. Victorian decorum forbade it. Poor Johnny Briggs, a Lancashire professional of the period, ended his days in a lunatic asylum. One way and another, there was a fair bit of unhappiness beneath the calm certainties of county cricket.

Fit, healthy, moderate in his vices – he liked to smoke a pipe with his evening drink – Hirst lived well into his eighties, unusual for a man of his generation when, with high infant mortality rates, the life expectancy of a British male at birth was still below 50. He was born a Victorian and died an Elizabethan, in May 1954. But it is probably as a great Edwardian, the years of his pomp as a cricketer, that he will be remembered.

Folk memory has the Edwardians playing croquet on sunlit lawns as the war clouds gathered in Europe, but folk memory is playing tricks.

Some of the wettest years on record occurred just before the Great War, notably the soggy summer of 1912, when cricketers spent half the season in the pavilion, watching the puddles grow. But it was certainly a time of peace, prosperity and steady economic growth. People of all classes enjoyed the simple pleasures of life, cricket not least of them.

The Edwardians were no fools, sleepwalking to disaster. They thought for themselves. Revolution was vaguely in the air, although, in the British way of things, it felt more like evolution, practical Darwinism rather than red-blooded Marxism. Men of a reforming bent did not rush to the barricades: they wrote pamphlets or formed trade unions. The true militants were the women – like the suffragette Emily Davison, who threw herself under the King's horse at the 1913 Derby. But if no comparable political cause united the men of the period, that does not mean their habits and attitudes were set in stone. The rock-solid Victorian world into which George Hirst had been born was changing around him.

The man himself was essentially unaltered. That was one of the things people admired about Hirst. He was not a slave to fashion or prone to jumping on passing bandwagons. But the Edwardian England in which he played his most productive cricket was not simply Victorian England with a new backside on the throne. It was a different animal. Life had suddenly become a mite more complicated, whether you were a cricketer, a farmer or a poet. A man could not simply aspire to be the same sort of man as his father before him. New ideas jostled for attention, as old ways of looking at the world came under the microscope. Little by little, morality was shifting.

Muscular Christianity, the great sledgehammer with which the Victorians had tried to crush the impulses lurking in boys' breasts, came to be viewed as the flawed ideology it was. There was an appetite for a new approach to male adolescence that was saner, gentler, more understanding of human frailty. Men who had been raised with Victorian harshness – beaten, brutalised, expected to be seen and not heard – wanted something better for their own children. It was no longer thought axiomatic that a boy ought to develop into a man as soon as reasonably possible. Indeed, one of the defining features of the Edwardian period was the proliferation of children's books which sought to preserve childhood as a haven of innocent escapism.

'Beyond the Wild Wood comes the Wide World,' Ratty tells Mole in Kenneth Grahame's *The Wind in the Willows*, published in 1908. 'And that's something that doesn't matter, either to you or me. I've never been there, and I'm never going, nor you either, if you've got any sense at all. Don't ever refer to it again, please.'

Growing up, toughening up, becoming a man, was pleasurably delayed – or, in the case of Peter Pan, who made his first appearance in 1902, put on permanent hold. The creation of J. M. Barrie, a mad-keen amateur cricketer – he ran a scratch team called the Allahakbarries, for which P. G. Wodehouse, Jerome K. Jerome, A. A. Milne and other overgrown schoolboys turned out – *The Boy Who Wouldn't Grow Up* spoke to a generation as surely as Harry Potter a century later. Peter Pan struck a chord because he reflected new sensibilities and new priorities in the raising of boys. He was emblematic of a generation that, little by little, was beginning to unbutton emotionally.

Different men express their emotions in different ways. That has been true since the dawn of time. But each generation of men shares its own emotional language, subtly different from the language of previous generations. Take one of the recurring litmus tests of manliness – crying. No statistics, alas, exist of how many men were caught blubbing in public (a) in 1810 (b) in 1910 and (c) in 2010. The figures would be quite revealing if they did. But it is a matter of simple observation that this is a field of masculine behaviour where attitudes change over time.

In Shakespeare's plays it is perfectly normal for a male character to cry at times of high emotion; indeed, tears are often a testament to his humanity, as when Coriolanus is moved to tears by his mother and his eyes 'sweat compassion'. But the centuries that followed saw the hardening of that quintessential English accessory – the stiff upper lip. By 1770, Oliver Goldsmith could write admiringly of 'the silent manliness of grief'. There was still the odd occasion when the floodgates burst – like the funeral of Nelson, when there were 'tears in every eye', according to newspaper reports. At a more banal level, the death of Dickens' Little Nell in 1841 was another cue for waterworks, from men and women alike. But by the late Victorian period, crying was widely regarded as a sign of womanly weakness, inadmissible in any circumstances. A man kept his tears in, and a boy was not a man until he had learnt the same trick. Now, little by little, teardrop by teardrop, the tide was turning.

One of the men in the vanguard of the change was the pioneering psychiatrist Henry Maudsley, born in Yorkshire in 1835. 'The sorrow which has no vent in tears may make the other organs weep,' wrote Maudsley, anticipating one of the great themes of modern psychiatry, the need to express feelings, not bottle them up. Maudsley was years ahead of his time in believing that for a man to cry was not just socially acceptable but, on occasion, medically necessary. He knew what he was talking about: his own mother had died when he was a small child, and he had been expected not to make a fuss about it. But he was not a lone voice. As the new century dawned, there was a growing reaction against perceived repressiveness. On the surface, life went on much as before. Below it, there were the first stirrings of discontent. If a boy was to grow into a man, it was not enough to break him like a colt, with repeated thrashings. He needed to be given a broader understanding of his place in the world.

One of the most significant milestones on the road to a more humane vision of manliness occurred in 1908, with the publication, originally in instalments, of *Scouting for Boys: A Handbook for Instruction in Good Citizenship* by Robert Baden-Powell, one of the best-selling non-fiction books of the entire 20th century. Its soldier-author was already a national hero after his exploits at the Siege of Mafeking during the Boer War. He had written military textbooks which drew on his experiences of scouting in Africa. Now he set his sights on higher things – a revolution in the way boys were brought up, a revolution that would cause ripples around the world.

Baden-Powell has been criticised, lampooned, even branded a warmonger. Some passages in *Scouting for Boys*, the seminal text of the Scout Movement, cause a definite queasiness today. 'Every boy ought to learn to shoot and obey orders.' It sounds like the ravings of a megalomaniac, a blueprint for fascism. Others induce paroxysms of laughter. 'A Scout smiles and whistles under all circumstances.' What miseries the non-whistlers must have endured! They probably spent hours in the bathroom, practising in vain. But many of Baden-Powell's precepts are just sound common sense, far more appealing, at an ideological level, than the fundamentalist values of the Muscular Christians who preceded him.

A little of the old sententiousness lingers. The tenth article of the Scout Law, which codifies how Scouts should behave, reads: 'A Scout should be pure in thought, word and deed.' No sex, please, gentlemen, this is a Scout camp. But it is perhaps significant that Baden-Powell only added it as a rider in 1911, three years after the first nine articles were published. Stamping out masturbation was not his priority: he was fired by loftier ideals. His thinking had been influenced, not just by Western Christianity, but by Burmese Buddhism, which he had observed at first hand. There were suddenly some new, kindlier, ingredients in the recipe for manliness.

In the Scout Law, dos are far more important than don'ts, which is appealing in any ideology. The famous injunction to do a good deed a day has been much mocked, but still holds good. You see the same sentiment encapsulated in that New Age sticker in car windows, 'Practise random kindness and senseless acts of beauty'. Dated in many respects, the Scout Law is surprisingly forward-looking in others. If you think the Edwardians lived in a stratified world, riddled with class prejudices, think again. 'A Scout is a friend to all, and a brother to every other Scout, no matter to what social class the other belongs,' wrote Baden-Powell. 'A Scout must never be a SNOB.' Even the fact that he capitalises the 'snob', signalling the strength of his loathing of snobbery, endears the man to you.

At the very heart of the Scout Law, impervious to passing fashion, is the Christian ideal of selflessness. 'A Scout's duty is to be useful and help others.' What parent, in any era, would mind their son pinning that to his bedroom wall? And if Baden-Powell's emphasis on the importance of obeying orders grates in 2012, in our more egalitarian times, he never preached slavish social conformity. 'A boy should take his own line,' he wrote, 'rather than be carried along by herd persuasion.' Another bullseye – and a line that would have gone down well in the Yorkshire dressing room of George Hirst, Wilfred Rhodes et al.

The senior professionals in the side were men of substance, not hired hands. You did what Lord Hawke said. If he told you to field at second slip, you fielded at second slip. If he told you to play for a draw, you played for a draw. But you didn't *grovel* to his lordship. Real men didn't grovel. They ploughed their own furrow in life.

Two years after the publication of *Scouting for Boys*, another classic hit the bookshelves, probably the single most quoted poem in the history of the language. 'If you can keep your head/While all about you are losing theirs…' The opening words of Rudyard Kipling's famous poem might have been written by a man who had been in the crowd at the Oval in August 1902, the zenith of Hirst's career. Pandemonium in the stands, a nerve-shredding Test against Australia at stake, and two unflustered Yorkshiremen, Hirst and Rhodes, keeping their heads to see their side home.

'We'll get 'em in singles,' Hirst reportedly said to Rhodes at the start of their immortal last wicket stand. Others might panic, but not the calm, methodical Hirst. He adjusted his pads between every ball, according to one observer at the Oval. He patted the pitch. He brushed aside stray bits of dirt. He refused to be hurried. If Kipling had been batting at the other end, he would probably have approached the same task in the same way. No fuss. No histrionics. No showboating. Just a good dose of British phlegm.

Kipling was not at the Oval in 1902: he was house-hunting with his wife in Sussex and putting the finishing touches to *The Just So Stories*, published that year. He actually wrote 'If' in 1895, although it did not see the light of day until 15 years later, as part of a miscellany called *Rewards and Fairies*. But his celebrated advice to boys, with its cheesy punchline, 'You'll be a Man, my son!', might have been written with George Hirst in mind.

Hirst needed no lessons in how to treat those twin impostors, triumph and disaster. He was equanimity personified. Right through his long career, he could get a century one day and a duck the next and be the same man in the pub afterwards. He was never too down on himself in lean seasons or too full of himself in times of plenty. Could he fill the unforgiving minute with 60 seconds' worth of distance run? Could he 'eck. Hirst ran in to bowl day after day, season after season, for more than 30 years. He never let up. He never complained. He was one of the great workhorses of sport. As for walking with kings and not losing the common touch, a man who could grow up above a pub in Yorkshire, leave school at ten and end up a much-loved cricket master at Eton was clearly blessed with human attributes that transcended class.

But it is probably one of the less well-known lines in the poem that best captures the prosaic values by which George Hirst lived. 'Don't look too good nor talk too wise.' You can almost imagine him reading the words, puffing at his pipe, and giving a vigorous nod of approval. Hirst always dressed neatly, right through his life. But to have worn anything that made him stand out from the crowd – a velvet waistcoat or flamboyant tie – would have revolted him. He was a cricketer, not a peacock. To show off in conversation – gild the lily when telling an anecdote or brag about his achievements – would have been equally unthinkable. He left that to others. For all his sporting prowess, he was a modest man in a modest age; if we still have a soft spot for the Edwardians, that ubiquitous modesty goes a long way towards explaining it. They did some extraordinary things, but would have thought it vulgar to mention them.

One of Hirst's most celebrated contemporaries, the supplier of a quotation as well-known as 'We'll get 'em in singles', was Captain Lawrence 'Titus' Oates, the polar explorer, who perished in Scott's expedition to the Antarctic in 1912. Oates was born in London, but raised in Yorkshire, where he joined the 3rd West Yorkshire (Militia) Regiment, in George Hirst's backyard, and was inculcated with the same quiet stoicism.

Oates had fought in the Boer War, and been badly wounded in the leg. He and Scott never hit it off. 'I dislike him intensely,' he wrote in his diary, 'and would chuck the whole thing if we were not a British expedition.' Scott, for his part, called Oates 'a cheery old pessimist'. But if he found him curmudgeonly, a stereotypical Tyke, he was forced to acknowledge his fortitude. Yorkshiremen were made of stern stuff. They *never* made a fuss – not even if they were 12,000 miles from home, stuck in a howling blizzard, at minus 40 degrees, with galloping frostbite.

'I am going out,' Oates told Scott, as he left their tent, to certain death, 'and I may be gone some time.'

What an exit line! And what a man! You want to give him a cricket bat and send him in to bat on a sticky wicket against Australia, with a nation on tenterhooks and George Hirst at the other end.

And how about those other shadowy figures who lurk in the background of the great men of the past – the women? If George Hirst had been dogged by tabloid hacks 24 hours a day, who knows what peccadilloes they might have stumbled across? A mistress called Gwendoline in Bradford? A one-night stand on a tour of Australia? A bit of hanky-panky with a maid behind the pavilion at Eton during a second XI match against Harrow? But if he behaved badly – to anyone, of either sex – there is no record of it. Indeed, his memory is as revered among his surviving family as it is among the Yorkshire cricketing public.

'I remember him as a very loving granddad who was a friend as well,' says his granddaughter Lindsay Watkins. When she was being bullied at school, her grandfather promptly wrote to her with some kindly words of advice: 'Do your lessons and stick up for yourself and all will come right in the end.' The values he bequeathed to her were prosaic but timeless: 'Always be courteous and respectful to others, whatever their station in life. Be cheerful, good-humoured, never criticise others, never boast. Have self-control, self-discipline.'

We have already caught a glimpse of Hirst the family man, taking the bus to visit his mother in Kirkheaton every Sunday. One does not imagine him being over-demonstrative in his affections when he greeted her. That was not the emotional language of the time. Equally, one can feel sure that he would have experienced no sense of contradiction between being a man's man and a solicitous son. Filial piety was prized by Edwardians of all classes – Lord Hawke attended Sunday morning church with his mother till the day she died. Hirst's mother certainly doted on him. In 1906, his most successful season, she travelled to Scarborough in the hope of seeing him take his 200th wicket – but was so overcome with anxiety that she left the ground before he had reached his milestone.

Communications between men and women were laughably formal by modern standards, but not without tenderness. Here is one of the great Edwardians, Yorkshire-born Herbert Asquith, signing off a letter to a woman friend, Mrs Harrison, after he had resigned as prime minister in 1916:

'Bless you, dearest,

Ever your loving,

H. H. A.'

Are modern text messages, with their folksy abbreviations, any more intimate?

There is a natural temptation to assume that relations between the sexes at the turn of the last century were deep-rooted in inequality. George Hirst, remember, was nearly 60 before women were finally granted equal suffrage. At cricket matches at Kirkheaton, his home town, the women's role was decorative and menial – to serve tea in the pavilion between innings. But inequality did not mean a lack of respect. Many men of the period viewed their mothers with a reverence bordering on devotion. They had been able to observe at first hand the sacrifices women had to make to hold their families together, while their menfolk were away from home.

One of Hirst's best-known contemporaries, born in the same decade, was John Masefield, later Poet Laureate. Masefield was just six when his mother died giving birth to his younger sister, prompting one of his most haunting poems:

In the dark womb where I began
My mother's life made me a man.
Through all the months of human birth
Her beauty fed my common earth.
I cannot see, nor breathe, nor stir,
But through the death of some of her…
What have I done, or tried, or said
In thanks to that dear woman dead?

Men triumph over women still,
Men trample women's rights at will,
And man's lust roves the world untamed.
O grave, keep shut lest I be shamed.

The author may be male, but the sentiments have a raw feminist timbre. In an age when home births were the norm, and infant mortality rates were distressingly high, a growing boy was in no danger of viewing his mother through a sentimental lens. He saw her whole. He probably thought, 'There, but for the grace of God…'

Not all men, inevitably, showed the same reverence to the mothers of their children as they did to their own mothers. In Glebe Street in Huddersfield, the suburban street where Hirst lived with his wife Emma and their three children, you would not have had to go very far to find a drunken brute beating his wife, while the neighbours turned a blind eye. Domestic tyrants were two a penny. But that does not mean they were the social norm. The great majority of young couples setting up home did so, one can confidently surmise, on the basis of love, affection and mutual respect.

George and Emma Hirst married in the 1890s, the decade which saw the publication of *A Duet With an Occasional Chorus*, a neglected but delightful novel by Arthur Conan Doyle, whom Hirst would have known. The creator of Sherlock Holmes was one of the most enthusiastic amateur cricketers of the age. His roots were very different to Hirst's. He was a Scots-born doctor and had been educated at a public school, Stonyhurst. But he was admired by his contemporaries for the same reasons as Hirst. He combined exceptional physical vigour with an enviably straightforward way of communicating. You knew where you stood with Doyle. On his gravestone in Hampshire are inscribed four words: 'STEEL TRUE, BLADE STRAIGHT'.

In Holmes and Watson and their little bachelor ménage in Baker Street, Doyle painted a portrait of a certain kind of male friendship – undemonstrative, unsentimental, but rooted in absolute loyalty – that has never been surpassed. He captures the distinctive flavour of Edwardian manliness – in particular, the absence of *fuss* – better than any historian. 'Wedlock suits you,' says Holmes, after his friend has moved out of Baker Street to get married. 'I think, Watson, that you have put on seven and a half pounds since I last saw you' – *not* a line you would expect to hear in 2012, when Holmes and Watson would work out in the Baker Street gym, discussing cases over a carrot juice, and when putting on two pounds, never mind seven and a half, would trigger panic. The surnames by which the friends address each other seem comical today, but the bonds of trust that unite them are timeless. So is their quiet, understated fortitude.

A Duet with an Occasional Chorus, though not nearly as familiar, is equally revealing of marital relations in suburban households of the era. The two main characters, Frank and Maude Crosse, have hardly moved into their new home before they are agreeing, and committing to paper, 20 principles for a happy marriage. They include:

4. Never be cross at the same time. Wait your turn.
5. Never cease to be lovers. If you cease, someone else may begin.
10. Permanent mutual respect is necessary for a permanent mutual love.
12. Let there be one law for both.
13. There is only one thing worse than quarrels in public. That is caresses.

The tone is light, tongue-in-cheek. But the subtext is crystal-clear. This is not a domestic hierarchy, but a partnership of equals. The couple are not intellectuals, members of a social elite: their charm lies in the very ordinariness.

The same spirit of egalitarianism seems to have animated George Hirst's marriage to Emma, according to his granddaughter, Lindsay Watkins: 'My grandmother must have been a strong woman. She had to cope on her own for long periods when her husband was away. They made a good partnership.' Visitors to the Hirsts' house in Huddersfield remember Emma doing most of the talking while her husband retreated behind a newspaper. He had his bugbears – they included swearing and women smoking – but he seldom raised his voice, unless it was to sing, which he did in a gentle tenor, with his daughter Molly accompanying him on the piano. Quaint old songs, as innocent and artless as the man who sang them, would ring around the family parlour:

I'll sing thee songs of Araby,
And tales of fair Kashmir,
Wild tales to cheat thee of a sigh,
Or charm thee to a tear…

Like so many of the vignettes of Hirst the cricketer, the image of Hirst the family man relaxing has a reassuring tranquillity. He is master of his house, but he is not a tyrant. He is just playing the role nature intended for him with humility and good humour.

As a professional sportsman, away from home for weeks at a time, even months at a time, George Hirst would have lived and breathed a male-dominated world. The sexes were far more sharply delineated than they are today. 'Men as a rule prefer to associate with men and women with women, except for such functional purposes as procreation,' declared anthropologist Ernest Crawley in 1902. Social institutions we take for granted today, such as the unisex health club, the workplace with equal numbers of men and women, or the pub packed with drinkers of both sexes, would have been unthinkable.

Many women did go out to work, but the man was the main breadwinner, ex officio. Even if the tools of his trade were a bat and ball, he remained a hunter-gatherer, a figure wreathed in primitive romance. 'Man is the doer, the creator, the discoverer, the defender,' wrote the great Victorian aesthete John Ruskin. 'He sallies forth to perform his rough work in the open world under conditions of peril and trial.' The perils might have shrunk with time. A hunter-gatherer no longer had to bring a dead bison home to his cave, slung over his shoulder. A decent living wage was enough. But the principle remained the same. And, just as importantly, the hunter-gatherer, like a cricketer, was part of a *team*. He was not foraging for himself, but for his nearest and dearest.

Family mattered to George Hirst. He treated men and women with the same respect, the way he treated everyone else. And, if the evidence of his surviving relatives is to be believed, he seems to have brought the same quiet integrity to the role of husband and father as he did to his cricket.

His manliness demanded no less.

CHAPTER 2
HERBERT SUTCLIFFE:
A NEW BREED OF
YORKSHIRE CRICKETER

*We're all in the same boat. We all come here and
we don't know why. We all go in our turn and we don't
know when. If you are a bit better off, be thankful.
An' if you don't get into trouble an' make a fool of
yourself, well, be thankful for that, 'cos you easily might.
What I say is – we're all human, aren't we?*

J. B. Priestley, *When We Are Married*

Timing is vital in cricket, on and off the field.

If George Hirst had been born a few years later, he might have been
one of the lions led by donkeys who perished in the Great War. That he
would have served his country with distinction, and without complaint,
can be taken as read – there never was a man more blessed with the
soldierly qualities of loyalty and courage. As it was, he missed the cut.
He was 45 by the time conscription was introduced in 1916, setting an
upper age limit of 41.

Some of his younger team-mates at Yorkshire were not so lucky. For
a few, the war proved a stepping-stone to higher things. Jack Wilson,
who had played nine games for Yorkshire before the war, became a
much-decorated air ace with the Royal Navy Air Service, then tried his

luck as a jockey and won the 1925 Grand National on Double Chance. But others never returned from the front.

The all-rounder Major Booth – 'Major' was a given name, not a military rank – lost his life on the first day of the Somme offensive in 1916. He was only five years younger than Hirst, but found himself in the wrong place at the wrong time. A treacly poem published in his local paper in Pudsey captures both his qualities as a man and the resigned, even wry, attitude to the slaughter in Europe, almost as if war was cricket by other means:

> *Cricket field or battle plain*
> *He e'er went in might and main.*
> *Things were hard, smooth or rough,*
> *Made of good old Yorkshire stuff,*
> *Major, he was e'er the same,*
> *Kept his end up, played the game.*
> *Good old Major.*

Booth was one of the 'Leeds Pals', a battalion of Kitchener's army raised in West Yorkshire. He died in the arms of Abe Waddington, the fast bowler, who played two Tests for England after the war. Booth's best friend, Roy Kilner, the popular left-arm bowler, also fought at the Somme, where he sustained a shrapnel wound to his wrist. Kilner's younger brother was killed at Ypres, and Kilner himself was dead before he was 40, after contracting an unexplained illness on a tour of India. War or no war, longevity was for the privileged few in working-class Yorkshire: it was not a birthright. Alonzo Drake, who had been a key member of the Yorkshire XI before the war, sickened and died at the age of 34.

If Hirst was lucky, Herbert Sutcliffe, born in Nidderdale on 24 November 1894, was even luckier. Having shown early promise as a cricketer, he might have expected to be playing for the Yorkshire first XI in his early 20s. Instead, he was called up in 1915 and served first with the Royal Army Ordnance Corps, stationed at York, then with the Sherwood Foresters. He was later commissioned into the Green Howards as a second lieutenant. It was akin to a death sentence – in the grim calculus of war, a commissioned officer of the period could expect to be killed or wounded within three weeks if sent to the front. But fate smiled on Sutcliffe. His unit was summoned to France and reached Etaples the day after the Armistice was signed. By the spring of 1919, young, fit and hungry for success, he was opening the batting for his county, just as George Hirst's career was drawing to a close.

Sutcliffe's subsequent career for Yorkshire and England, spanning the inter-war period with the same neatness he brought to his batting, marks him down as one of the most prolific batsmen in the history of the game. His Test average, 60.73, speaks for itself – only Don Bradman seriously eclipsed it. But for reasons of personality, as much as anything else, he was never loved as George Hirst was loved. He was just too complex, too awkward. He came from a new generation of men, not totally sure of their place in the world.

The Yorkshire cricketing faithful were in awe of him. He was much the most prolific batsman the county had yet produced. But even those most patient of cricket fans would sometimes get exasperated by his imperturbability, his adamantine refusal to give the opposition bowlers a sniff of a chance. One of the few times he got out to a reckless shot was while playing against Essex at Leyton in 1932, when he took an ungainly swipe and was bowled off his pad – with the scoreboard reading 555 for 0, a new world record for an opening partnership.

At other times, Sutcliffe was uncompromising, immovable. He epitomised the tough, efficient brand of cricket which had been developed under Lord Hawke and which continued without remission up to the Second World War. In the 1930s alone, Yorkshire won the county championship seven times, with Brian Sellers proving as ruthless a captain as Lord Hawke. But their cricket was not always easy on the eye.

The Roses matches of the Sutcliffe era were particularly dour. 'Runs were severely discountenanced,' remembered Neville Cardus. 'No fours before lunch on principle was the unannounced policy.' At one such match, Sutcliffe was barracked by a Yorkshire fan: ''Erbert, coom on. What dost tha think thi are? A bloody war memorial?' It is a telling metaphor. Sutcliffe had such a cold, monumental quality that people sometimes forgot he was a human being. His GP once told him he had the lowest blood pressure in Pudsey. Those who watched him in his pomp, steering England calmly through a crisis against Australia, would have readily believed it. His powers of concentration were unrivalled. Don Bradman reckoned he had the best temperament of any cricketer he had ever played against. But, as Geoffrey Boycott would later discover, calmness at the crease is never quite as captivating as its opposite: the romantic impulsiveness that lures a batsman into an expansive cover drive or a cheeky late cut. Men who strenuously eliminate all risk are not sexy.

Sutcliffe did have his occasional lighter moments. On one tour of Australia, the local rednecks in Brisbane presented him with an engraved ashtray in token of the good humour with which he had dealt with their barracking while fielding on the boundary. But it is one thing to be jocular in the outfield. At the crease, with a new ball to see off, Sutcliffe was never jocular: he would have thought it a sin against the gods of cricket. Batting partners who got themselves out to self-indulgent shots could expect an absolutely filthy look from the other end. That was not how the game was meant to be played.

Jack Fingleton, one of Sutcliffe's Australian opponents, captures both the respect in which he was held and his masterful, slightly prissy, demeanour at the crease: 'I like most the spit and polish of Sutcliffe when he is master of the situation and knows it. I see him in his element at Lord's, where none can match the outraged indignities he suffers when, with Lord's packed, somebody has the misfortune to move in the members' pavilion as the bowler runs to deliver the ball. Up shoots Sutcliffe's traffic arm, his planked palm daring anything to move between his end and Buckingham Palace. He draws away from the wicket, makes vigorous sweeps with his bat to the pavilion, and all eyes follow it to discover some hapless wretch (possibly a Baronet) who had dared to move in his seat at such a moment in British history.'

Like Geoffrey Boycott and, to a lesser extent, Len Hutton, Sutcliffe exuded a perfectionism that bordered on the fanatical. I got a glimpse of that perfectionism when a friend showed me an old autograph book that had originally belonged to his father. One page has been signed by the entire Yorkshire XI who played against Surrey in a match at the Oval in the early 1920s. Every signature is legible down to the last letter – what a contrast with the hasty scrawl of the modern superstar – but the runaway winner, in terms of calligraphy, is the 'Herbert Sutcliffe', neatly underlined. It could go into the Book of Kells with no questions asked.

At the crease, Sutcliffe tried to wrest control of a match by keeping his own emotions strictly under control. He wore down the opposition by force of will. But as he squirreled away the runs that would add up to another century in the scorebook, there were much darker passions smouldering underneath. How else to explain Sutcliffe's mastery of that most flamboyant of cricket shots, the hook? He would defend dourly for two hours, get a bouncer and hit it out of the park. In fact, he scored more sixes in his career than any other Yorkshire batsman. It was almost as if the hooked six acted as an emotional safety valve from the responsibilities of building an innings.

'In outward appearance, he resembled a respectable business executive with a well-appointed home in a fashionable London suburb,' wrote Ronald Mason in an anniversary tribute in the *Yorkshire CCC Year Book*. 'But when some unwary bowler served him a short one, there was this sudden, blinding unmasking: he leaned outside the line of flight and released the shattering violence of his power-driven hook and there was no more suburban gentility about – only hard Pennine rock and the relentless strength which his native hills and his native people alike embody.' Shades of Heathcliff in *Wuthering Heights*.

Opposition quickies could not bully Sutcliffe, however fast they bowled. His powers of concentration were supplemented by physical courage. He never flinched. He never backed away. He played the game as hard as anyone. Indeed, among the senior professionals on the 1932–33 tour of Australia, he was one of the staunchest supporters of the bodyline tactics deployed by the England captain, Douglas Jardine. There was nothing you could teach Herbert Sutcliffe about playing hardball on the cricket field. It was part of his inheritance.

He did come from Yorkshire.

What *does* make a Yorkshireman a Yorkshireman? Now might be as good a place as any to address a question that runs through this book. Different people would answer the question in slightly different ways. But certain words would inevitably recur. 'Practical.' 'Level-headed.' 'Cautious.' 'Phlegmatic.' 'Hard-working.' 'Laconic.' 'Undemonstrative.' 'Blunt.' 'Down-to-earth.' Roundhead virtues all, though none the worse for that. The Roundheads, lest we forget, won the Civil War. The Cavaliers were too busy looking in the mirror and straightening their ruffs.

'You'll never meet a Tyke who isn't *honest*,' says my friend Andy from Bradford, who has been calling a spade a spade since 1955. 'Harold Wilson?' I murmur, teasing. Andy gives a grudging nod, then comes back strongly. 'Ay, but 'arold were *different*. If he hadna' gone to bluidy Oxford…'

I am reminded of the old joke about Yorkshire, probably dating from the days when Fred Trueman was holding forth in a pub in the Dales and nobody else could get a word in edgeways: 'You can always tell a Yorkshireman, but you can't tell him much.' Wise outsiders avoid getting drawn into arguments with the natives.

To the true-born Yorkshireman, manliness goes with the territory the way roast beef goes with Yorkshire pudding. In his classic 1961 memoir *Weekend in Dinlock*, the American writer Clancy Sigal, summing up his impressions of a Yorkshire mining village, was emphatic about one thing: 'Above all, the Dinlock collier regards himself as A Man, in every single department of his life. The slightest traces of femininity, of softness, of sexual ambiguity, are ruthlessly rooted out, or suppressed… A man is judged by how good a miner he is, how consistent a provider, how fair a mixer, how tough… The miners are cordial but formal with each other, intimate but restrained, frank but never inquisitive, honouring a code of personal conduct as elaborate as that of the medieval knight… But the thing that impresses me, again and again, is the sinewy humour of these men. They are neither grim nor bitter nor angry.'

Others have spoken less affectionately of God's own county. 'Everything in West Yorkshire is slightly unpleasant,' wrote the poet Ted Hughes, who spent the first seven years of his life in the village of Mytholmroyd. 'Nothing ever quite escapes into happiness.' It is a moot point whether traditional Yorkshire strengths outnumber traditional Yorkshire failings. 'We are bad at expressing our pleasant feelings, but

I have noticed that we give tongue to the other kind with great force and frequency,' observed the Bradford-born writer J. B. Priestley, a contemporary of Herbert Sutcliffe, in 1933.

Ranulph Fiennes, the explorer, has had so many bad experiences of whingeing Yorkshiremen that he has more or less barred them from his expeditions: 'People from Yorkshire, we have found, are dour and nurse a grudge. One thing you can't put up with on expeditions are people who search for trouble, then nurse it when they have found it.' Had he been sharing a tent in Antarctica with Ray Illingworth?

Labour politician Roy Hattersley, raised in Sheffield, believes that a Yorkshireman's most distinctive feature is 'his suspicion that the tender virtues are not really virtues at all'. From Catterick to Doncaster, there is an aversion to displaying emotion that can border on the psychotic.

Being from Yorkshire can often be as much a state of mind as a geographical fact – although if you miss the geography, you miss Yorkshire. It is easily the biggest of the English counties and, if its inhabitants sometimes come across as cocky, that simple fact may explain it. Yorkshire is a world within a world, with a siege mentality to go with its sense of self importance. The sort of Yorkshireman who will tell you Geoffrey Boycott's batting average in 1971 (100.12) will also tell you that there are more acres in Yorkshire (3,906,940) than there are letters in the Bible (3,566,840). And you can bet it was a Yorkshireman who did the arithmetic.

For almost all its history, Yorkshire County Cricket Club refused to admit players born outside the county borders – it didn't need 'em. The geography of the county – all those rugged hills and windswept moors, punctuated by drab industrial towns – seems to affect its inhabitants in other ways. If Jane Austen had lived in Yorkshire, she would not have written *Pride and Prejudice*. She would have written *Jane Eyre* or *Wuthering Heights*.

Tough landscapes breed tough inhabitants. Bernard Ingham, Margaret Thatcher's Yorkshire-born press secretary, saw that link clearly: 'They don't come much more angular, taciturn, single-minded, stubborn, opinionated, more gallows-humoured, determined or industrious than true Pennine people.' It is certainly not an environment for softies, or for men who want to wear the latest fashions, or for breezy optimists who think that, because the sun is shining at breakfast, the weather is set fair for the day.

Realistic expectations about the future are intrinsic to the Yorkshire ethos. It is not a county where people are encouraged to get their hopes up. They are expected to keep their heads down, work hard and show respect to their neighbours. Big-headedness – unless, of course, it is the big-headedness that insists there is no better county in England – is a cardinal sin in Yorkshire. 'We were never encouraged to think that we were better than anybody else,' remembers gardener Alan Titchmarsh, who was brought up in Ilkley in the 1950s. 'If anything, we were taught that we were just the same. The most important thing in life seemed to be to blend in.'

In some parts of the county, bourgeois respectability is endemic – actor Michael Palin, who grew up in a middle-class part of Sheffield, remembers the family television set being covered by an antimacassar – but you do not have to dig too deep to find the Yorkshire grit beneath the tweeness.

'If I had to sum up what is good about Yorkshire in one word, it would be self-sufficiency,' says broadcaster Michael Parkinson, the son of a miner, born in Barnsley in 1935, when Sutcliffe was in his pomp. 'The mining village where I grew up was a tight, closed community, but people looked after each other. They dealt with grief, poverty, drunkenness, in a pragmatic, supportive way. They didn't look for handouts from the state because they knew they weren't going to get them. They were not cosseted, like the people of today, but they created a safe, secure environment for children to grow up in.'

Yorkshire's reputation for social conservatism, Parkinson says, is a myth. 'Most parts of the county are Labour strongholds. There is a tradition of non-conformism going back hundreds of years. In the mining village in which I grew up, there must have been half a dozen Methodist chapels.' And you can forget the idea that Yorkshire is a male-dominated world, according to Parkinson. 'It's a matriarchal society, no question. The men may talk tough, but a lot of that is quite superficial. I have known strong Yorkshiremen weep at the sound of a brass band. In the home, certainly when I was growing up, it was the women who called the shots. They were more organised. They looked further ahead.

You can take the boy out of Yorkshire, but you cannot take Yorkshire out of the boy. Michael Parkinson moved down south nearly 50 years ago, but there is no mistaking the Yorkshire vowels, the combativeness, the direct way of talking or the earthy common sense – as bracing as a stiff nor'wester howling across the moors.

In the cricket world, one of the best-known of all Yorkshiremen was the England off-spinner Jim Laker, who was brought up in Saltaire, near Bradford, but later moved south and ended up playing for Surrey. When he took 19 for 90 against Australia at Old Trafford in 1956, he did his native county proud, not just with his record haul of wickets, but because of the downbeat way he celebrated his achievement.

If he took 19 wickets in a Test today, he would have to kiss each of his team-mates 19 times, making nearly 200 kisses in all – it makes you wince just thinking about it. As it was, he exhibited no more emotion than a sheep-farmer rounding up his flock in the Yorkshire Dales. After taking his final wicket, Laker threw his pullover over his shoulder, strolled off the field, gave a few interviews, then drove back to London, stopping en route at a pub in Staffordshire, where not a soul recognised him, even though his name was on everyone's lips. When he got home, he was greeted by his Austrian wife – who was puzzled why the phone had not stopped ringing – with the deathless words, 'Jim, did you do something good today?' Not being a man to make a fuss, Laker probably said, no, he just got lucky.

He brought the same qualities to the commentary box when he retired from playing. No histrionics. No extravagant praise. No flamboyant metaphors. Just matter-of-fact observations about the game, delivered in a voice so flat and leeched of emotion that it could have been a Bradford undertaker talking. A fine commentator? Or a boring commentator? Cricket fans could never agree. But there was no doubt which county Laker came from. The qualities that make a Yorkshireman – like the qualities that make a Scotsman or Welshman – are ingrained from birth.

Herbert Sutcliffe's life story is both highly personal, with an undertow of real sadness, and emblematic of the confusions and uncertainties to which men who reached adulthood at the time of the Great War were prey. An era of exceptional self-confidence was followed by an era of exceptional diffidence. It was as if the road map of masculinity had got mislaid in the mud of Flanders. Men were unsure which way to turn. Too many of the emotional cornerstones of their life had been smashed beyond repair.

Very few men of any class were unaffected by the war and its aftermath, although some coped better than others. For the sculptor Henry Moore, a Yorkshire-born contemporary of Sutcliffe who was injured at the Battle of Cambrai and subsequently served as a physical training instructor, the war passed 'in a romantic haze of trying to be a hero'. But Moore was an exceptional case. For most, the sheer scale of the loss of life was mind-numbing.

Ted Hughes' father William was one of only 17 survivors of his battalion in the Lancashire Fusiliers. The rest were slaughtered at Gallipoli. They have passed into military folklore as 'the battalion which won six VCs before breakfast'. But when the subject of the war came up, William Hughes would lapse into silence. Of men who were aged between 20 and 24 in 1914, more than 30 per cent were killed. There had never been a war like it. Even those who had not been at the front were left feeling shell-shocked and disorientated.

The case of Arthur Conan Doyle, doughtiest of Edwardians, the epitome of sturdy British common sense, was not untypical. Doyle's son died of pneumonia in 1918 while convalescing from wounds sustained in the Battle of Somme. Doyle's brother died a year later, also of pneumonia. It was all too much for the creator of Sherlock Holmes, who started dabbling more and more in spiritualism, attended séances and wrote a book insisting that the famous photographs of the Cottingley fairies – a blatant hoax, with hindsight – were genuine.

There is an emotional rawness in the Sherlock Holmes stories of the 1920s that was not there before the war. In *The Three Garridebs*, published in 1924, Watson is shot and wounded, drawing a quite un-Holmes-like reaction from his friend: 'You're not hurt, Watson?

For God's sake, say that you are not hurt?' Poor long-suffering Watson is pathetically grateful: 'It was worth a wound – it was worth many wounds – to know the depth of loyalty and love that lay behind that cold mask.'

The gulf between men's feelings and their ability to articulate them had never been greater. Beneath the calm surface of daily life, horrors were lurking. As county cricket resumed after the war, there were careworn faces in every dressing room. Relief that the fighting was over was accompanied by overwhelming feelings of loss. Happiness lay in the past, not the future. The most sanguine of men were vulnerable to depression – and Herbert Sutcliffe was not naturally sanguine.

How could he be? His life had begun so inauspiciously that, even if he had wanted, he could never have been jolly and carefree as an adult. His father died when he was four, after suffering complications from an injury on the rugby pitch. His consumptive mother followed six years later. The orphaned Herbert and his brothers were raised by their Aunt Harriet in Pudsey, in an austere church-going household, where they slept in an attic above a bake-house. It must have been light years from the sunlit Edwardian childhood of folklore, and it left its mark.

Sutcliffe would later raise his own children in the same spartan way, making them endure long Sunday services in a freezing church before sitting down for lunch in a draughty parlour where there had been no fire all week. 'His word was law,' remembered his son Billy, hinting at a strictness that would seem excessive today. 'He perhaps showed the better side of his personality outside the family.'

If Sutcliffe was unusual in being orphaned so young, he was not unusual in being raised in a strict household. For every kindly Victorian paterfamilias, there was another whose ideas on child-rearing were dismayingly primitive. Large families tended to preclude individual displays of tenderness. Many households were run on quasi-military lines.

One of the most infamous sons of Yorkshire in the 1890s was John Christie, the serial killer, who murdered at least six women in his flat in Rillington Place, London. Born in Halifax in 1899, Christie was one of seven children and had a troubled relationship with his father Ernest, an austere, uncommunicative man who displayed little affection towards his children and would beat them for trivial offences, such a taking a tomato from a plate without asking. Herbert Sutcliffe was not abused in the same way, but he was certainly raised in an environment where children were at no risk of being pampered.

If Sutcliffe learnt from his Aunt Harriet that life was a serious business, he brought a similar earnestness to the cricket field. His opening partnership with Jack Hobbs became the stuff of cricketing legend, but there was never any doubt which was the Roundhead and which the Cavalier. Hobbs had an impishness and lightness of touch which won him friends wherever he went. Sutcliffe seemed dour in comparison: an accumulator of runs, not an artist. It was the same story at Yorkshire, where his opening partner was Percy Holmes, a jaunty, uncomplicated batsman who thought cricket should be played for fun – not a sentiment Sutcliffe could possibly have echoed.

Even after the success he achieved on the cricket field, he never entirely lost his careworn air. He was self-confident, but not in a cheerful way. Little things would throw him into a rage. He was uptight and prickly. Nor did he lose his emotional reserve. Understatement – the clipped monosyllables of the strong, silent man – was the only language he knew.

His dry-as-dust memoir, *For England and Yorkshire*, published in 1935, must be one of the most unrevealing sporting autobiographies ever written. There is no mention of the family tragedies that blighted his childhood: the book opens with him batting for Pudsey St Lawrence as a 14-year-old. And the prose is so ponderous that it hurts to read it. 'It has fallen to my lot to be closely associated with the men who have captained England in Test cricket... and I have seen sufficient to have a fair understanding of the strain the work can put on a man.' The dullness of the pedagogue never lifts.

In some contexts, his sangfroid could be rather touching. When he and Percy Holmes opened the innings for Yorkshire, they would say 'Well, good luck, old man', as they walked to their respective ends. Holmes and Sutcliffe might as well have been Holmes and Watson, their friendship was so exquisitely undemonstrative. There was an absence of histrionics from which the modern glove-punching, badge-kissing batsman could learn. The trouble was that Sutcliffe had no other language to deploy in times of stress. He was the prisoner of his own reticence.

Like many naturally aloof men, he was at his warmest with pets. Pets were easier to talk to – they made fewer demands. Sutcliffe kept pedigree boxer dogs and, in the words of his biographer Alan Hill, 'idolised them with a devotion bordering on fanaticism'. The owner of a fish-and-chip shop near Headingley remembered him ordering haddock and chips for himself and a piece of haddock apiece for his dogs, who were called Master and Son. He spoiled the animals the way he would never have spoiled his children. On one occasion, Master was so indulged at the Scarborough Festival that, after careering around the tea tent, licking the dresses of the women, he ran on to the pitch and urinated on the stumps.

It is a delicious story, because it is so out of character. When not besotted with his dogs, *nobody* took cricket more seriously than Sutcliffe. Sadly, his relations with human beings tended to be more constrained. He was perfectly sociable; he was just reluctant to let his hair down. Some people found him pompous. They hesitated before teasing him because they could not be confident he would take it in the right way. A lot of the anecdotes told about him touch on his awkwardness in communicating with other people.

The cricket writer David Frith recalls talking to Sutcliffe during a one-day county match shortly after he had lost his wife, who had been badly burned in a domestic accident and died soon afterwards: 'We sat in comfort for a long period during the afternoon, and I listened enchanted to a stream of reminiscence, delivered in his soft and carefully enunciated voice. All the while, he was fortifying himself with gin and tonic. Suddenly, as if relating another tale from a Test match of the 1920s, he told me that his wife had just died. His voice wavered and his eyes moistened as he told me of the harrowing accident.'

It is a touching vignette and, in fairness to Sutcliffe, there is nothing particularly surprising or unexpected about the story. He was a man of his times, hard-wired to be stoical in bereavement. With odd exceptions, men of Sutcliffe's generation were no more capable of talking fluently about their feelings than their fathers before them. If anything, they were less capable, particularly if they had fought in the Great War and been witness to the horrors of the trenches. The repressions of the Victorian era had been given a new overlay of gravitas.

There was often a whole world of sadness behind those stiff upper lips. Bearing adversity with fortitude became a substitution for communication. Far too much went unsaid, a point well made by J. B. Priestley: 'If we openly declare what is wrong with us, what is our deepest need, then perhaps the death and despair will by degrees disappear.' The sentiment is noble, but utopian. Deepest needs? Yorkshire cricketers of the inter-war period didn't have deepest needs – certainly none they were prepared to share with their team-mates. They just got on with winning county championships, relentless in their efficiency.

'Antagonism personified,' was how J. M. Kilburn described George Macaulay, one of the senior professionals in the side. Macaulay had a fiery temper, was witheringly sarcastic about fielders who dropped catches off his bowling, and thought nothing of deliberately bowling head-high beamers.

Another of Sutcliffe's contemporaries was the batsman Arthur Mitchell, the *ne plus ultra* of Yorkshire dourness. His nickname was Ticker because of his habit of talking to himself, but his conversations with other people were downbeat and prosaic. 'Gerrup,' he once growled at a slip fielder who had taken a diving catch. 'Tha's making an exhibition of thiself.' Mitchell's son was once asked what his father would have made of cricketers kissing each other at the fall of a wicket. 'He didn't even kiss my mother,' came the reply.

Emmott Robinson, a card-carrying eccentric who played for Yorkshire from 1919 to 1931 before joining the coaching staff, was similarly dour, competitive to a fault and given to interminable post-mortems when his team lost. One of his favourite maxims was 'Never take a risk if you can win without.' Neville Cardus relished Emmott Robinson as the embodiment of his county – 'a grizzled, squat, bandy-legged Yorkshireman with... shrewd eyes, a hatchet face and grey hairs, most of them representing appeals that had gone against him for leg before wicket.'

Not all Yorkshire players of the era were equally grey. As Cardus put it: 'By nature's law of compensation, there are usually one or two rich genial spirits in the Yorkshire XI, to allow cheerfulness occasionally to creep in.' Batsman Maurice Leyland was fabled for his joviality and dry wit. Wicketkeeper Arthur Wood was another colourful extrovert, addicted to rhyming slang. 'Had any France and Spain?' he would ask the groundsman, if the wicket looked damp. When he was called up for his first Test match, against Australia at the Oval in 1938, he was so excited that he got a taxi from Leeds to London. After Len Hutton had scored his record-breaking 364, he came in to bat with the score on 770 for six and joked, 'I was always the man for a crisis.' But such levity was the exception. Whether you were winning or losing, cricket was no laughing matter. And if your private life went pear-shaped, you certainly didn't burden your team-mates with the details.

Herbert Sutcliffe ended his days in a nursing home, lonely, arthritis-ridden and increasingly reliant on gin. He died stroking a dog called Billy, named after his son, a Yorkshire cricketer in his own right, from whom he had become estranged. It was a melancholy end to a life of high achievement from which true happiness was too often absent. Nobody rhapsodised about Sutcliffe's smile the way they rhapsodised about Hirst's. They remembered him for other reasons. If he stood out from his contemporaries at Yorkshire, it was not just because of his qualities as a cricketer – the machine-like accumulation of runs, the imperious centuries – but because of how he conducted himself off the field, particularly in matters of dress and deportment.

In his own quiet way, Sutcliffe was a New Man, before the term had been popularised, someone determined to do things differently, and to *look* different. Compared with George Hirst, he represented a generational shift as surely as Kevin Keegan and his perm represented a generational shift from Bobby Moore and the short-back-and-sides World Cup winners of 1966.

Where Hirst seemed happy in his own skin, unchanging, the still centre of the turning world, Sutcliffe was a man on the move. The adrenalin of ambition ran through his veins. To fulfil his boyhood dream and play cricket for Yorkshire and England was not enough. He could see, just by looking around the Yorkshire dressing room, that the lot of a professional cricketer had as many downsides as upsides: 20 years in work, if one was lucky; pretty meagre earnings; then a wintry old age, cash-strapped, living off memories. Sutcliffe wanted something better, for himself and his family, and set about achieving it with the same quiet determination he brought to his batting.

He was not well-read or well-educated. He had left school at 13 and been apprenticed to a shoe company before getting clerical work at a local textile mill, where he learnt bookkeeping. But the latter skill stood him in good stead throughout his life. He had an excellent head for figures, allied to meticulous working habits. Soon after making the grade for England, for whom he made his debut in 1924, he set up a successful sports shop in Leeds. His cricketing star was in the ascendant – he scored a mountain of runs on his maiden tour to Australia in 1924–25 – and he had the business nous to capitalise on his celebrity. A. A. Thomson called him 'the merchant prince of cricket, a man both polished and powerful'. He accumulated wealth the way he accumulated runs, by thoroughness and hard graft. Colleagues at Yorkshire remember him dealing with his business correspondence in the pavilion when not batting. He would concentrate on his work to the exclusion of all else, then glance up and say 'How are we doing?'

By the mid-1930s, Sutcliffe was in a position to buy Woodlands, a large detached property on the outskirts of Pudsey, with views across the valley. It set him back £2,000, a small fortune at the time, and boasted three bathrooms – riches indeed, when many Yorkshire houses still had an outside lavatory. But he had arrived. He was still a professional cricketer – a player, not a gentleman, in the quaint argot of the game – but he could look the gentlemen in the eye. He was as good a man as they were, and he made sure that they knew it, addressing them by their first names – which George Hirst, brought up to refer to amateurs as Mr So-and-So, would have regarded as a liberty.

He also spoke their language. Where Hirst retained his broad Yorkshire accent, even during his years coaching at Eton, Sutcliffe shed his as soon as he decently could, with the help of elocution lessons. Neville Cardus, with a hint of a sneer, remembers him speaking 'not with the accents of Yorkshire but of Teddington'. Sutcliffe had not been to a public school, but sounded as if he might have done. He no longer drove down to London, noted one contemporary, but 'motored' down. He even expected his wife to follow his lead, chiding her when she reverted to the broad vowels of her native Pudsey when there were guests present. A simple case of snobbery? Or something more innocent? It certainly underscores the fact that, from boyhood onwards, Sutcliffe was building a professional persona, the way he built an innings, bit by bit.

The contrast with George Hirst and his generation manifested itself in other ways. Male fashion was undergoing a revolution; men were taking liberties that would have been unthinkable before the Great War. In 1928, the 17-year-old Thomas Stevens – later to achieve immortality as Terry-Thomas, playing the archetypal English bounder in a string of much-loved movies – turned up for his first day of work as a clerk at Smithfield Market sporting an olive-green pork pie hat, a taupe double-breasted suit decorated with a clove carnation, a multi-coloured tie and yellow gloves, holding a cigarette-holder in one hand and a silver-topped cane in the other.

The following year, the Men's Dress Reform Party was formed, with the objective of campaigning against the retention of stiff collars, starched shirts, clunking leather shoes and other Victorian encumbrances. The campaign – spearheaded by a Yorkshireman, William Inge, Dean of St Paul's, who predicted that one day 'everyone would simply wear a tunic over which a cloak could be thrown in warm weather' – made slow but steady progress. The wearing of hats, once all but obligatory, declined sharply in the 1930s. Looser shirts became the norm. And if the revolution never quite achieved the far-reaching goals its founders had set, Sutcliffe, for one, was in the vanguard of change.

George Hirst always dressed extremely neatly, like most Yorkshire-men, but he was not a dandy; he just faded into the background. Sutcliffe set his sartorial sights higher. His fluttering silk shirts – made from consignments of silk from Thailand that he ordered specially for his sports shop in Leeds – were one of the wonders of the sporting age. His flannels were immaculate. His buckskin boots gleamed in the sun.

He could have been a fashion model. Throw in a head of shiny black hair, meticulously parted, and you had the complete package. To his less talented contemporaries, it seemed unfair that someone should score quite so many runs while looking quite so dashing. But Sutcliffe didn't mind being complimented on his looks, particularly by women. In fact, he actively cultivated his looks. Go through back numbers of *Wisden* and you will probably find that he spent 43.21 minutes a day in front of a mirror, compared with 0.3 minutes for W. G. Grace and 57.82 minutes for Kevin Pietersen.

Yorkshiremen were still wary of putting on airs in public, but behind the scenes, it was another matter. In Winifred Holtby's 1935 classic *South Riding*, adapted for television in 2011, a well-heeled Yorkshireman of the Sutcliffe type washes his hands before tea, giving a simple-seeming task the solemnity of a religious ritual: 'He removed his coat and hung it on a special padded hanger. He slid the links through the cuffs of his delicate lavender grey poplin shirt and rolled up his sleeves, baring his slender blue-veined forearms. He turned a hot and a cold tap and watched the rising steam bedew his stainless fittings. The water was artificially softened. It gushed out into the pale green porcelain basin. The soap was of a deeper green, with a faint herbal fragrance... He regarded his fine toothbrushes, his loofahs, shaving tackle, disinfectants and mouthwashes. Everything was in order – neat, expensive, the thoughtfully designed equipment of a man of sensitive taste.'

Sutcliffe's physical vanity did not go unnoticed. Arthur Wood, the mischievous Yorkshire wicketkeeper, nicknamed Sutcliffe 'Beautiful Herbert'. He simply could not fathom how a mere cricketer could take his appearance so seriously. Sutcliffe was once fielding at first slip and, as the ball flew between them, Wood dived to his right and deflected it on to Sutcliffe's face, knocking out his two front teeth. 'I could never understand why he was so bloody mad about it,' Wood said later. 'After all, I did apologise.' To Wood and his unsophisticated ilk, a cricketer with 80 per cent of his teeth was ahead of the game.

Off the field – like Walter Hammond, his England contemporary, with whom he had a lot in common – Sutcliffe wore Savile Row suits, which would once have been unthinkable for a professional cricketer. The suits, like his accent, confirmed his social standing. They also established him as something of a heart-throb, a matinée idol who happened to play cricket for a living. One young woman of the period, completely uninterested in cricket, admitted to having fantasies about dancing the Charleston with the famous Herbert Sutcliffe.

There was no question of him growing a moustache, however, or even attempting to. It is easier to imagine Brian Close in a tutu than the debonair Sutcliffe with fungus on his upper lip. Fashions were changing, and changing fast. In the photograph of the Yorkshire team that played The Rest of England at the Oval in 1919, George Hirst is one of the few players still sporting a 'tache, and even that is a shadow of its Edwardian self. Most of the others, Sutcliffe included, are smooth-faced. It is almost as if men no longer had to prove their manliness by sprouting facial hair. The age of Rudolph Valentino had arrived.

Rudolph Valentino probably seems like an interloper in a cricket book, like those fake umpires who once gatecrashed a Test at Headingley. But of all Herbert Sutcliffe's contemporaries, none, arguably, did more to challenge and re-define prevailing notions of manliness than the Italian-born actor, who became one of the biggest, most charismatic, stars of the silent cinema.

Valentino was born six months after Sutcliffe, in May 1895, and died in August 1926, at the zenith of Sutcliffe's career. England were chasing their first Ashes series victory against Australia since before the Great War and, on the morning of 17 August, as Hobbs and Sutcliffe resumed their opening partnership on a rain-affected pitch at the Oval, the cricketing nation held its breath. Both men went on to score centuries, with Sutcliffe registering a monumental 161, a super-human feat of skill and concentration in testing conditions. The Ashes had been regained, with a Yorkshireman taking centre stage.

Sutcliffe's performance would have gone largely unnoticed in New York, but events taking place in the same week in New York did not go unnoticed in England. The movies had made the Latin Lover, as Valentino was nicknamed, a world-famous celebrity, with an army of adoring female fans that ran into millions. When he was admitted to the Polyclinic Hospital in Manhattan on 15 August, his condition did not seem life-threatening: the diagnosis was acute appendicitis and gastric ulcers. But as complications set in, with Valentino finally passing away on 23 August, mass hysteria swept the city.

Windows were smashed at the funeral home where his body was laid out. Despondent fans were reported to have committed suicide. On the day of his funeral, 100,000 people lined the streets. His body was then taken across the States by train for a second funeral in Beverly Hills. It was quite an exit, as over-the-top as the man himself. In the media, and on Capitol Hill, the tear-stained scenes provoked much pious tut-tutting: they just seemed so un-American. Thousands of miles away, the Vatican took fright at the excesses that followed Valentino's death, issuing a statement condemning the 'collective madness, incarnating the tragic comedy of a new fetishism'.

Nobody in strait-laced Yorkshire, one can be confident, would have thought the death of a mere movie star a suitable occasion for suicide. But they had certainly heard of Rudolph Valentino: he had become a global phenomenon. In Pudsey, where Herbert Sutcliffe lived, there were already two cinemas up and running as early as 1920, nearly ten years before the coming of the talkies.

West Yorkshire had played a prominent role in the early years of film. By the turn of the 20th century, Bamforth & Co., a film company founded by portrait photographer James Bamforth from Holmfirth, was churning out so many films that the region briefly produced more movies than Hollywood, mainly feather-light comedies with a wholesome message. In 1915 alone, there were more than 70 Bamforth films, including *Always Tell Your Husband*, *No Fool Like an Old Fool* and *Troubles of a Hypochondriac*. They must have offered welcome relief from the grim news from the front. But the technical quality of the films, shot on a shoestring, was inevitably poor.

In the long term, there was no stopping the Hollywood invasion. By the 1920s, Pudsey cinema-goers were no longer watching Yorkshire-made films, but ones starring Charlie Chaplin, Douglas Fairbanks and That Man, Rudolph Valentino. Chaplin played the clown, the loser, the perpetual underdog; a fine actor, but not exactly a poster boy for shaggy moustaches. You laughed at Charlie, but you didn't want to *be* Charlie. But it was the contrast between Fairbanks and Valentino, polar opposites in almost every way, that got people talking. There was no longer a single template for manliness, but two different templates, mutually exclusive. You could be a Fairbanks or a Valentino. You could not be both. The new medium of cinema had posed men a fresh conundrum.

The pencil-moustachioed Fairbanks, swashbuckling hero of movies like *The Thief of Baghdad*, *Robin Hood* and *The Mask of Zorro*, projected the same kind of uncomplicated virility as Clark Gable and Errol Flynn would do in the 1930s. As he was not required to talk, he let his body do the talking. He was the sort of actor who looked good in tights and did his own stunts. He was naturally athletic. In *The Three Musketeers*, he did a one-handed handspring to catch a sword that had audiences gasping in admiration.

Valentino, soft-skinned, full-lipped, almost feminine in appearance apart from his trim sideburns, offered something quite new, something which conservative-minded men, on both sides of the Atlantic, found hard to comprehend. All right, he was handsome, in a Mediterranean sort of way. But manly? No way, José. In fact, he probably batted for the other side, with those poncey clothes. So why, oh why, were so many women swooning over him?

Because 'he makes the love-making of the average husband or sweetheart look tame, flat and unimpassioned,' explained one American housewife, interviewed in 1922. *Not* what you wanted to hear if you were Mr Typical American from Des Moines, Iowa, with a 46-inch waist and a bald patch. This pomaded upstart from Italy was dangerous.

On screen, Valentino wooed women with an ardour that matched their fantasies. He looked them deep in the eyes. He kissed them as if he meant it, hard on the lips. He was a beautiful, loose-limbed dancer. The famous tango scene in *The Four Horsemen of the Apocalypse* would have seduced a nun. He held all the cards – in an age when most men did not know what the cards were.

Like movie stars who followed, Valentino trod the primrose path of celebrity, albeit with mixed emotions. In 1923, in a foretaste of future obsessions, *Prospect* magazine published a series by him entitled 'How You Can Keep Fit'. There was a string of ghosted memoirs. But he was also embarrassed by the attention he received. 'Women aren't in love with me, but with the picture of me on the screen,' he once complained. 'I am merely the canvas on which women paint their dreams.' But wittingly or unwittingly, he had unleashed forces which shook the accepted order of things. He had become a talking point.

Was he the real deal, sexually, or a phoney? Heavyweight boxing champion Jack Dempsey, who worked with Valentino, reckoned him 'the most virile and masculine of men'. But it was not masculinity as it had previously been conceived: it reeked of the boudoir, not the smoking room. To the Victorians, it had been axiomatic that what made a man attractive to a woman was the fact he was fundamentally different from her. But suppose that was not what women really wanted? Suppose their deepest need was for a man who understood them, and could relate to them, not one who kept aloof from all things feminine? 'It is fatal to be a man or woman pure and simple,' wrote Virginia Woolf in *A Room of One's Own*, one of the seminal feminist texts of the 1920s. 'One must be a woman manly or man womanly.'

As Valentino fever spread, and movies like *The Sheikh* became box-office sensations, men increasingly hedged their bets in the Fairbanks-or-Valentino debate. They were right about one thing. Valentino almost certainly did bat for the other side. There is evidence of male lovers, as well as two wives. He seems to have been a textbook bisexual, although the term was not yet in vogue. But they were quite happy to imitate aspects of his appearance. If women wanted Latin smooth, why not give them Latin smooth? It was worth the cost of a razor to get a woman into bed.

Slicked-back hair, unthinkable before Valentino, became fashionable across the world. A new word was coined for the men who adopted the look – 'Vaselinos'. They never formed a majority, but there were enough of them to enjoy safety in numbers. The look even reached Yorkshire, where Herbert Sutcliffe's sleek coiffure was more Valentino than Fairbanks. 'Herbert was immaculate,' remembers one contemporary. 'There was a polish about him. His hair was lavishly brilliantined.'

There was never any suggestion of bisexuality in his case. But he was surely one of the first Yorkshire players to use a deodorant – radical stuff in the 1920s. He also sprinkled eau-de-cologne on his flannels, which was not so much radical as reckless – the fashion equivalent of a batsman dancing down the pitch with his eyes shut and trying to hit a leg-break over midwicket.

Sutcliffe may not have consciously modelled himself on Valentino, but he reflected social changes which the movie star had helped bring about. And he in turn influenced others. One Yorkshire supporter who idolised Herbert Sutcliffe as a boy remembers plastering his hair down before going out into the back garden to practise Sutcliffe-style cover drives. Post-Valentino, there were suddenly new options for men, new forks in the road, new decisions to make.

Today, the metrosexual man has become such a familiar figure that one forgets quite how revolutionary a figure Valentino was. Just as the French tennis player Suzanne Lenglen caused a sensation at Wimbledon in the 1920s, wearing dresses that exposed far more flesh than had previously been thought acceptable, Valentino planted a stick of dynamite under polite society in the United States. Right to the end he was ruffling feathers, challenging long-held assumptions about how men should conduct themselves. On 18 July 1926, in an episode that encapsulated his career, an editorial in the *Chicago Tribune* deplored the placing of a pink powder machine in a men's washroom on Chicago's North Side. Blame for this 'degeneration into effeminacy' was laid squarely at the feet of Valentino, who was in town promoting a new film. The actor, outraged, challenged the writer of the editorial to a boxing match – a fight one would have paid a king's ransom to see. But, alas, the gauntlet was not taken up. A month later, Valentino was dead.

Herbert Sutcliffe may not have made as many women swoon as Rudolph Valentino, but he was no slouch in that department. He married Emmie, a Pudsey Grammar School girl, in his mid-twenties, but retained a keen eye for the ladies all his life. There is no firm evidence of philandering: just an unabashed enthusiasm for female company, stretching into old age. Even in his eighties, wheelchair-bound, Sutcliffe was flirting so energetically with female patients at his nursing home that the staff were horrified.

He seems to have taken a particular fancy to Australian women. 'Never get married until you've been to Australia,' he told his son. 'You'll find the women there are absolutely magnificent.' On his own first tour of Australia, in 1924–25, he was already a married man, so he must have suffered pangs of regret, not to mention moments of temptation. Did he succumb? We can only speculate. On one tour of Australia, the England wicketkeeper Les Ames came across Sutcliffe having dinner in the team hotel with two attractive young women. When Ames was introduced to the women, he could not help blurting out, 'Where there is a pretty lady, you will find Herbert' – a remark which later earned him a ticking off from his team-mate. Ames might have been tactless, but he was only articulating what many felt.

In general, Sutcliffe's dealings with women seem to have been marked by exaggerated gallantry, not sexual innuendo. He was a holder-open of doors, a payer of compliments, not a pincher of bottoms. One of his female correspondents, Australian again, remembers getting a letter from the cricketer in which he apologised for some small oversight. 'It surely must have been your vivaciousness which was responsible for my brain not functioning properly.' The sentence could have come straight out of a Jane Austen novel. In its old-fashioned way, it is rather charming. Most women would rather get a compliment like that than a text message from Shane Warne congratulating them on their awesome breasts and asking for their room number. But it also has a clumsiness that is symptomatic both of Sutcliffe and the times he lived in.

Feminism, a sideshow before the Great War, made huge and lasting gains in the years that followed. Women were not just granted the vote for the first time, achieving full equality at the ballot box in 1928, but were placed on the same footing as men when it came to marriage. In Edwardian England, thanks to antediluvian laws, a man could divorce a woman on grounds of adultery, but not the other way round. That anomaly was removed in the Matrimonial Causes Act of 1923, which also placed restrictions on the access that divorced men could have to their children.

The foundation stones of modern divorce may have been laid, but the fact that it was easier to extricate oneself from a bad marriage did not make it any easier to contract a good marriage. Indeed, the more independent and assertive women became, the harder some men found it to form strong relations with them. Proposing marriage – which, in Victorian England, would have involved a man-to-man discussion with the father of the bride, mainly about money – was suddenly a major stumbling block, particularly for those uncomplicated types whose lifestyles meant they had limited dealings with women. For many, it was easier to charge German lines than to open one's heart to a member of the opposite sex. In John Buchan's *Mr Standfast*, published in 1919, Richard Hannay, the quintessence of English phlegm and fortitude, dithers for six whole months before declaring his love for Mary. 'You can't live my kind of life, for 40 years, wholly among men, and be any good at pretty speeches to women.'

His predicament was all too common. The tongue-tied bachelor, terrified of women, became a stock comic character in the 1920s and 1930s, reaching his apotheosis in the pathologically drippy Gussie Fink-Nottle in the novels of P. G. Wodehouse. Poor timid Gussie, happiest in the company of his newts, only summons the nerve to propose to Madeleine Basset after Bertie Wooster has spiked his orange juice.

Men and women might have been equal under the law, but they do not seem to have been any better at communicating with each other than their Victorian grandparents. In Middle England between the wars, there were so many mixed messages, such reluctance to call a spade a spade, so many unsatisfactory encounters in the bedroom, that D. H. Lawrence was moved to write: 'I am sure no other civilisation, not even the Romans, has showed such a vast proportion of ignominious and degraded nudity, and so much ugly, squalid, dirty sex. Because no other civilisation has driven sex into the underworld and nudity to the W.C.' To the high-minded author of *Women in Love* and *Lady Chatterley's Lover*, both published in the 1920s, sex and marriage were alike sacred: 'The only stable happiness for mankind is that it shall live married in blessed union to woman-kind – intimacy, physical and psychical, between a man and his wife.' The reality was more humdrum. Most couples just muddled through.

If Lawrence's fierce determination to talk frankly about sex made him a man in a million, the liberalisation of the divorce laws at least made it easier for people to acknowledge the reality that the Victorians had tried to brush under the carpet – that marriage, the supposed cornerstone of society, could sometimes be a prison.

One of the most successful plays of the inter-war period was J. B. Priestley's *When We Are Married*. It was first performed in 1938, but set in bourgeois Edwardian Yorkshire, which Priestley remembered with less than affection. As three middle-class couples gather to celebrate their silver wedding anniversaries, they discover, to their horror, that they were not legally married in the first place. While they struggle to come to terms with the fact that they have been living in sin, they are also forced to confront the shortcomings of their marriages. Wives suddenly see their husbands for the stuffy bores they are. A henpecked husband dreams of regaining his freedom. The genie of independence has been let out of the bottle.

While comparatively few marriages ended in the divorce court, there were the first glimmerings of a new social order, in which men and women alike followed their hearts, not their heads, and social attitudes became a mite less rigid. Leading an unconventional lifestyle was no longer social death, and while homosexuality remained a criminal offence, it no longer provoked the sort of horror it had done 30 years earlier. The Yorkshire-born Shakespearean actor Henry Ainley, an older contemporary of Sutcliffe, was married three times, as well as being romantically infatuated with the young Laurence Olivier. Another Yorkshire acting great, Charles Laughton, born in Scarborough in 1899, was married but, according to his wife, homosexual. The lavender marriage became part of the social furniture of the times. Some of the highest in the land sailed close to the wind, certainly by Victorian standards. George, Duke of Kent, younger brother to Edward VIII and George VI, had a string of lovers of both sexes. His intimates ranged from Noel Coward to Barbara Cartland, with whom he had a child.

More and more men, whatever their sexual orientation, did their own thing in their private lives, without giving a damn what other people thought. One of Sutcliffe's most colourful contemporaries was Percy Shaw, the inventor of cat's eyes, who was born in Halifax in 1890. Shaw never married, lived alone and, in later life, became a paid-up eccentric, removing the carpets and most of the furniture from his house and, despite his natural stinginess, keeping three televisions permanently turned on, with the sound turned down. Weird he might have been, but he could always be sure of a warm welcome in his local pub.

With so many social changes afoot, and the country still struggling with the aftermath of the Great War, not to mention the economic hardships of the Depression, it is not surprising that masculinity itself became a moveable feast. I have already looked at Rudolph Valentino and the revolutionary impact he had on men of his generation. But there were plenty of others jostling for attention. Heroes leapt out from every bookshelf, every advertising hoarding, every cinema screen.

Boys' weekly magazines – sometimes known as the 'penny dreadfuls', even though most of them cost tuppence – were at the zenith of their popularity. By the time of the Second World War, noted George Orwell in an essay in *Horizon*, there were ten such titles on the bookshelves of every newsagent: *Magnet, The Gem, Wizard, Rover, Triumph, The Modern Boy, Skipper, Hotspur, Champion* and *Adventure*. It was not quite an embarrassment of riches, more an embarrassment of mediocrity, but it illustrates the growing influence of a popular culture which transcended class and marginalised parents and teachers.

In terms of content, the magazines had changed very little since the turn of the century. Many of them were still set in minor public schools, with their rough-and-ready application of justice and stock comic characters, like the evergreen Billy Bunter. Racial stereotyping was ubiquitous. If a Chinaman appeared, it was a racing certainty that he would be pig-tailed and untrustworthy. A Frenchman would gesticulate and wear a beard. A Swede would be kindly but stupid. A black man would be loyal, but in a lumbering, clumsy way.

Orwell – educated at Eton, just before George Hirst became cricket coach – could discern only two major developments in the stories that appeared in the magazines during the 1920s and 1930s, compared with their Victorian precursors. One was the increasing prominence of characters who, either physically or intellectually, could be classified as supermen. Whereas the first wave of boys' stories had no main character, but revolved around a group of equals – classmates, say – there was now a fascination with air aces, master spies, boxing champions and the like. It had become manly to excel at something, not just be a loyal member of a group. The other – in part, as a result of trends in America, where boys' magazines had a much more bloodthirsty subtext – was the increase in casual violence, described with relish. ('He volleyed blows with bewildering speed for so huge a fellow.') Little by little, the ideal man was becoming less of a gentleman.

In other respects – to Orwell's obvious disappointment – conservatism ruled. Any change in attitudes was incremental. Fathers raised sons in their own image, with only minor tweaks. The old-world values of George Hirst retained their currency. On the cricket field, they were embodied by Jack Hobbs, Sutcliffe's opening partner for England, one of the most loved of all English sportsmen, modest and dashing in equal measure. Off it, they could be seen in such fictional characters as Beau Geste, the creation of P. C. Wren, and a throwback to the age of chivalry.

Wren's hero, who made his bow in 1924, combined 'the inconsequent romanticism and reckless courage of a youthful d'Artagnan with the staunch tenacity and stubborn determination of a wise old Scotsman'. It is a beguiling recipe, and it struck a chord with readers nostalgic for the moral certainties of the pre-war world.

If Wren traded off the past, others were looking to the future, crafting a new kind of role model for a new generation – characters like Bulldog Drummond, who anticipates James Bond in his harsh brand of virility, solid at the core, but rough around the edges. 'He has the appearance of an English gentleman who fights hard, plays hard and lives clean... His best friends would not have called him good-looking, but he possesses that cheerful type of ugliness which inspires immediate confidence... Only his eyes redeem his face. Deep-set and steady, with eyelashes that many women envy, they show him to be a sportsman and an adventurer, a man who goes outside the law when he feels the end justifies the means.'

The Bulldog Drummond novels, written by Herman McNeile under the pseudonym Sapper, ran from 1920 to 1937, pretty much coterminous with Herbert Sutcliffe's career. Bestsellers in their time, and successfully adapted to the screen, they are largely unreadable today, if only because of the inevitable jingoism and racism, but they catch the flavour of the age. If they had a message for their readers, it was surely that a man could no longer afford to be nice if he wanted to get his way – a sentiment which Douglas Jardine, England's captain on the Bodyline tour, would surely have echoed.

Bodyline – certainly in the systematic way it was used – could never have been dreamed up in the Edwardian era. The tactic would have been seen as ruthless, unsporting, a breach of good cricketing manners. But Jardine was not an Edwardian. He was part of a new generation, with changed priorities. Playing the game was no longer enough: one had to win, whatever the cost. Beau Geste, wedded to the chivalric code of an earlier age, would have been appalled by bodyline. Bulldog Drummond, one can feel equally sure, would have given the tactics a fair wind, just as Herbert Sutcliffe did.

After all, if the interests of the British Empire were threatened – and it did not matter whether it was by a dastardly Russian Jew, bent on world domination, or by an upstart Australian batsman scoring 300 runs in a day at Headingley – the proper course was to stop the bounder, by fair means or foul.

Like Valentino and Fairbanks on the screen, Beau Geste and Bulldog Drummond represented contrasting versions of manliness, one idealised, the other sharper-edged. The characters are so different that it is hard to believe that their creators were contemporaries – just as it is hard to believe that the novels of P. G. Wodehouse belong to the same period as the novels of D. H. Lawrence. But a healthy pluralism was one of the defining features of the age. After the comparative simplicity of the Victorian era, there was suddenly a bewildering variety of influences in play.

One of the most vivid fictional characters of the age was Tarzan – a figure lurking on the boundary edge, not quite at the heart of the action, but too striking to be ignored. He belonged to the world of light entertainment. But he also gently challenged men – and women – to re-evaluate what it meant to be a man. If the Frankenstein movies conjured a dystopian future in which a man could be assembled in a laboratory – rendering all arguments about manliness null and void – Tarzan set the imagination racing in the opposite direction.

The fogies of the day were still clinging on to Victorian formality. 'A sturdy and virile man is perfectly capable of withstanding the rigours of a stiff shirt,' wrote a contributor to a debate on male fashion in June 1932. 'The man who, alone in the jungle, changes into his dinner jacket does so to convince himself he is not a savage. Soft, sloppy clothes are symbolic of a soft and sloppy race.' Now, suddenly, the fogies had to contend with a man in a jungle who not only did not own a dinner jacket, but owned nothing apart from what he had been born with. It was a jolt to the system.

Edgar Rice Burroughs' noble savage first appeared in a novel published before the Great War; was the subject of umpteen sequels and magazine spin-offs; and also featured in several silent movies. But it was the 1932 classic, *Tarzan the Ape Man*, starring Johnny Weissmuller, which cemented the character in the public imagination. 'There is hardly an American male of my generation who has not at one time or another tried to master the victory cry of the great ape as it issued from the chest of Johnny Weissmuller,' wrote Gore Vidal, who watched the movie as a boy. In Britain, as the England cricket team prepared to sail to Australia on the Bodyline tour, cinema audiences across the country flocked to see the film, riveted by this compound of man and ape, with his rippling muscles, natty loincloth and trademark yodel.

Was he sub-human or superhuman? The answer, intriguingly, seemed to be both. Few fictional characters in any genre have pressed quite so many buttons at the same time. To men, still dressed in the constricting clothes of the period, Tarzan offered a vision of back-to-nature simplicity, a utopian ideal that stretched back to the Garden of Eden. To women, he represented kindness without complications: the kind of man who would protect them from a lion or snake, but not expect them to make fancy conversation before mating. He just got on with things, as men were meant to, swinging cheerfully from creeper to creeper.

Tarzan was hardly a sex symbol to rival Rudolph Valentino, even if you liked Johnny Weissmuller's bulging pecs. In his screen incarnation, the character was far coarser than the noble aristocrat of Burroughs' novels. He talked in pidgin English, whereas the original Tarzan had spoken a range of European languages fluently. His chat-up lines – even if he never actually uttered the line 'Me Tarzan, you Jane' – were rudimentary. But, subliminally, he challenged some of the conventional wisdom of the time. Post-Darwin, it had seemed as if science might carry all before it. Man was master of his destiny, to an extent he had never been before. Diseases were being eradicated. Mass industries were supplanting agriculture. Nature had been tamed. But suppose things were not quite that simple? Suppose the sophistication to which the modern metropolitan man aspired was just a veneer?

An upwardly mobile professional like Herbert Sutcliffe might take elocution lessons, dress immaculately, live in a fine house, drive a flash car, enjoy the respect of his peers, earn pots of money, have women eating out of his hand. But, at the end of the day, was he any more than a glorified ape?

The more society tried to constrain and civilise people, the more people dreamed of escape. The seven-year-old Ted Hughes, bored out of his skull during services at the Methodist Zion Chapel in Mytholmroyd, used to imagine himself as a wolf running wild in the woods. He and his brother Gerald, ten years his senior, spent a large part of their childhood camping out, fishing and shooting and trapping animals.

Just a few miles from Woodlands, Sutcliffe's grand house in Pudsey, a young man called Burt Haley was also taking a leaf out of Tarzan's book. Devastated by the scale of the losses during the Great War, from which so many of the men from his village had not returned, then embittered by life on the dole, Haley spent seven years, from 1927 to 1934, living in a tent in a wooded valley near Shelf. He had been a Boy Scout before the war, and Baden-Powell would have admired his resourcefulness, surviving in the wild, living off leaves, berries and animals he had trapped. But he would have been horrified by the fact that, on hot days in summer, Haley went around stark naked.

At one point, he was challenged about his lifestyle by the village policeman:

'What's th'idea of camping in a wood… like that… by thisen…
What's the game?'
'It's no game at all. I love it.'
'Well, tha must be daft.'

Daft or not daft, Haley, like Tarzan, offered a vivid alternative to the bourgeois conventions of the time. A kindly local vicar, ex-Cambridge, came to visit Hale and suggested that, if he came to church decently attired – the vicar proposed a cricket shirt – he might find the answers to the questions that were troubling him. Thank you, but no thank you, said Hale. He had found the answers he was seeking in the woods.

Burt Hale was hardly a typical man of his generation. In time, he would emerge from the woods, get a job, meet a nice girl, marry, settle down and live happily ever after. But the sense of confusion he experienced was widely shared. As war loomed in Europe, the most self-assured of men was prey to nagging doubts.

CHAPTER 3
HEDLEY VERITY:
A VERY ENGLISH WAR HERO

In peace there's nothing so becomes a man
As modest stillness and humility;
But when the blast of war blows in our ears,
Then imitate the action of the tiger,
Stiffen the sinews, summon up the blood;
Disguise fair nature with hard-favor'd rage.

Shakespeare, *Henry V*

At the military war cemetery in Caserta, Italy, 16 miles from Naples, a simple gravestone marks the last resting place of Captain H. Verity of the Green Howards. Date of death: 31 July 1943. An inscription at the bottom of the stone commemorates 'a gentle man of action, not forgotten'.

The grave is immaculately maintained by the Commonwealth War Graves Commission, but there is nothing to mark it apart from the hundreds of other graves on the site. It is a touchingly ordinary memorial to an extraordinary man: modest, unassuming, incapable of arrogance, but a giant of his sport.

The strong silent man enjoys a special place in British life, and Hedley Verity fitted the description like a glove. He was quite shy, but was lucky enough to live in a country where shyness, provided it is not a euphemism for weakness, is no barrier to being admired. A shy man with the strength to persevere – think of the success of *The King's Speech*, which had cinema audiences bursting into applause by pressing those buttons so skilfully – can achieve heroic stature.

Men of a certain age still have fond memories of Wilson of *The Wizard*, a cartoon-strip character in the Roy of the Rovers mould who made his debut in July 1943, just a few days before Verity died. The two men had much in common. Wilson, born in the fictional Yorkshire village of Stayling, not only performed extraordinary sporting feats, such as running the three-minute mile, but in personality was 'an unassuming, totally dedicated loner who wanted no glory or publicity'. It could be a word-for-word description of Verity, who was as modest as he was determined. 'His character and disposition never changed amid all his triumphs,' remembered one of his captains. 'He just remained Hedley Verity.' Even his surname is redolent of the homespun honesty he encapsulated.

He used to appeal so quietly, according to an Australian opponent, that often only the umpire and the batsman at the non-striking end could hear him. His 'polite inquiries' were part and parcel of the man – unimaginable today, but oddly endearing, like something out of an Ealing comedy. Anyone who doubts that the past really is a foreign country could do worse than ponder those whispered, almost timid, appeals.

No batsman who faced Verity in his pomp forgot the experience. He was a left-arm spinner, as accurate as Rhodes, but faster. In recent times, the closest equivalent would be Derek Underwood. His career statistics – nearly 2,000 career wickets at an average of less than 15 – speak for themselves. It was supposed to be a golden age for batsmen. The likes of Bradman and Hammond would arrive at the crease with the air of bankers checking into a country house hotel for the weekend. But Verity did his best to make their stay uncomfortable. Even when the wicket was giving him no assistance, he was master of his craft, wearing down batsmen with his accuracy. On turning pitches, he was unplayable, scything through teams like a force of nature.

He was not a flashy player, whether he was batting, bowling or fielding. He just set calmly about his business, doing what he was paid to do, plying the trade he had taken years to master. He did not empty bars when he came on to bowl, or turn eyes in the street outside the ground. There was nothing striking in his appearance. He was fit rather than muscular, trim rather than handsome. His ears were too big and his hair started receding while he was in his twenties. If George Hirst was an all-purpose man of action, and Herbert Sutcliffe was a matinée idol in cricket flannels, Hedley Verity was the boy next door, someone you could depend on.

As a man, he sounds as if he was more fun to be with than Sutcliffe. He had a lighter touch. He was less inclined to be pompous. 'Hedley could always see the funny side of things,' remembered Len Hutton, Verity's junior by 11 years. The older man used to tease Hutton about his youthful infatuation with the Hollywood pin-up Joan Crawford. He also played golf with him and gave him driving lessons. He was by all accounts a gentle, considerate man, as well as a devoted husband and father.

Verity was ten years younger than Sutcliffe, although their careers at Yorkshire overlapped. Very different men in some ways, they shared the same almost superhuman concentration on the job in hand. You didn't expect to get Sutcliffe out with a long-hop, any more than you expected Verity to bowl a long-hop. He took his responsibilities seriously, whether in war or peace.

A sea of purple ink has been expended on his remarkable exploits on the cricket field, including bowling figures of ten for ten in an innings in a county match – his spell included a hat-trick and 113 consecutive dot-balls – and 14 wickets in a day in the 1934 Lord's Test against Australia. But nothing in his short life became him like the leaving it, wounded in action during the Allied landings in Sicily. Eyewitnesses, who were a few yards from the cricketer when he was hit, told the story:

> The objective was a ridge with strong points and pillboxes. Behind a creeping barrage Verity led his company forward 700 yards. When the barrage ceased, they went on another 300 yards and neared the ridge, in darkness. As the men advanced, through corn two feet high, tracer bullets swept into them. Then they wriggled through the corn, Verity encouraging them with "Keep going, keep going". The

moon was at their back and the enemy used mortar-fire, lights and firebombs, setting the corn alight. The strongest point appeared to be a farmhouse, to the left of the ridge; so Verity sent one platoon round to take the farmhouse, while the other gave covering fire. The enemy fire increased and, as they crept forward, Verity was hit in the chest. "Keep going," he said, "and get them out of that farmhouse." When it was decided to withdraw, they saw Verity lying on the ground, in front of the burning corn, his head supported by his batman… So, in the last grim game, Verity showed, as he was so sure to do, that rare courage which both calculates and inspires.

Verity's wounds were not at first thought to be life-threatening. Along with other wounded prisoners of war, he was transferred to the Italian mainland and treated in a military hospital under the auspices of the Italian Red Cross. But complications set in after a chest operation and he died a few days later. As news of his death filtered back to England, the tributes were unstinting and heartfelt. They were typified by the eulogy in the *Bradford Telegraph and Argus*: 'Wherever good cricket is appreciated, wherever sportsmanship is accepted as an indication of character, wherever men are honoured not because they are wealthy or gifted, but because they are in the true sense of the word men, here the name of Hedley Verity will be honoured.'

The tone may be florid, but the substance is revealing of the attitudes of the time. A man's highest calling was exactly that – to be a man. In a simple three-letter word, eternal virtues were thought to reside. The word alone was sufficient, just as it had been for Hamlet mourning his dead father: 'He was a man, take him for all in all…' George Hirst, in a letter of condolence to the Verity family, took up the same theme: 'Anyone who came into contact with Hedley had but one thought: he may be a good bowler but he is certainly a fine man. I will cherish his memory as long as I live.' Don Bradman, in a tribute in *Wisden*, was unable to recall Verity uttering 'a word of complaint or criticism'. Considering that they had been opponents during the Bodyline series, the most acrimonious in Ashes history, with tempers fraying in the Australian sun, that spoke volumes.

On the battlefield, by the standards of the time, Hedley Verity did nothing particularly exceptional. There was no question of a posthumous gallantry medal, indeed his actions pale in comparison with the exploits of the three men in his regiment, the Green Howards, who were awarded VCs during the war. Lieutenant Basil Weston led an attack on a heavily defended Japanese position in Burma, fell wounded in the entrance to an enemy bunker, then blew himself up with a hand grenade, taking the occupants of the bunker with him. Lieutenant Colonel Derek Seagrim was killed in action in Tunisia, shortly after carrying out two audacious attacks on enemy machine-gun posts, leading from the front under sustained fire. Warrant Officer Stanley Hollis's heroics during the Normandy landings included capturing a German pillbox in the face of heavy machine-gun fire, then deliberately exposing himself to further fire, so that two of his men could escape to safety.

Captain H. Verity was just doing his duty, in the service of his country, like millions of others, laying his life on the line because that was what was required of him. But that kind of matter-of-fact courage is often more touching than blood-and-guts audacity. It shows the steel in a man who would not otherwise stand out from the crowd. It makes the humdrum sublime.

The British Empire's finest hour, in Churchill's famous phrase, was no historical accident. It was rooted in the human qualities of the generation to which Hedley Verity belonged – and which he came to epitomise.

Compared with Herbert Sutcliffe, orphaned as a boy, Hedley Verity had a stable, happy childhood, in the bosom of a close-knit family where discipline and hard work mattered but where there was also room for laughter and merriment. He was born within a stone's throw of Headingley cricket ground, on 18 May 1905, and grew up in the village of Rawdon, seven miles west of Leeds. He was a bright, inquisitive boy and attended Yeadon and Guiseley Secondary School, later Aireborough Grammar School – a step up the educational ladder from the rudimentary schooling which Hirst and Sutcliffe had enjoyed.

His father, Hedley Verity Sr, was a coal merchant, lay preacher and chairman of the urban district council. He was a kindly man, with a strong work ethic and quiet determination that he bequeathed to his son. 'I have bred a better man than myself,' he used to boast, when that son became the outstanding spin bowler of his generation.

Hedley Jr was close to his sister Grace, who later became a schoolmistress at the Rawdon elementary school, where her charges included the young Brian Close. But the 'real steel of the family', according to one surviving family member, was the cricketer's mother Edith, who stood at five foot nothing, but could be a tigress in defence of her nearest and dearest. Like her husband, she was ambitious for her son and, when he started to show promise as a cricketer, followed his progress with a gimlet eye.

Other cricket mums might content themselves with ironing shirts and making sandwiches. Not Edith. There is a story told about her sitting on the boundary at a village match. When her son came on to bowl, she clapped her hands, summoned one of the fielders, like Queen Victoria giving orders to a footman, and said, 'Tell our Hedley he hasn't got a fielder *there*,' indicating a vacant area on the leg side. If her precious boy dropped a catch or gave away his wicket cheaply, she was the first to give him a tongue-lashing. Not since W. G. Grace's mother Martha, who taught her son the rudiments of the game in an apple orchard in Gloucestershire, had one woman done so much to mould a future England cricketer.

Edith Verity seems to have been quite overpowering and, not surprisingly, her son grew up with an air of diffidence which never totally left him. He was a studious, self-contained child, an introvert rather than an extrovert. When not playing cricket, he could be found marshalling his toy soldiers on the kitchen table or with his nose deep in the children's encyclopaedia that he had badgered his father to buy. The steel of purpose was there, but hidden beneath the surface. He had none of the cockiness of the alpha male. What he did have, in abundance, was the determination to better himself, even if it took time. Above his bed, as he grew up, there was a plaque which might have been his motto: 'They told him it couldn't be done. He made up his mind that it could – and he did it.' In a life strewn with obstacles, from Don Bradman to German machine guns, he had to dig deep into his reserves, again and again.

Very little came easily to him. Even making the grade as a Yorkshire cricketer, for all his natural talents, was a slow, arduous progress. Verity was a left-arm spinner and, if you were a left-arm spinner in Yorkshire in the 1920s, you stubbed your toe against the immovable stumbling block that was Wilfred Rhodes – past 40, but seemingly ageless. The job was taken, and it was 1930 before it would become vacant. After leaving school – where he had been too keen on sport to do himself justice academically – Verity worked for a time at his father's coal depot at Guiseley. There was talk of him getting secretarial and accountancy qualifications. He needed to grow up, get a proper job, settle down – that was the refrain at home. It was only after he had convinced his parents that he was determined to become a professional cricketer, and had the necessary perseverance to achieve his ambition, that they gave him their blessing.

He would be 25, comparatively old, before he made his county debut, and with opportunities at Yorkshire scarce, had to learn his craft across the Pennines in Lancashire league cricket. But evidence of his determination can be found in his fitness regime. He spent long hours skipping in his back garden and, in days when jogging was unheard of and a cricketer training in a gym would have been a laughing stock, took three-mile evening runs which left him physically exhausted.

British men of the period were not fit by today's standards. We look at team photographs of the 1920s, see those whippet-thin bodies and reach the wrong conclusion. Most of them were thin for the wrong reasons. During the First World War, only 36 per cent of those examined for recruitment to the army were graded A1 (fully fit for combat) while 31 per cent were C3 (unfit for combat). Beer, cigarettes and poor diet took their toll. Unless you made a conscious effort, you were a heart attack waiting to happen.

Hedley Verity, looking after his body with scrupulous care, was years ahead of his time. Those solitary runs around the back streets of Rawdon betokened a new kind of manliness, rooted in athleticism, not the *mens sana in corpore sano* mantra of the Muscular Christians. The body was now a machine, not a temple. Verity did practise the virtues of moderation and self-discipline. He was a member of the Band of Hope, a temperance movement that started in Leeds in the mid-19th century and, at its peak, had three million members. But his self-discipline was allied to the kind of hard-training mentality you associate with a boxer, not a vicar.

It was a dour lifestyle, but then times were dour. The Yorkshire in which Verity spent his formative years was a grey, anxious place. People soldiered on, but they had no illusions of living in a time of plenty. The legacy of the war was everywhere. When J. B. Priestley, who had been wounded in the war, returned to his home city of Bradford in 1933, he found it much changed, mainly for the worse. The people were much as before: 'They stand on their own feet, do their jobs with a will, stoutly resist stupid opposition but give way to affection… and are grand lumps of character.' But the tribe of which they were part was hidebound, frozen in time, run by whiskery churchgoing elders who thought nothing had changed since Victoria was Queen.

'Young people no longer want the good old-fashioned English Sunday,' Priestley wrote, 'any more than they want the good old-fashioned English side-whiskers, thick underclothing or heavy meals.' And it was young men who were the big losers. 'They are far more subdued, far less enterprising and ambitious than the girls, who seem to have mysteriously acquired all the dash and virility.'

The men who had returned from the front were simultaneously proud of what they had achieved and uncertain what to do next. 'How queer it was,' reflects Priestley, surveying the faces at a regimental reunion, 'that these chaps from Bradford and Halifax and Keighley, warehousemen and wool-sorters, clerks and tram-conductors, should have gone out and helped destroy the power of the Hapsburgs, closing a gigantic chapter in European history.' But peace, Priestley reckoned, had emasculated them. 'They have found their manhood stunted, their generous instincts baffled, their double instinct for leadership and loyalty completely checked.' Instead of standing tall, they shrank from view and kept their heads down. They became strangers in their own communities.

A middle-aged Bradford woman gives Priestley an earful on the subject: 'Where are the *men*? Yes, I know there was a war – but even that doesn't explain it… What do they *do* with themselves? They don't go to the pubs every night, as they used to. It's not that. It isn't even the pictures, because they're mostly women there too. Do they just sit at home and play with the wireless, or what? I tell you, it's a mystery to me, and nobody I know can explain it.'

Hedley Verity, introspective rather than outgoing, a loner by temperament and inclination, was one of the 'missing men' the woman was talking about. He had not fought in the First World War, but shared the diffidence of those who had. The rough working men's clubs and pubs of the West Riding held no appeal for him. He preferred jogging on his own, his head filled with dreams.

At least he was purposeful in his introspection. He knew what he wanted to do with his life. Professional cricket offered an avenue for advancement that would not have been there 100 years before. One can almost hear Verity giving himself pep talks as he pounded the streets, waiting for Rhodes to retire, so he could take his place. 'Wilfred'll be 'ard act t'follow, but t'bugger is nigh on 50, 'e can't go on for ever…'

If he was a late developer as a cricketer, he made up for lost time when his chance came. Within a year of his Yorkshire debut in 1930, he had won his first cap for England, in a Test against New Zealand. The following year, he was one of *Wisden*'s five Cricketers of the Year, along with his great friend Bill Bowes, the bespectacled fast bowler. In Yorkshire folklore, the names of Verity and Bowes, skittling sides in tandem, are as securely linked as those of Hirst and Rhodes, the master all-rounders, and Holmes and Sutcliffe, the all-conquering opening batsmen.

Bowes became a cricket writer after he retired and, in his autobiography *Express Deliveries*, eloquently captures the undemonstrative human qualities which Verity brought to the cricket field: 'He never altered his expression, or his attitude to life and cricket, from the first ball he bowled to the last. He tackled every job studiously and quietly. If you saw nothing but his poker face, it would be impossible to tell whether his ball had been knocked for six or had spreadeagled the stumps.' Another Yorkshire great, Len Hutton, remembered him for similar reasons: 'He always impressed me as a man. If you dropped a catch off him, he just smiled. I never saw him agitated at a turn of events in a game.'

One of the few occasions when Verity did lose his cool was in a match at the Oval, when Surrey, having passed 500 on a shirt-top wicket, delayed their declaration until after lunch on the second day. Verity was so disgusted that he resorted to leg theory, with every single fielder on the leg side, then bowled two balls underarm, before being ticked off by his captain. But even this rare lapse from good sporting manners shows the character of the man. He took his cricket very, very seriously.

In his efficiency, which simultaneously awed and chilled, Verity had a lot in common with Herbert Sutcliffe. The name of the game was not being more brilliant than the opposition, but making fewer mistakes. If he could not overpower batsmen with his spin, he would bore them out with his accuracy and meticulous field placings. He regarded bowling as a science of which he was a perpetual student – 'the ever-learning professor', as R. C. Robertson-Glasgow put it in his obituary of Verity in *Wisden*.

Sutcliffe's ambitions extended beyond the cricket field. He channelled a lot of his energies into his sportswear business. He enjoyed the social trappings which his wealth brought. Verity had no such ancillary goals. He just wanted to be a cricketing professional, in the fullest sense. In the Golden Age of cricket, when George Hirst was in his prime, the game was still largely played for fun. Hirst and other county professionals made a living out of cricket, and counted themselves lucky to do so, but they did not spend long hours analysing the nuts and bolts of the game. In Verity, one can glimpse a new type of cricketer, and perhaps also a new type of man: identifying an area of potential expertise, then refining that expertise with single-minded intensity, as if it were one's whole purpose in life. Being a man was now as much about learning as doing.

Verity certainly played for the right county. Fifty years before sporting academies became fashionable, Yorkshire County Cricket Club was a university of cricket, with battle-hardened senior players schooling their younger team-mates in the rudiments of their craft. Verity's early mentors included the recently retired Rhodes, fount of all wisdom when it came to left-arm spin, and Emmott Robinson, sage and perfectionist. Bill Bowes remembers county matches in the early 1930s at which he and Verity were collared after play by Rhodes and Robinson and given a debriefing in a hotel bedroom: 'A shaving stick, toothbrush, hairbrush and the contents of a dressing-case would be pushed around the eiderdown to represent the fieldsmen, as our mistakes of the day were discussed in detail. They were hard and demanding taskmasters, but they were always right. How could any young man, coming into such an atmosphere, get a swollen head?'

It is a slightly potty scene, like an episode of *Dad's Army*, but it captures the intense flavour of Yorkshire in its championship-winning heyday, when a team game was raised to the level of an art form, with hours of thought given to how each player might best contribute, so that the whole would be greater than the sum of the parts. Verity might have been a virtuoso spin bowler, but he subordinated his own efforts to those of his team. 'Remember you are representing Yorkshire, not just yourself,' Sutcliffe used to tell younger team-mates. Verity followed the advice to the letter. In 1931, when he took ten wickets in an innings against Warwickshire – a feat which had eluded Rhodes – he almost did himself out of the record by diving to try to take a catch off another bowler and gashing his arm.

If Verity was a consummate team man, it is his individual skill people remember: the little variations on a theme that would lure a batsman to his destruction. Cricket is such a technical game that some of its most successful exponents – Geoffrey Boycott, to name but one – have had a touch of the mad scientist in their make-up. But no modern Test batsman, studying his dismissals again and again on his laptop, embraced the science of cricket as earnestly as Hedley Verity. The boy who had played with toy soldiers on the kitchen table brought the same intensity of purpose to his adult calling. Every fielder had to be placed just right. To concede cheap runs was a crime. Cricket was not show business, but a war of attrition.

Verity's uncompromising attitude perhaps explains why, along with Sutcliffe, he was one of Jardine's most loyal lieutenants on the Bodyline tour. At a human level, the mild-mannered Verity was not totally happy with bodyline tactics and the rancour they aroused, with Australian fans baying their disapproval. But, as a young bowler making his first overseas tour, he was only too delighted to find himself serving under a tough, determined captain who took the science of cricket – where you placed your fielders, down to the last square foot of turf – as seriously as he did.

Jardine played for Surrey, the apotheosis of southern languor, but once said that one of his regrets in life was that he had not been born in Yorkshire. Hard-as-nails Tyke cricket fans understood Jardine perfectly – they gave him a standing ovation in Sheffield in 1933, on one of his first public appearances after the Bodyline tour.

Jardine certainly found a soulmate in Verity. On the boat trip out, he briefed him privately in his cabin, explaining the containing tactics which he would have to deploy on the flat wickets of Australia, drying up the runs at one end while Larwood and the other fast bowlers rested. History doesn't relate whether hairbrushes were shuffled around on an eiderdown, but they probably were. Verity followed the tactics scrupulously and, while his bowling figures for the series were unremarkable, they were a vital ingredient in a famous victory. Jardine was vocal in his appreciation, calling him 'the oldest head on young shoulders playing in England today' and praising 'the Yorkshire grit which impelled Verity always to give of his best'. The bowler reciprocated by calling his second son Douglas. It was an unlikely alliance – the two men could hardly have been more different in background and personality – but it had borne fruit.

Verity kept a journal during the Bodyline tour and, if it is bland in content, it is written with a literary polish rarely found in the jottings of professional sportsmen. Here he is enduring a rough boat journey from Hobart to Launceston: 'A freshening breeze and squalls of rain at about 3 pm, as we went down the river, gave promise of a rough night… We pitched and rolled; shipped seas over the front; and spray continually swept the boat deck and went right over the top of the funnels… Down below all night: pitch and toss; groans from every timber and plate; a sudden jerk and splash; followed by rumbles overhead as we hit and shipped a heavy sea, which went the length of the deck…'

It is not *Moby Dick*, but there is an economy of language and vivid use of detail that are reminiscent of Robert Louis Stevenson. The journal certainly puts the Twitter generation to shame. It reveals an intelligent, thoughtful young man, eager to learn and fascinated by the new worlds he was discovering.

On the field, Verity's finest hour came with the bat. The hero of the fourth Test at Brisbane – which England won to retain the Ashes – was little Eddie Paynter from Lancashire who checked himself out of the hospital where he was languishing with tonsillitis, took a taxi to the ground in his pyjamas and played a match-winning innings of 83. But Paynter's bravado would not have been possible without staunch support from Verity. He only scored 23 but, defending with Boycott-like immovability, batted for two-and-a-half hours in enervating heat. 'I think I can claim to have been on top of the bowlers and mastered everything they attempted,' he wrote in his journal. It was the closest he ever came to boasting.

A year later, again under Jardine's captaincy, Verity toured India, where he became bosom friends with the young Gloucestershire batsman, Charles Barnett. Their friendship was 'a literary affair', according to one amused observer, who nicknamed them David and Jonathan, they were so inseparable. On the boat journey out, while their team-mates played deck quoits, Verity and Barnett would be found with their noses buried in books. Verity read and re-read Kipling, one of his favourite authors. He also read T. E. Lawrence's *Seven Pillars of Wisdom*, a challenging book by any standards.

One passage in the book must have particularly resonated with the studious Verity: 'All men dream, but not equally. Those who dream by night in the dusty recesses of their minds wake in the day to find that it was vanity, but the dreamers of the day are dangerous men, for they may act their dream with open eyes, to make it possible.'

From boyhood onward, Hedley Verity was a dreamer: the sort who says little but whose face tells of a rich inner world. He could often be seen with such a far-away expression on his face that some of his team-mates likened him to a man in a trance. Norman Yardley, a fellow officer in the Green Howards, who went on to become Yorkshire captain after the war, used to talk about 'Verity's daydreams'. But the dreams were not the kind that dissolve on waking: they had a hard, practical edge to them. He might look a bit dopey on occasion, semi-detached from what was going on around him. But people under-estimated his determination at their peril.

By the time war was declared, on 3 September 1939, Hedley Verity was at the peak of his powers. In the very last first-class match he played, against Sussex at Hove, his bowling analysis was 6-1-9-7, which would have been extraordinary in normal circumstances. But nobody was concentrating on the cricket pages. As the Yorkshire coach travelled back up north, there had to be an unscheduled overnight stop at Leicester – a blackout had been ordered across the country and it was thought inadvisable to drive through the darkness.

If the war caught some people on the hop, Verity was ready. That he lost his life in the fighting was happenstance, an accident of war. But that he was *prepared* to lose his life was no accident. He had kept tabs on Hitler almost as closely as he kept tabs on Bradman. And he knew what had to be done to stop him. 'As early as 1937 he was certain that war was coming and said it would last for six years,' remembered his friend Bill Bowes. If only Verity had been employed by the Foreign Office, not Yorkshire County Cricket Club…

At the time of the Munich crisis in 1938, he had a meeting with Lieutenant-Colonel Arnold Shaw of the Green Howards in the pavilion at Headingley. The two men had first met five years earlier, when Shaw had hosted a reception during the England tour of India. Now, with Europe lurching towards war, Verity wanted to know how he could best prepare himself to serve his country, if the need arose. Shaw responded by giving him a collection of military manuals, which Verity, the perpetual student, read from cover to cover. On the 1938–39 England tour of South Africa, he could be seen boning up on army tactics and manoeuvres. Cricket had been a serious business. Now there was even more serious business to be conducted.

By the end of 1939, he had been gazetted in the Green Howards and was attached to the 1st Battalion under the command of Colonel Shaw.

Its first posting was to Northern Ireland, on training exercises. There was even time for the odd cricket match. But Verity had no illusions about the seriousness of the challenge ahead. 'This is no chuffing garden party,' he wrote to his sister Grace. 'This fellow Hitler means it, if we don't stop him. We have got to stop him.' To his young sons, Wilfred and Douglas, he issued what sounds, with hindsight, like a personal credo. 'Always remember to do what's right,' he wrote, 'and to fight for what's right, if necessary.'

In training, he was far from a model soldier. The skills of his new profession did not come easily. 'To watch him stripping a Bren gun, you would think he had two right hands, mainly consisting of thumbs,' joked one colleague. Verity had little appetite for square-bashing: he was more interested in the finer points of military tactics. But when it came to the big picture, he knew where he stood. His attitude to the enemy was simply stated. 'They started it, now let them take it,' he told his commanding officer.

The same steely resolve could be seen among many of his Yorkshire team-mates. They had been a formidable fighting machine, the most successful in the history of the county championship. They had shown loyalty to colleagues, resilience under pressure. Now they had to exhibit those qualities in a new arena.

The first Yorkshire player to be called up was Herbert Sutcliffe, who had been a reservist before the war. He joined the Royal Ordnance Corps and attained the rank of major, but did not see service outside Great Britain and was discharged in 1942, at the age of 48, having undergone two operations for sinus trouble. Len Hutton, Sutcliffe's protégé as opening batsman, was called up to the Army Physical Training Corps, promoted to sergeant instructor, but damaged his wrist in a fall in 1941, necessitating a series of operations which left his left arm two inches shorter than his right. Verity's great friend Bill Bowes – appropriately for one of the fast bowlers who had formed the England attack in the Bodyline series – joined the Royal Artillery. He was promoted to lieutenant and served in North Africa, but was captured at Tobruk in 1942 and spent the rest of the war as a POW, losing four-and-a-half stone in the process.

Other Yorkshire cricketers in uniform included Maurice Leyland, Arthur Wood, Norman Yardley and Frank Smailes, the fast bowler. Many of them passed through the Green Howards depot in Richmond, prompting Verity to boast: 'I reckon we can put out a team from this depot to beat any county side in England.' George Macaulay, born in 1897, served his country twice – in the Royal Field Artillery in the First World War and in the Royal Air Force in the Second. He died of pneumonia in 1940, while stationed at Lerwick.

Even the non-combatants did their bit. The Batley-born batsman Edgar Oldroyd – well described by R. C. Robertson-Glasgow as 'one of those small, tough, humorous, militant men... who bounce and argue their way down time's corridors' – was 50 when war was declared but volunteered as an air raid warden. He took his responsibilities so seriously that, when he heard a siren go off in the night in 1947, two years after the end of the war, he immediately got out of bed, dressed and put on his helmet, ready for duty.

At first blush, it seems the most natural thing in the world that young men who had excelled at sport should also have been among the first to serve their country at a time of war. But we should not take that link for granted. In the First World War, Yorkshire, or parts of it, had been a hotbed of conscientious objection. As documented in Cyril Pearce's *Comrades of Conscience*, there was particularly strong opposition to the fighting in Huddersfield, where George Hirst lived. It was not just a few isolated individuals: Quakers and socialists found common cause.

After conscription was introduced in 1916, special tribunals had to be convened to hear the cases of those refusing to go to the front. One of them, Arthur Gardiner, argued his corner so eloquently that he was absolved from service for two months while his case was given further consideration. After the war, far from becoming a pariah – the fate of many conchies – he went on to become Mayor of Huddersfield.

One of Hedley Verity's best-known Yorkshire contemporaries was the actor James Mason, born in Huddersfield in 1909. He was studying architecture at Cambridge when war broke out, and declared himself a conscientious objector. His family found his attitude incomprehensible and severed all contact with him for a long period. Mason was not quite a social outcast, but he paid a price in his professional as well as his private life. Noel Coward refused to cast him in his Second World War classic *In Which We Serve*, arguing that it was wrong for a man who had refused to wear a uniform in real life to wear one in a film.

A united front was presented to the enemy. British propaganda was subtler than the German equivalent, but still seems artless today. There is an old BBC film, shot to raise morale, of three young men from Huddersfield, with ear-to-ear grins, cycling across the moors to the strains of *Ilkley Moor Baht 'At*. It conjures an innocent, wholesome world, pastoral in its unscrubbed charm, under threat from the forces of oppression. But the reality was more complex.

Not all the conscripts who turned up at the Green Howards depot in Richmond were spoiling for a fight with Hitler. Many of them would have been happier staying at home. Going to war might have felt romantic in 1914. It did not feel romantic now. Training could be pretty haphazard. One sergeant major tried to encourage his recruits to take their responsibilities seriously by organising a rifle-shooting competition with a small cash prize. The competition was won by a local gypsy, who absconded with the cash and was never seen again.

Barry Davitt, a furnace-man from Sheffield, was dumb insolence personified, if his account of his experiences at Richmond is any guide: 'Never mind this slop about King and Country. It's a load of old codswallop. You're fighting for yourself… We are herded into a barrack room and the sergeant introduces himself and impresses upon us that, although we are the worst-looking bunch of humanity he has had the misfortune to see, he will make soldiers out of us – that is what *he* thinks.

'Our first day is spent being inspected by doctors. The fashion seems to be nudity, as we are very rarely dressed. Someone wants you to cough, somebody wants you to look at something, somebody wants you to pass urine, and so it goes on…'

After a 6 a.m. parade in teeming rain, a close encounter with the dentist from hell, a brisk cross-country run and a difference of opinion with a butch PT instructor who wants to get rid of his beer belly, Davitt is left to muse: 'Is this the beginning of the end?'

At least Hedley Verity, ever single-minded, knew his priorities. From the moment war was declared, his focus was on one thing – winning. When his unit was training in Northern Ireland, his wife Kathleen was able to slip across the Irish Sea to spend time with him, leaving her sister in charge of their three children. But the call to arms could not be long delayed. In early 1942, the 1st Battalion of the Green Howards sailed from Liverpool to India, from where it would eventually make its way to Egypt, via Persia and Syria, preparatory to the Sicily landings in the spring of 1943.

While in India, Verity had such a debilitating bout of dysentery that his doctors wanted to send him to a more congenial climate. But he was not to be sidetracked, insisting on rejoining his battalion before being declared fit. When he met up with his men on manoeuvres, he was still looking so weak that he was asked if he had got clearance from his doctor. 'No, but I'm not waiting any longer,' said Verity.

He could no more have cried off sick than he could have asked to be excused playing for Yorkshire because he had a headache.

The Green Howards are no more. The famous foot regiment – with a history dating back for more than 300 years – was amalgamated with other regiments in 2006 and is now part of the drably named Yorkshire Regiment. Administrative efficiency has done for the Howards what it did to the Ridings. It is not only Yorkshire County Cricket Club that has withered in the winds of change.

There is still a regimental museum in Richmond, North Yorkshire, and anyone curious to know more about the Green Howards, and the men who served with them, will get rich pickings there. Faded black-and-white photographs show soldiers slogging their way across the plains of Sicily in punishing heat. How they must have longed to be walking in the Dales or along the beach at Scarborough! But there is a grim determination on their faces. Hedley Verity's fellow Green Howards included Middlesbrough and England footballer Wilf Mannion, known as the Golden Boy, and Miles Smeeton who, along with his wife Beryl, became a celebrated explorer and round-the-world sailor. But it is the unsung heroes of the regiment, their names long forgotten, who bring a lump to the throat; fighting and dying thousands of miles from home.

There have also been some fine memoirs of the Second World War by soldiers of the Green Howards. The most recent is the excellent *Fighting Through – from Dunkirk to Hamburg* by Bill Cheall, published in 2011. Edited by Cheall's son Paul, it is one of those extraordinary books, typical of the genre, where the most harrowing events imaginable are described in the most soldierly, matter-of-fact prose. 'All my six-and-a-half years in the army did not change my character and principles,' writes Cheall, a grocer from the village of Normanby, near Middlesbrough. 'I always minded my own business, had my pals and got on with the job.' It could be a Yorkshire cricketer speaking. No posturing. Just an honest day's work done, without complaint, for scant reward – two shillings a day (10p) when Cheall joined the Green Howards in 1939.

Cheall was younger than Verity, and their paths did not cross – Verity was in the 1st Battalion, Green Howards, Cheall in the 6th – but they both took part in the invasion of Sicily, crossing from North Africa on the HMT *Orontes* in July 1943. Cheall, who had also fought at Dunkirk, later took part in the D-Day landings as well. He had a crowded war, and the Sicily chapters seem like a pastoral interlude compared to some of the other horrors he saw. There are some beautiful vignettes of Mount Etna, glowing in the moonlight, and of hillsides refulgent with orange and lemon trees. But he captures the human landscape even better: the square-bashing and the sing-songs; the interminable journeys, by boat and train, to destinations unknown; the comradeship and the cups of tea; the larking about and the lurking terror. The book is a homage to the 'good north-country lads' that Cheall served with – many of whom never returned. Just boys when they enlisted, they had a man's job to do and they knew it.

Cheall's account of the preparations for the D-Day landings suggests that, despite a few backsliders, the needs of the regiment were paramount: 'There was to be no slacking or scrounging, and it would be stamped on in no uncertain terms. Nobody was allowed to go sick unless his condition was serious. Some of the lads used to play hell, and there was no shortage of foul language, but that was all part of the rough life we led – we did not pretend to be angels, but they were really grand lads and tough nuts to crack.'

Like Verity, Cheall was a devout Methodist and his religious faith informs his account. Others were not churchgoers, but in the solemnity of war, fell into line: 'I knew many lads who had tough characters, and didn't give a damn for anything or anybody, but they closed their eyes as soon as the Padre said, "Men, let us pray" – there were no objectors.' We think of the stiff-upper-lip generation that won the war as stoical, come rain or shine. We could not be more wrong, if Cheall is to be believed: 'Over the years, I saw some lads who, after being in battle, just gave vent to their feelings, and wept and trembled, out of control. These boys were not discriminated against in any way because we were all aware that lads of a particular nature just could not help showing their feelings in the aftermath. They had endured a very traumatic experience and they were by no means cowardly, because they had fought well and extreme tension had built up within them.'

For some, it all became too much. Poet and novelist Vernon Scannell of Leeds was not lacking in physical courage – he had been an amateur boxer before the war – but was so disgusted by the scale of the slaughter at Wadi Akarit, in the Western Desert, that he just walked away: 'I didn't think. It wasn't something I'd planned. I just turned around and walked like a machine or a ghost or something. It was unreal... I remember all those dead bodies lying out there... and got out and walked. It was like a dream. Why didn't anybody stop me? I just floated down that fucking hill like a ghost or the invisible man.'

Scannell was court-martialled as a deserter, but went on to write some of the most haunting poetry of the war, including 'The Walking Wounded':

> ... *A humble brotherhood,*
> *Not one was suffering from a lethal hurt,*
> *They were not magnified by noble wounds.*
> *There was no splendour in that company.*

If there was no splendour, there was certainly solidarity. From every page of Bill Cheall's memoir, one catches the flavour of rough-and-ready friendships, laced with humour: men of few words sharing such extraordinary experiences that the bond between them would last for a lifetime.

While male comradeship was the glue that held everything together, women were not forgotten. Soldiers wrote tear-stained letters to their wives or went to their deaths with photographs of their sweethearts in their pockets. At one point in his memoirs, Cheall asks a friend to type out the words of 'Lili Marlene', so he can commit them to memory. The song had got under his skin – and he was not alone.

Originally a German song, recorded by Lale Andersen in 1939, 'Lili Marlene' became such a hit when it was broadcast on Radio Belgrade that soon soldiers on both sides were getting their nightly fix. 'Husky, sensuous, nostalgic, sugar-sweet, her voice seemed to reach out to you as she lingered over the catchy tune and the sickly, sentimental words,' wrote the diplomat Fitzroy Maclean, who listened spellbound to 'Lili Marlene' while serving in the Western Desert. English translations soon followed. It was more than the catchy tune that transcended national boundaries. The central conceit of the song – a soldier haunted by memories of a woman kissing him under a lamp post outside his barracks – had universal resonance. It spoke to a whole generation of men at war.

Hedley Verity had always been a dreamer, his mind a-wander. It would have been no different in wartime. As Siegfried Sassoon wrote of the soldiers of the Great War:

Soldiers are dreamers; when the guns begin,
They think of firelit homes, clean beds and wives.
I see them in foul dug-outs gnawed by rats,
And in the ruined trenches lashed by rain,
Dreaming of things they did with balls and bats.

But reveries on past glories could not be allowed to deflect from the main objective – the defeat of Nazism. 'Keep going, keep going, keep going…' The last instructions Verity gave to his men in Sicily before he was shot were of a piece with the man.

When you go home,
Tell them of us and say,
For their tomorrow
We gave our today.

The famous words of the Kohima Epitaph were not composed until 1944, a year after Hedley Verity's death, but if they still bring a lump to the throat, it is because of men like Verity and the sacrifices they made in such cruel, capricious circumstances.

The vagaries of cricket pale beside the fortunes of war. Edna Johnston of Sunderland married her husband, 'Shaky' Stewart, a sergeant major in the Green Howards, in 1939 and lost him, in near-farcical circumstances, on the very last day of war. He had survived the carnage at Tobruk and El Alamein, but fell off the top of a truck in Syria while lighting a cigarette. What a contrast with the experience of John Gandah of Durham, who was only four years old at the end of the war, but has never forgotten the homecoming of his elder brother, another Green Howard, who had been captured in Sicily and spent the rest of the war as a POW: 'When my brother came through the door, I remember hiding behind the easy chair in our sitting room, as I was confused at all the excitement and shouting and crying that was going on, and mostly I was a bit scared of this tall, very thin stranger who was my brother George that I had never seen before… Then the serious rejoicing started with my sister's boyfriend playing the accordion and my grandmother, all four foot eleven of her, banging a tambourine and singing "Where did you get that hat? Where did you get that hat?" There was a lot of eating and drinking and laughter that day. I even had a sip of beer out of my brother's glass, but my mother did not say a word. Her precious boy was home and he could do no wrong.'

There was no singing and dancing in the Verity household in Rawdon, not even a coffin draped in a Union Jack, just memories of a good man cut off in his prime. For what kind of tomorrow *did* Verity give his today? Was post-war Britain a better place than pre-war Britain? And, if it was a better place, has it remained a better place?

Hedley Verity would hardly recognise the Rawdon of 2012. The surrounding countryside is unspoiled. There are still bluebells in the woods through which he jogged. There are still some lovely views across the valley. But the town centre is such a shrine to 21st-century life at its most girlishly vacuous that a man of Verity's generation would run screaming down the road to Leeds. A home fit for heroes? More like a home fit for hedonists, fops and popinjays.

There are three hairdressers so close to each other that they resemble a cordon of Yorkshire slip fielders. A beauty salon offers 'lash perming', 'eyebrow sculpture' and 'semi-permanent make-up'. The florists are 'designer florists'. (Have they invented a new brand of gladioli?) Another shop advertises 'custom-made eyewear' – otherwise known as glasses.

Try and buy tea in the delicatessen and you will be offered a choice of three-fennel tea or mint-and-chilli. Try and hire a morning suit for a wedding and, if the mannequin in the window of the menswear shop is any guide, you will have to wear a white waistcoat with grey swirls. Even a traditional-looking butcher has a sign in his window reading 'Male and Female Models Required'. Throw in a French patisserie, where you couldn't get a bacon butty for love nor money, a bar called Nabu, packed with women reading *Hello!* magazine, and a clutch of boutiques with foreign names, selling dresses at prices that would have given Mrs Verity heart seizure, and you have an environment through which Hedley Verity would have walked uncomprehending, stunned by the frivolity of it all.

One of the men sitting at a pavement cafe looks not unlike Verity *c.* 1936, when he had just turned 30. He is similar in height and build and has an unassuming air: he does not say much and, when he does open his mouth, his girlfriend has to crane forward to hear what he is saying. But what would Verity have made of his matching ear-studs, spiky hair, salmon pink T-shirt and yellow shoes?

Perhaps Verity would have adapted with time. The men who fought in the war were nothing if not versatile. But Verity was a serious man at heart: happier working than idling. What would he have achieved with his life if he had survived the war? Cricket fans have naturally focused on the additional wickets he would have taken for Yorkshire and England. He was 40 by the time the war ended and, taking Wilfred Rhodes as a precedent, might still have had a few productive seasons to look forward to. Don Bradman's 1948 Invincibles might never have earned that tag if Verity had been bowling at Headingley when the Don and his men famously chased down 400 on a turning pitch.

But it is what Verity might have accomplished after retiring from the game that is really intriguing. With his tactical acumen, he might have been a superb coach and mentor to younger players, like George Hirst before him. He could have served as an England selector, as Herbert Sutcliffe did. But suppose he had tried to spread his wings and make a mark beyond the cricket field?

His son Douglas reckons he might have wanted to stay on in the Army. He had developed an appetite for leadership and military challenges. As a stalwart of his local Congregationalist church, he might have become a lay preacher, like his father. But there is another possibility. One woman who billeted Verity in Omagh, when he was training with the Green Howards, remembered him saying: 'After the war I would like to go into politics to make this world a better place to live in.'

Just idle chatter? Or evidence of more serious ambitions? Verity did not get actively involved in politics before the war. But he was not a man for idle chatter either. All through his life, he had set himself goals and worked tirelessly to achieve them. One can perhaps see him as a sedulous and effective backbench MP, harrying ministers on behalf of his constituents, the way he had once harried Australian batsmen. His very name on the ballot paper would have brought voters flocking to the polls.

One Yorkshireman of Verity's generation who both fought in the war and went on to have a successful career at Westminster was Denis Healey, one of the most formidable politicians of the post-war era. He was born in 1917, grew up in Keighley and represented his Leeds constituency for more than 40 years.

Intellectually, Healey is a heavyweight, where Verity was no more than a light-middleweight. He went to Bradford Grammar School, then got a double first in Greats at Balliol College, Oxford. He was terrifyingly well-read, not to mention having an extensive knowledge of art, music and the cinema. But in his general studiousness, his hunger to learn and go on learning, he could have been first cousin to the cricketer.

War challenged Healey, the way it challenged Hedley Verity. As a bright academic boy, he had been in his own words, 'an individualist intellectual'. Now he was suddenly faced with the need to be part of a team effort. The account of his wartime service in his autobiography *The Time of My Life* is bracingly free of cant or sentiment: 'Unfashionable though it is to admit it, I enjoyed my five years in the wartime army. It was a life very different from anything I had known, or expected. Long periods of boredom were broken by short bursts of excitement. For the first time I had to learn to do nothing but wait – for me the most difficult lesson of all ... A dumb, animal endurance is the sort of courage most men need in war. I was constantly amazed by the ability of the average soldier, and civilian, to exhibit this under stress.'

Healey served in the Royal Engineers and, like Verity, took part in the Allied landings on Sicily in 1943. Later he saw action in Italy, was beachmaster at the Anzio landings, and attained the rank of major. The most valuable legacy of his war service was 'the knowledge that I depended on other people and other people depended on me'. That knowledge, in turn, created 'the sense of comradeship so characteristic of wartime and so lacking in peace'. No military operation, he realised, had any chance of success without concerted planning – a lesson he carried forward into his political career. Certainly there was room for initiative, bravery, individual acts of daring, but those qualities alone would never carry the day. The individual had to subordinate himself to the common cause. If Healey despised the every-man-for-himself rapaciousness of the Thatcher years, it was partly because of lessons he had learnt 40 years earlier on the beach at Anzio.

Hedley Verity, who was both the ultimate autodidact, forever learning, and the ultimate team man, doing his bit for his side, would surely have echoed Healey's sentiments. Yes, it was good to have talent, something that set you apart from the crowd. But that talent was worthless unless it was used in the service of a greater good, whether it was Yorkshire County Cricket Club, a successful Ashes campaign or the defeat of Nazism. There is a touchingly direct link between the young cricketer shuffling hairbrushes around on eiderdowns to work out his field settings and the captain in the Green Howards leading his men into battle after months spent studying military tactics. One belongs to comedy, the other to tragedy. But they share the same intensity of purpose.

Verity probably comes across as a greyer figure than the other cricketers featured in this book. Partly that is because he was so shy; he shunned the limelight whenever possible. Partly it is because he died young. But it also reflects the age he lived in. One of the paradoxes of the men who served in the war is that, for all their courage, they were also extraordinarily similar: they dressed the same, talked the same, had the same general outlook on life. Individual traits were flattened by the need to form a united front against the enemy.

If it had not been for the two great wars, the social conformity which had been one of the hallmarks of the Victorian era would surely have been relaxed faster than it was. Even in the Edwardian era, the discarding of corsets, literal and metaphorical, was well advanced; more individual self-expression was now admissible. But war, and the disciplines of war, retarded that progress. Every man in every regiment knew that he was part of a larger whole. It was no time for personal agendas. You had to march into battle together.

To their children and grandchildren, the men who fought in the war, and were lucky enough to return, were frustratingly opaque. They had lived extraordinary lives, but rarely talked about them. Reticence was second nature to them. As men, they could sometimes seem colourless as a result. There was none of the flamboyance, the jauntiness, the self-assertiveness that in peacetime makes a man the envy of his peers. But the unobtrusiveness of their virtues should not diminish them. Their willingness to function as a unit, putting self aside, was their lasting memorial.

Long before he put on his soldier's uniform, Hedley Verity was a good team man in a great Yorkshire XI. The three most productive periods in the county's history – the years before the Great War, the 1930s and the 1960s – were only possible because there was harmony in the dressing room and a strong team ethic on the pitch. When all that evaporated in the 1970s and 1980s, it resulted in a period of internecine warfare that made Yorkshire a laughing stock throughout the cricket world. There were some good players in the side, and some strong personalities, but they lacked the humility that is the integral aspect of manliness in a team sport.

The coming of war reinforced attitudes and principles that had been instilled in Verity since he first walked through the door of the Yorkshire dressing room. Fitting in was more important than standing out. It was not a time for show ponies.

He rose to the challenge, as if he had been born to face it.

CHAPTER 4
FRED TRUEMAN:
MODESTY OUT OF
THE WINDOW

*Yorkshire greats are invariably born with the awkward gene
that is characteristic of Yorkshire species. Their DNA is richly
endowed with gritty determination, a wilful refusal to give up
and a sheer bloody-mindedness that eventually prevails.*

Bernard Ingham, *Yorkshire Greats*

Nobody who studies the history of Yorkshire County Cricket Club can
fail to be struck not just by the value of teamwork, but by the power
of community. In its heyday, a strong county side was underpinned
by strong local sides, in a way that was never true of, say, Surrey or
Gloucestershire. The great players have not grown up in isolation.
Again and again, a town or village has produced a brace of them in
quick succession.

George Hirst and Wilfred Rhodes, the two pre-eminent English
all-rounders of the first half of the 20th century, both came from
Kirkheaton, a semi-rural community with a population of under 5,000.
Herbert Sutcliffe of Pudsey begat Len Hutton of Pudsey. In the village
of Rawdon, people were still mourning the loss of Hedley Verity
when they realised they had another England great in their midst –
all-rounder Brian Close, the human punchbag, whose England career

spanned four decades, from the 1940s to the 1970s, and about four million bruises. He had quite a modest record on paper, but made an indelible impression on his contemporaries, players and fans alike.

His judgement was often questioned: he would lose his wicket to poor shots or get drawn into needless controversies. But nobody ever doubted his passion for the game. He was a cricketing obsessive, mulling over events on the field long after stumps had been drawn. Stories of his obsession grew with the telling. In one such story, dating from the time when Close was Yorkshire captain, he rings up one of his bowlers, Tony Nicholson, at two in the morning to tell him he has worked out what is wrong with his bowling action. A bleary-eyed Nicholson picks up the phone and says, 'Skipper, do you know what time it is?' On which Close turns to his wife Vivienne and says, 'Tony wants to know what time it is. T'clock's on your side.'

If Close was daft as a brush, in the nicest possible way, nobody, friend or foe, ever questioned his physical courage. Long after the scorebook had been closed, people would be shaking their heads in wonder at his fearlessness, whether facing fast bowlers or fielding at short leg, under the nose of the batsman. There was no helmet. In fact, there was not even a cap. Protection would have spoiled the fun for Close. Latterly, there was not even any hair to deaden the thud of the cricket ball. As Eric Morecambe joked, 'You know the cricket season has arrived when you hear the sound of leather on Brian Close.'

Rightly or wrongly – and there are women who find this aspect of male behaviour slightly pathetic, like the way men judge each other by their cars, their mobile phones or the size of their penises – the ability to shrug off pain has always been one of the hallmarks of manliness, perhaps *the* hallmark of manliness. Whether you are on the battlefield or the sports field, or just sitting in the dentist's chair, if you can grit your teeth – think John Wayne with an Apache arrow in his leg – while the next man is howling like a banshee, then you are better than the next man. Brian Close, following in a great Yorkshire tradition, made a career out of being better than the next man in this respect.

England fans of a certain age will remember him, in the twilight of his career, taking 95mph bouncers from Andy Roberts and Michael

Holding on the chest without flinching. It was mad. Couldn't he just duck? But it was also sublime: the flannelled fool re-invented as war hero. A decade earlier, it had been Wes Hall and Charlie Griffith using him for target practice. After the 1963 Lord's Test, in the course of which he took a terrible battering, photos of his bruise-mottled body were splashed across the sports pages. When he returned to play for Yorkshire the next day, he went around the dressing room showing off his wounds.

In a tough county, he was the toughest of them all, a figure from a cartoon strip, and loved for the same reasons. In one county match, when he had to take over as wicketkeeper, he insisted on keeping without gloves. There never was a sportsman more careless of life and limb. Even at the wheel of the car, he was recklessness personified. Stories abound of him taking reluctant passengers on white-knuckle rides with a buccaneering smile on his face. Close, who turned 80 in 2011, shrugged off their protests, the way he shrugged off bouncers in the ribs.

It says a lot for Frederick Sewards Trueman, born in Stainton on 6 February 1931, that he could elbow a larger-than-life figure like Brian Close out of the limelight. The two men made their debuts for Yorkshire in the same match, against Cambridge University in 1949, when *Wisden*, in a rare lapse, described Trueman as a 'spin bowler'. Had the reporter been overdoing things in the beer tent? It was the last time anyone made *that* mistake. Fiery Fred – broad of beam, hair tousled, face contorted with fury as he charged in to bowl – was not just a great fast bowler, but the definitive fast bowler, the standard for the breed.

He was the first bowler to take more than 300 Test wickets, and was equally destructive for Yorkshire, but the statistics, with Trueman, are more than usually irrelevant. His greatness began where the statistics end. If connoisseurs of fast bowling purred at the sight of his classical, side-on action, casual observers were struck by his aura of physical indestructibility – a quality he shared with Close. He looked like the last man in Yorkshire you would want to get into a fight with.

From the time of his birth, when he weighed in at 14lb 1oz, only a few ounces shy of the national record, Trueman always seemed to be throwing his weight about. If he was not terrorising opposition batsmen, or flailing his bat, blacksmith-like, at the end of an innings, he was making the headlines with some spectacular social gaffe. Stories of his brashness stuck to him, whether they were true or not. One story, palpably ridiculous, had the young Trueman turning up at Yorkshire wearing a tie with a naked woman on it. 'I have no idea where the story came from,' said Trueman. 'If I had ever worn a tie like that, my father would have pulled it so tight I would never have breathed again.' But that didn't stop the canard, and scores of similar ones, gaining popular currency.

Not since W. G. Grace had a cricketer been such a magnet for apocryphal stories. Years after Trueman had hung up his size 12 boots, people would come up to him, get his autograph and ask, 'Fred, did you *really* say…?' In retirement, he became an outspoken commentator on *Test Match Special*, when his catchphrase was 'I don't know what's going off out there', as well as a popular after-dinner speaker. He still threw his weight about and people still loved him for doing it. When Prime Minister Harold Wilson called Trueman 'the greatest living Yorkshireman', he was not being glibly populist. He was acknowledging a living legend.

If Hedley Verity had an apt surname, the same could be said of Fred Trueman. Both men were fundamentally honest: they said what they meant and meant what they said; there was no beating about the bush, no speaking with forked tongues. But there the resemblance ends. Temperamentally, they were poles apart.

Before Trueman came bristling on to the scene, just about the only generalisation you could safely have made about Yorkshire cricketers, from the geniuses to the journeymen, was that they did not brag about their achievements. Hirst, Sutcliffe and Verity were as modest as they were gifted. That was what was expected of professional sportsmen of the period. They had been blessed with a skill, and they were grateful for that skill, but they did not pat themselves on the head for being a cut above the rest; it would have felt like hubris. That instinctive modesty extended far beyond Yorkshire and far beyond the cricket field. If one takes arguably the three most celebrated English sportsmen of the first half of the 20th century – Jack Hobbs, Stanley Matthews and Gordon Richards – the common denominator is humility. They were idolised not least because they seemed so down-to-earth. They treated the autograph-hunter as an equal. They performed extraordinary sporting feats, then faded quietly into the background. The more the press lionised them, the more they insisted they were just ordinary mortals.

There was no danger of Fred Trueman fading into the background, playing down his achievements or missing an opportunity to blow his own trumpet. 'People saw me as not only a genuine fast bowler, but also dramatic, comic, earthy, nostalgic and, in some way, epic and heroic,' he wrote in his autobiography. It was a lot of boxes to tick, but he ticked them with relish. When John Arlott told him he was planning to write his biography, and asked if he could suggest a title, Trueman came up with the answer, as if he had been rehearsing it for years – 'T'Definitive Volume of t'Finest Bloody Fast Bowler That Ever Drew Breath'. He was only half-joking. A few years earlier, Michael Parkinson had got a similar reply when he mooted the idea of a Trueman biography. 'It was the combination of athlete and comedian that made him the most charismatic cricketer of his time,' Parkinson wrote in a tribute in *Wisden*. 'He loved adulation, fed it assiduously.'

Modesty, as far as Trueman was concerned, was for wimps. English self-deprecation? He didn't do English self-deprecation. He left that to Peter May and Colin Cowdrey and the other amateurs. A man's man should be cock of the walk. He should stick up for himself and not let anyone push him around. If a fight was in the offing, he should get his retaliation in first. Trueman could talk, and talk, and talk – a quality that amused Bill Bowes, a Yorkshire fast bowler from a less loquacious era: 'He talked in the field to anybody who would listen. He talked in the dressing room to such an extent that his Yorkshire team-mates seldom answered back because this was encouragement… he could invariably be found talking in the dressing room of the opposing team… Fred's unhappiest moments on the cricket field were when his skipper sent him down to the fine-leg boundary, 20 yards in from the spectators, where he could find no one to talk to.'

Among his Yorkshire-born contemporaries, probably the only one with a comparably outsize personality is the actor Brian Blessed, he of the bushy beard and booming voice, the ham's ham, born in Mexborough in 1936. The stentorian Blessed, a miner's son who left school at 14, has earned such a cult following that there is now a Brian Blessed Centre for Quiet Study at York University, named in his honour. He made three unsuccessful attempts to climb Everest and, in June 2011, hungry for a fresh challenge, stood for the post of Chancellor of Cambridge University – an undertaking of Truemanesque cockiness, if ever there was one.

For a much-loved sportsman, blessed with the common touch and a ready smile, Trueman was also oddly belligerent, a taker of offence, a picker of quarrels, a brooder on ancient slights. He had insecurities which people failed to see because of the carapace of toughness and invincibility. He was also, heart and soul, a class warrior – conservative in outlook, but with a militant edge. Where Herbert Sutcliffe was quietly determined to show the amateurs in the Yorkshire side that he was as good as they were, Trueman set out to show them that he was *better* than they were. An MCC or Old Harrovians cap was more likely to attract a bouncer than a baggy green Australian cap. As the era of Gentlemen and Players limped to its inevitable end, nobody willed its demise more fervently than Fiery Fred.

A rebel in his youth, forever clashing with the authorities, Trueman in retirement became a professional Yorkshireman, living up to an image which he had helped to mould, but which had then been distorted by others – to the point when it was impossible to pin down the real Fred Trueman, if there was such a thing. The word 'celebrity' does not sit easily with Hirst, Sutcliffe or Verity, celebrated men though they were. But Fiery Fred was a celebrity, long before the word achieved its current ubiquity.

In 1990, when Trueman's daughter Rebecca married the son of movie star Raquel Welch, to the delight of the tabloids – the marriage crashed and burned, as might have been predicted – it felt like a culmination of a process that had begun 30 years earlier, when Trueman stood at the end of his run-up, pawing the ground, before charging in to hurl a bouncer at an Australian batsman, with the crowd baying him on. It made wonderful theatre, but it was the theatre of hyperbole. Like all great showmen, Trueman relied on exaggeration to achieve his effects. Batsmen were intimidated before they got to the crease by the image of this dark-haired destroyer, bristling with menace, emitting strange curses.

Off the field, people wanted Trueman to act like the larger-than-life character of popular mythology: the blunt Yorkshireman who kow-towed to nobody, told off-colour anecdotes in the bar and could drink for England. It was a good act, polished by years of practice, but half the time, that is all it was – an act. The real Fred Trueman was both more banal and more complex than the stage Yorkshireman he impersonated with such aplomb.

In the 1990s, it was discovered, to general amusement, that the great England fast bowler, John Bull with a cricket ball in his hand, was actually Jewish, under strict Orthodox law – his maternal grandmother was a Jew who had given up her baby for adoption. *Oy vey* and *ee bah gum*! Trueman cheerfully embraced his new-found status as T'Greatest Jewish Fast Bowler That Ever Drew Breath. But the episode underscored the gulf between the myth and the reality.

Cricketer David Green, who played for Lancashire and Gloucester-shire, made a telling observation about Trueman: 'If anyone offered him a drink – and thousands did – he would generally accept. But at the end of the evening, those clearing up would find numerous pint pots, each with an inch or so sipped off the top, concealed behind curtains, under chairs or behind plant pots. Hence the many occasions on which one would hear a cricket follower say: "Do you know I was with Fred Trueman last night? I watched him drink 14 pints, and look at him this morning, fresh as a daisy."'

The figures in *Wisden* don't lie. Trueman was one of the all-time great fast bowlers, by any yardstick. John Woodcock of *The Times* caught Trueman to a tee: 'On his day, he displayed, to the highest degree, the beauty and the skill and the manliness and the terror of his calling.' But many of the stories about him are apocryphal or exaggerated. His career overlapped with an age when the coverage of sport in the press was in a state of transition: from the relatively sober reportage of the 1930s to the kind of hysteria-drenched headlines that are the norm today. Little by little, it was becoming impossible for a sporting celebrity to enjoy anything resembling a normal life. Everyone wanted a piece of Fiery Fred, the way they wanted a piece of George Best.

As a man, Trueman was *sui generis*, although nobody would have dared use the expression to his face – they would have got a mouthful for using Latin instead of plain English. But he was also a man of his times – in his vigour, in his bloody-mindedness, in his eagerness to kick over the traces and make a new start. There were plenty of Fred Truemans in the 1950s, as Britain emerged from war and rationing and cheap grey suits into a brighter world. None of the other Fred Truemans sent the stumps skittling at Headingley or Lord's, but they identified with the man who could: part hero, part anti-hero, but irreducibly virile.

'He was a man's man,' Trueman wrote of his father Alan in his 2004 autobiography, *As It Was*. It is one of those expressions that trip off the tongue of men of a certain age, seems to be largely self-explanatory, but gets murkier the more you try to dissect it. Just as calling a man manly is semantically akin to calling a dog canine, calling him a man's man is tautology on stilts.

If a woman called another woman a woman's woman, she would spend the next ten minutes explaining what she meant; but one of the hallmarks of a man's man is that he does not explain, he simply asserts. 'A man's man' is of a piece with that other wonderfully circular cliché from the male phrase-book, 'A man's gotta do what a man's gotta do'. A man is either a man's man or he isn't. If he is not sure, he probably isn't, and if he asks a man who *is* sure he's a man's man what he needs to do to be admitted to the club, he is wasting his breath. All he will get is a manly grunt.

Peering through the fog into the world of the self-styled man's man, one can glimpse certain recurring themes: physical toughness; economy of speech; sobriety of appearance; a lack of flourish or complication; dry-eyed self-sufficiency. But you will never pin down the man's man. He maintains his mystique, his aura of impenetrability.

'Once met, you will always know them,' wrote the Yorkshire-born playwright Alan Bennett of a certain type of Englishman, 'for their hand is firm and their eye is clear and, on those rare occasions when they speak, it is well to listen, for they choose their words dangerously

George Hirst: 'Manliness was his birthright. He was virility made flesh.'

Robert Baden-Powell, founder of the Scout Movement. His *Scouting for Boys*, published in 1908, marked a revolution in child-rearing.

Heavy formal clothing was de rigueur at cricket matches, right up to the First World War.

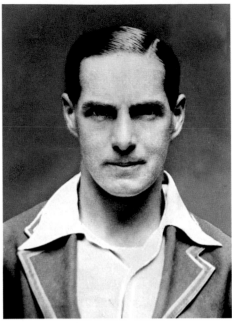

Herbert Sutcliffe took his appearance so seriously that one of his team-mates nicknamed him 'Beautiful Herbert'.

Rudolph Valentino: no star of the silent screen had such an adoring female following – or posed men so many riddles about their sexuality.

Yorkshire carried all before it in the 1930s, winning seven county championships with dour, remorseless cricket.

Yorkshire cricketers in the Green Howards: team spirit was paramount, whether in the dressing-room or on the battlefield. Hedley Verity is on the far left and Herbert Sutcliffe in the centre.

Hedley Verity: 'He used to appeal so quietly that often only the umpire could hear him.'

Yorkshire-born Denis Healey, who saw war service in Italy and was later Chancellor of the Exchequer, remembers 'the sense of comradeship so characteristic of wartime and so lacking in peace'.

Fred Trueman: 'Connoisseurs of fast bowling purred at the sight of his classical, side-on action.'

Fred with a pint of beer in his hand – the quintessential stage-prop for a man's man of his generation.

After the grey days of rationing, the Teddy Boys sparked a revolution in male fashion.

Geoffrey Boycott: another chanceless century in the score-book – but could his mam have played the bowlers with a stick of rhubarb?

Boycott, like Trueman, grew up in a Yorkshire mining village, which he remembers with affection.

The England team that won the Ashes in 1970–71 – note the steadily lengthening hairstyles.

Darren Gough wearing ear-studs – a first for a Yorkshire fast bowler and a portent of fashion excesses to come.

Gough with his *Strictly* partner Lilia Kopylova: 'I prefer it when the woman is in charge. I think that is the way it should be in life.'

Roy of the Rovers: 'Even in the last redoubt of male escapism, all was not well.' When Roy's wife Penny walked out on him in the early 1980s, it was reported on the BBC news.

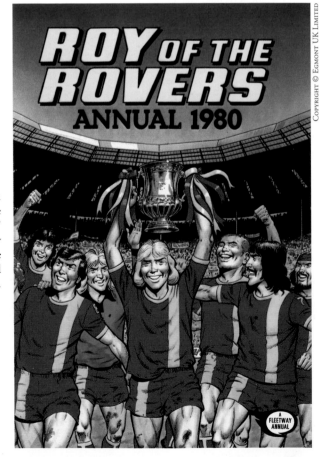

Michael Vaughan and the England cricket team at the Oval in 2005: 'A stirring reminder of how many different forms manliness could take in 21st-century Britain'.

Vaughan 'artballing': is it art? Or just a nice little earner for fading sporting celebrities?

David Beckham with his wife Victoria: the high priest of metrosexuality, never knowingly underdressed.

The Ashes-winning team of 2010–11: they thrashed the Aussies, they bristled with manliness – and one of them even flew home to the UK to attend the birth of his child.

'Fancy dress' day at Headingley: never mind the cricket, the Saturday of the Headingley Test match has become a fancy-dress party to rival the Rio Carnival.

well.' A few well-chosen manly words is a step up from a grunt, but it is still not very enlightening.

Rock-solid in some respects, the man's man is infuriatingly elusive in others. It is a protean phrase, subject to infinite interpretation. I once asked a woman in the pavilion at Lord's – an MCC member of some standing – what she understood by a man's man. 'A hairy chest,' she said, without hesitation. 'Think Sean Connery in his thirties.' Quite so. Her views on men's exfoliating creams were trenchant and lapidary.

Fred Trueman – who, from published photos, would have scored poorly on the hairy-chest test – judged his father a man's man because he was '...physically strong, worked hard, loved sport... worked impossibly long hours to put food on the table and heat in the hearth... a teetotaller, God-fearing, stickler for discipline... even in my thirties, I never dared answer him back... encouraged his children to be honest, respectful and forthright... average take-home pay was 37 shillings a week...' It is easy to smile. Tinker with the script and you have a passable imitation of the famous *Monty Python* sketch in which four Yorkshiremen vie with each other for the honour of having had the most impoverished childhood. ('House? You were lucky to live in a house. We used to live in one room, all 26 of us, no furniture and half the floor missing.') But if it is a sentimentalised childhood, there are nuggets of truth beneath the sentiment.

Just as cricket can be a simple game, once you have mastered the basics, the progression from boyhood in the Yorkshire in which Trueman grew up was only complicated if you made it complicated. With the coming of war, close-knit northern communities closed ranks more than ever. It was a time for solidarity, not for putting on airs. Traditional British values were under threat, so those values had to be defended and re-asserted. Continuity was more important than experimentation.

Trueman's father was an ex-miner who got a job with a local racehorse-owner. His working life revolved around horses, not the colliery. But the village of Stainton in which Trueman and his six siblings were raised, on the county border with Nottinghamshire, was also a mining community of the old school, peopled by men and women who were tough, resourceful and devoid of social pretensions. A growing boy, even one with precocious sporting talent, was expected to defer to his elders and betters. 'Teenagers were respectful in those days,' Trueman wrote. 'I was brought up to respect not only my parents, but my fellow man, irrespective of colour, race, creed or financial status, and to respect other people's property, particularly their homes.'

At home, his father's word was law. If Hedley Verity's mother was the dominant member of the family, Fred Trueman grew up in a strict patriarchy, where children stepped out of line at their peril. At the age of 17, he started smoking a pipe – a habit that stayed with him for life. But when he came home with a pipe in his mouth, he got short shrift from his father, who told him he was welcome to smoke, but not in the house. Trueman meekly did as he was told – as he always did where his father was concerned. He was only eight when war was declared in 1939 – his father served in the Home Guard – but inherited many of the values of the wartime generation. Family came first and community second.

'People were plain speaking,' Trueman wrote, 'and for a person to speak his or her mind was considered a mark of how open and upfront they were: an indication that they were not devious, deceitful or, to use modern-day parlance, had a hidden agenda. Having been brought up in an environment with such an attitude, it is little wonder that such attributes became a part of my character in manhood.'

Plain speaking did indeed become Trueman's stock-in-trade. Many of the best Trueman stories involve him being blunt to the point of rudeness. But there is a significant difference – and Trueman himself acknowledged as much – between plain speaking and emotional frankness.

In the spring of 1949, when a telegram arrived at the Truemans' house to inform Fred that he had been picked to play for Yorkshire against Cambridge University – his county debut and a moment of unbridled joy for the young fast bowler – the only member of the family to register no excitement was his father: 'He kept his thoughts to himself. I could see from the way he kept putting the telegram down, only to pick it up a few minutes later and read it again, that he was very proud. But he didn't say anything. That was typical of working men of the time. The only time they gave vent to their emotions was at funerals and, even then, it was restrained.'

Alan Trueman was no automaton. He may have kept his feelings in check when his son made his Yorkshire debut, but when Trueman was awarded his county cap, two years later, and brought the cap home, the mask slipped. 'Dad's face puckered up,' Trueman remembered. 'I thought: "Good God! He's going to cry." Then he pulled himself together... He just studied the cap and gently ran his coarse fingers over the material, pausing at the county's white rose emblem before emitting a sigh of satisfaction.' The tears remained unshed.

The young of Trueman's generation were nurtured, but not mollycoddled. If a teenage boy was miserable, for whatever reason, he was expected to snap out of it: there was no interest in delving into the whys and wherefores. In the cricket world, team spirit might have been paramount, but it was team spirit rooted in equality – all men together – and made no concessions to youth and inexperience. Trueman's team-mate Brian Close, who made his England debut as a teenager, was thoroughly miserable on his first tour of Australia in 1950–51. He was the baby of the side, but nobody liked babies or knew how to handle them. None of the older players – not even his Yorkshire colleague Len Hutton, the senior professional in the side – was willing to take him under his wing. Close felt so lonely and isolated that he sometimes cried himself to sleep.

The Yorkshire of the 1930s and 1940s, about which Fred Trueman waxed so sentimental in his autobiography, seems stunted today: far too many stiff upper lips, not nearly enough people willing to unbutton. Everyone mucked along fine when the going was good. It was when the going was not so good – when someone got into trouble or had personal problems – that the fault-lines in the community were exposed.

Fortitude, per se, is a universally admired quality. My own late father – not a Yorkshireman, but an Ulsterman, although the two tribes have much in common – offered a shining example of it. Born in 1924, a decade before Trueman, he was ill as a boy, had his left leg amputated and went around for the next 60 years on crutches, undaunted, uncomplaining, nor expecting sympathy. But there is a fine line between fortitude and the kind of mulish pride that dams up pain and blocks off communication.

One of Trueman's most remarkable contemporaries at Yorkshire was the bowler Bob Appleyard. As a cricketer, what made him stand out from the herd was his versatility: he could bowl off-breaks and fast-medium swingers, using a similar action, and regularly bowled both in the same innings, to the bemusement of the batting side. But his life beyond the cricket field was even more extraordinary: a tragedy on a Shakespearean scale, but without an audience.

His mother left home when he was seven, his sister died of diphtheria, and he spent a lot of time with his grandmother. In September 1939, he returned to the family home in Bradford, walked into the bathroom and found the bodies of his father, stepmother and two younger sisters in a room thick with gas. At the inquest, it was stated simply that his father had been disturbed by the recent outbreak of war. Appleyard, 15 at the time, was taken in by his stepmother's parents. But it is symptomatic of the times he lived in, and of the culture of reticence in the Yorkshire dressing room, that he never breathed a word about the tragedy to his team-mates throughout his playing career, which ran from 1950 to 1958. The truth only emerged in 2003, when Appleyard was nearly 80, with the publication of his biography, *No Coward Soul*, by Stephen Chalke and Derek Hodgson.

In a stoical age, personal tragedies tended to be glossed over or consigned to history. Alan Bennett, who grew up in Leeds in the 1930s, only discovered 40 years after the event that his maternal grandfather had drowned himself in a canal, overwhelmed by depression. Honest-to-God Yorkshire folk didn't talk about such things. What would the neighbours think? 'It is an odd family that censors its own history,' Bennett reflected. As a boy, he had always been told that his grandfather had died of a heart attack: it was only when his mother started suffering from depression herself that the truth came out. But by the standards of the time, the Bennetts were *not* an odd family, certainly not in their reluctance to talk about mental illness.

Bennett's father Walter, a butcher, was cripplingly shy, with a pathological horror of what he called 'splother' – people making a fuss.

Almost anything which could be deemed out of the ordinary, or which might get people talking, or which would make him conspicuous, failed the splother test. When he married Bennett's mother in 1928, he was so terrified of the happy day being marred by splother – bridesmaids, a cake, a photographer, etc – that he insisted the ceremony be held at 8 o'clock sharp, so that he could report to work at 8.15 as usual, and not have to field questions about his whereabouts. Bennett remembers him as a loving husband and father, but painfully undemonstrative – 'I never saw my father so much as kiss my mother's hand.' He abhorred attention, whatever form it took. He was so terrified of being conspicuous that his wardrobe consisted of two suits, known as 'my suit' and 'my other suit', which he wore day in, day out, even on the beach at Blackpool. An open-neck shirt would have been a liberty.

Like Alan Bennett, his junior by four years, Fred Trueman grew up in a dour world, where everyone knew their place, you didn't show off, or betray emotions, and you *certainly* didn't wash your dirty linen in public. But by the time he had forced his way into the Yorkshire team, that world stood on the brink of revolutionary change. Just as the Edwardians rejected some of the starchier dogmas of their Victorian predecessors, the generation who reached manhood in the 1950s were not content just to be clones of their fathers, however much they had admired and respected them.

They wanted to rewrite some of the rules – and they did.

If the 1950s were less obviously glamorous than the 1960s, they offered an exciting foretaste of what was to come. Long before the Beatles burst on to the scene, social attitudes were changing. Prime Minister Harold Macmillan, moustachioed relic of the Edwardian age, was on the way out years before he actually left Downing Street. Whether you were Fred Trueman, Alan Bennett or a plumber's apprentice in Scarborough, you could hardly fail to notice that you were living in a world of urgent change.

The first outward manifestation of change was dress. In the 1920s and 1930s, Herbert Sutcliffe and others of a dandyish disposition had cut quite a sartorial dash. The fluttering shirts which Sutcliffe wore were made of silk imported from Thailand. But the war nipped *that* sort of thing in the bud. Clothes rationing was introduced and continued for several years after the war. Men were no longer in military uniform, but they looked so similar that they might as well have been.

Anyone who tried to stand out from the crowd was viewed with suspicion, if not hostility. Roy Hattersley remembers as a boy seeing Don Bradman's 1948 Australian side arrive at their team hotel in Leeds. When he rushed home, bubbling with enthusiasm, and told his father he had seen Neil Harvey wearing a purple suit, yellow shirt and green tie, his father was not amused. Purple, he pronounced, like an Old Testament prophet, should only be worn by ambulance drivers on duty. Even in a heatwave, a certain decorum was expected. 'Whatever the weather, our men must dress in a grey suit, collar and tie,' declared the manager of a London department store in July 1955. 'The public expects them to look smart. If we allowed them to dress anyhow, the place would look very tatty indeed.'

As Fred Trueman's career took off, and he had a bit more expendable income, he invested some of the money in smartening up his wardrobe, although he was hardly a peacock: 'The new items of clothing I treated myself to were stylish for the day, but what you might call standard, even formal.' In photographs of him taken early in his career, you have to look very closely to see anything that marks him out from the crowd: here a wider-than-average tie; there a dark suit of an expensive cut, not an off-the-peg one.

Signs of a more radical approach to fashion first emerged in London, with the Teddy Boys, a phrase coined by the *Daily Express* in 1953. The original Teddy Boys were well-heeled young men aping the more flamboyant fashions of the Edwardian era. They wore drainpipe trousers, often exposing their socks, drape jackets, sometimes with velvet-trim collars, and suede shoes or, as they became known, brothel-creepers. Other items of clothing included brocade waistcoats, 'Slim Jim' ties and white shirts with high, loose-necked collars. Greased-up hair with a quiff at the front and a 'duck's arse' at the back was also de rigueur if you wanted to be taken seriously in Teddy Boy circles.

Initially confined to the metropolis, the Teddy Boys quickly struck a chord with the wider public. We take it for granted today that teenagers will try to make fashion statements that differentiate them from their parents, but the Teddy Boys of the 1950s were the first British generation to do so in such a striking, eye-catching, concerted way – and remembered quite fondly for that reason. But they were not just clothes horses. As the Teddy Boy craze spread, with working-class Teds taking over what had started as a middle-class party, it became as much associated with anarchic acts of violence as with dandyism. There was a notorious incident at a cinema in the Elephant and Castle in 1956, when Teds ripped up the seats and started dancing in the aisles. Similar scenes were repeated across the country. The movie that sparked the frenzy was the ground-breaking American classic *Blackboard Jungle*, featuring the Bill Haley hit 'Rock Around the Clock'. Music, too, was entering a revolutionary era, with Elvis Presley about to galvanise a generation.

It is hard to imagine Fred Trueman, still less Alan Bennett, ripping up cinema seats, but even Yorkshire, the land of flat caps and whippets and neatly pressed Sunday suits, was not immune from change. There is a very funny scene in Bennett's memoir *Untold Stories* in which the normally shy young writer decides that, if he wants to be part of the in-crowd, he needs to wear narrow-bottomed trousers, as popularised by the Teddy Boys. He scours Leeds for a tailor prepared to make the necessary alterations, but draws a blank:

> Despairing of finding an understanding seamstress, I decide to have a go myself, and painstakingly chalk out the necessary line, and sew along it, taking them down to under 14 inches around the ankle. In these extraordinary trousers, which must have made me look like the late Max Wall, I parade before my parents.
>
> 'You can't go out like that,' Mam said. 'People will think you're one of them.'
>
> Whereupon Dad, who was even more shocked than she was, said (and the question must have had a long gestation), 'You're not one of them, are you?' 'Oh, Dad,' I think I replied, as if the question was absurd. 'Don't be daft.' But I never wore the trousers.

Thus was the delicate issue of homosexuality finessed in 1950s Yorkshire. Alan Bennett today is unashamedly 'one of them' but has no regrets about not admitting as much to his parents, even when presented with such an obvious cue. It would have caused them needless unhappiness. 'If I had said "Yes", prey to the prejudices of their generation, they would have assumed I hung around public lavatories, interfered with little boys, or even got done up in drag, none of which I ever had any inclination to do.'

A time-traveller from the 21st century to 1950s Yorkshire would probably think what a homogenous world it was, with the overwhelming majority of men talking the same, dressing the same, living in similarly furnished homes. But there were some screaming extroverts lurking behind the lace curtains of those drab terraces in Leeds and Bradford – and their day in the sun was imminent.

Sartorially, none of Fred Trueman's Yorkshire contemporaries left a bigger mark on his times than Jimmy Savile, DJ, philanthropist and eccentric, born in Leeds in 1926. He would not achieve national prominence until the 1960s, when he presented *Top of the Pops*, but he was catching the eye long before then. Everything about the man was unconventional, not to say weird. He lived with his mother, whom he called the Duchess, until her death, then kept her bedroom just as she had left it, dry-cleaning her clothes every year. His dyed hair, gold jewellery and luridly coloured tracksuits made him stand out wherever he went. In the Yorkshire of the 1930s, when showing off was the eighth deadly sin, Savile would have been a social pariah; in fact, he would probably have been arrested for causing a breach of the peace. Now, with memories of war receding, and a brasher generation of men growing in confidence, Britain was ready for him.

At Yorkshire County Cricket Club, needless to say, nobody would have dared push the frontiers of fashion as far as Savile. Conservatism ruled. One of Trueman's team-mates was all-rounder Ken Taylor, who played football for Huddersfield Town in the winter, and was also a distinguished artist. When he turned up at the start of one season wearing a beard, standard issue in bohemian circles, club chairman

Brian Sellers told him, 'Take that bloody thing off or you'll never play for Yorkshire again.' But even in the land of beardless wonders, lantern-jawed types who said it with their chins, there were small concessions to changing times. Fred Trueman briefly succeeded Denis Compton as one of the faces of Brylcreem, a distinction later enjoyed by David Beckham and Kevin Pietersen, which says it all.

If changes in men's fashion were the outward face of changing attitudes, the revolution of which they were the harbinger cut much deeper. Independent-minded young men did not just want to look different from their fathers: they wanted to show that they thought about the world differently. Trueman was so in awe of his father, and had so much respect for him, that in the home he had none of the attributes of the rebellious teenager. Outside, it was another matter.

One early clue to the obstreperousness that became a feature of his career came when he was called up for National Service in 1951. 'I am patriotic through and through, and had no qualms about serving my country,' Trueman said in his autobiography. 'But I have to be honest and say that, just for the hell of it, I tried to pull a flanker at the medical.' Asked if he had any physical deficiencies, the cricketer told the doctor: 'I think I may be slightly colour-blind.' The doctor roared his head off and told him he was not buying *that* – he had seen Trueman play for Yorkshire against Essex the previous day and take a brilliant catch in poor light. The cricketer was passed fit and told to report for duty with the RAF.

Trueman was only trying it on, and did not resent having to do National Service, which he rather enjoyed, but somehow it is hard to imagine Herbert Sutcliffe or Hedley Verity or other Yorkshire players of that generation acting in such an underhand way. They would have thought it unpatriotic, a betrayal of the unwritten rules of the tribe. The days when men did as they were told by figures in authority – even strong, successful men like Sutcliffe and Verity – were numbered. Little by little, it was becoming every man for himself, which would have far-reaching consequences.

One of the senior pros in the Yorkshire team of the 1950s was the spin bowler Johnny Wardle, who had so many run-ins with the Yorkshire committee that the club parted company with him on acrimonious terms in 1958. The team spirit that had made Yorkshire so dominant in the 1930s was slowly evaporating. Surrey was now the dominant county, winning seven championships on the bounce, while Yorkshire began to churn out strong-willed individuals – Brian Close and Ray Illingworth, to name but two – who could start an argument in an empty room. With modesty a thing of the past, there was too much testosterone, not enough *esprit de corps*. The club would rally impressively in the 1960s, but the seeds of future discord had been sown.

If Teddy Boys caught the mood of the mid-1950s, the same was even more true of the 'Angry Young Men' – a ragbag of writers and intellectuals who moved in circles far removed from cricket, but articulated ideas which would have been meat and drink to the young Fred Trueman. They were a disparate group – more a media creation than a Bloomsbury-style literary circle, meeting in each other's homes – and included not just marquee names like John Osborne and Philip Larkin, but the Yorkshire novelist John Braine, author of the 1957 classic *Room at the Top*, and the philosopher Stuart Holroyd, born in Bradford in 1933. Thematically, their work covered the waterfront, from the class war to the battle of the sexes, not forgetting politics and education. But they were well named. Anger – not the sudden flying-off-the-handle outburst, but the kind of resentful rage that burns for years on end – was their common denominator.

One of the first works associated with the Angry Young Men was Kingsley Amis's *Lucky Jim*, published in 1954, when Fred Trueman was still seething after his first overseas tour with England, which took him to the Caribbean. After the happy triumphalism of Coronation Year, when Everest was scaled and England regained the Ashes at the Oval, with Trueman in the XI, there was cordite in the air. In the Caribbean, the Test series against the West Indies finished 2-2 – an honourable draw, in the circumstances, with England having to come from behind against formidable opponents, who included the three Ws, Worrell, Walcott and Weekes – but there were so many unsavoury incidents, on and off the field, that it became the most rancorous overseas tour since Bodyline.

At the thick of the action – young, brash, bellicose, opening his mouth before putting his brain into gear, usually with an expletive on his tongue – was Fred Trueman. His relations with his captain, Len Hutton, deteriorated from bad to awful, with Hutton insisting on formalities such as being called 'Skipper', which Trueman thought were plain daft. Throw in spats with umpires and various diplomatic incidents at cocktail parties and comparisons with bulls and china shops became inevitable. At the end of the tour, Trueman's good-conduct bonus was withheld, which enraged him, and no explanation was given, which enraged him even more. By the time the new season started, with Trueman left out of the England side, he was fit to burst. If the Angry Young Men had been looking for recruits, he would have joined up on the spot.

Jim Dixon, the protagonist of Amis's novel, is a young history lecturer at a redbrick university – about as far from a Yorkshire fast bowler on a tour of the Caribbean as it is possible to get. But as he tries to hack it in a world for which he is hopelessly unprepared – putting his foot in his mouth, drinking too much, making botched overtures to women, blundering from crisis to crisis – his frustrations are the frustrations of young men the world over. His elders and betters expect him to conform, the way the men in blazers running England cricket expected Trueman to conform, but there is a voice inside his head screaming at him to do the exact opposite. He dreams of mutiny, even when making small talk. 'What wouldn't he give for a fierce purging draught of fury or contempt, a really efficient worming from the sense of responsibility?' His gradual emancipation from the tyranny of politeness and respectability gives the novel its cutting edge.

What made the Angry Young Men of the 1950s so distinct was the historical circumstances. Their fathers might have been stuffy and pompous and set in their ways, and possessed all the other attributes which drive teenagers up the wall, but they had also fought for King and Country and seen off Hitler and the Nazis. Quite simply, they were a generation of heroes. How the hell was the next generation meant to follow *that*? For young German men of Fred Trueman's generation, the only way to go was up. They duly got their heads down, worked hard and turned their country into the economic powerhouse of Europe. In Britain, the opposite dynamic applied. The young men of the era did not just have a hard act to follow, they had an impossible act to follow; they were doomed to be forever second best in the history books. No wonder so many of them were angry.

One of the seminal works of the Angry Young Men was John Osborne's *Look Back in Anger*, first performed at the Royal Court in 1956, the year of the Suez Crisis. If Jimmy Porter, Osborne's disaffected anti-hero, had played cricket, he would undoubtedly have been a fast bowler, with the head-high bouncer his weapon of choice. Parts of the play seem dated now, but it offers telling insights into why men like Amis and Osborne were quite so hot and bothered. Their wings had been clipped by an accident of history. As Jimmy Porter puts it: 'People of our generation aren't able to die for good causes any longer. We had all that done for us, in the 1930s and 40s, when we were still kids. There aren't any good, brave causes left. If the big bang does come, and we all get killed off, it won't be in aid of the old-fashioned grand design. It'll just be for the Brave New-nothing-very-much-thank-you. About as pointless and inglorious as stepping in front of a bus.'

Fred Trueman – patronised, if unintentionally, by Len Hutton, Norman Yardley and the other senior Yorkshire players who had served in the war – would have known exactly where Jimmy Porter was coming from. A strain of anti-authoritarian bolshiness – Jack was as good as his master, particularly if his master was wearing an MCC tie – ran deep in Trueman's character. And with Britain becoming less deferential by the minute, his willingness to ruffle feathers in high places enhanced his popularity more than it diminished it. In the war, the men of spirit had been soldiers, facing danger with fortitude. Now many of them were class warriors, standing up for the working man. Some of the battles into which they got drawn were largely symbolic, but they were fought with rare intensity by young men determined to put their virility to the test.

Among the Yorkshire-born sportsmen of his generation, probably the closest to Fred Trueman in terms of personality was the showjumper Harvey Smith, born in the West Riding in 1938. A stage Yorkshireman in the Trueman mould, trading on his bluntness, Smith is best remembered – and remembered with affection, however much people tut-tutted at the time – for directing a V-sign at the judges at an equestrian event. Fred Trueman would never have gone so far – he would have been too scared of incurring the wrath of his father – but there were times when you could see his fingers twitching. Luckily, as a fast bowler, he had other ways of letting rip.

Arguably the angriest of all the Angry Young Men – against stiff competition – was the poet Philip Larkin, who was born in Coventry in 1922, but spent most of his life in Hull, where he lived from 1955 till his death in 1985. By day, Larkin was a librarian at the University of Hull; out of hours, he festered, juggling lovers, dabbling in pornography, incubating increasingly racist views. He never married or had children and his most famous poem, 'This Be the Verse' (*They fuck you up, your mum and dad/They may not mean to, but they do*) is so bleak in tone that one cannot imagine Fred Trueman, most dutiful of sons, echoing its sentiments. Where Larkin was pessimistic, not to say misanthropic, Trueman was a natural optimist, convinced he was going to take a wicket every time he ran in to bowl. But the poet and the cricketer did share one attribute – a conviction, hardening as they got older, that the world was going to the dogs.

Larkin once confessed to a friend that he had stopped going to Test matches because there were too many black people – he used a stronger word – in the crowd. Trueman, for his part, found plenty of other things about modern Test cricket to irritate him. Indeed, of all the grizzled old pros in the commentary box, moaning that things had been better in their day, when players did not need agents and fitness coaches and nutritionists and sports psychiatrists, he was the uncrowned king. If he had ever put his thoughts about modern fast bowlers into poetry, they would have had a Larkinesque mordancy. Once an Angry Young Man, always an Angry Young Man.

If Fred Trueman became an arch-conservative once the fires of his youth had burnt themselves out, he also evolved and matured as a human being. George Hirst and Herbert Sutcliffe lived into their eighties, but were essentially the same men in old age as they had been when they were 30; their outlook on life never changed. The same could not be said of Trueman, for all his reactionary views. He grew up in one kind of world and he died in a different world and, in at least one important respect, he adapted. Not only did he divorce and remarry, which was far commoner among his generation than among his parents' generation, but he was prepared to share the experience with all and sundry, in a way that would once have been unthinkable.

His 2004 autobiography has an emotional frankness that you simply do not encounter in sporting memoirs of the 1950s, when he was in his pomp as a player. At times, particularly when his marriage to his first wife Enid is on the brink of collapse, the ageing Trueman lets it all hang out like a child of the Flower Power generation. Coming from one of the hard men of sport, raised in a tough school, it is a touching document. The prose is suspiciously polished, and the hand of the ghost writer is not hard to detect, notably when Voltaire is brought on to bowl, with a most un-Truemanlike quotation, but the sentiments – and the sentimentality, if one is being cynical – are fascinating.

In a typical passage, Trueman describes the misery he endured after the breakdown of his marriage: 'Night after night I sat alone in hotels or the houses of close friends and cried like a child. I was convinced that life for me was finished, that there was nothing for me to look forward to. In truth I had very few close friends that I could open up to. Over the years, I had made a concerted and successful effort to build a wall to keep people out.'

On the subject of love – a four-letter word he would never have heard used in the Yorkshire dressing room – Trueman holds forth at some length, the sage of the tribe, pipe in hand: 'I've learnt from life that love can take many forms. There is the grand passion, which is electric, stimulating and fulfilling. But that sort of love simply can't be enduring all the time. There is also another type of love in a long-term relationship. Though it does not involve grand passion, it is stronger, in many ways more comforting. It's a companionable love in a relationship that does the ironing, gets the weekly shopping in, knows what clothes to buy for the children. A love which checks the car insurance and never forgets birthdays… It's a perceptive and common-sense love that knows which picture should go where, what curtains should go with the three-piece, what colour the bathroom should be painted. It is the love that decorates your dull facade, that delves into the toolbox and applies the nuts and bolts to keep yourself together.'

Too much information, Fred. Cricket fans who remember the great fast bowler at his belligerent best will find his ruminations on curtains – even the revelation that he lived in a house with curtains, not a cave in the Pennines, feeding off raw meat – dismayingly banal. But it is the ease with which Trueman glides from a masculine world to a feminine one that is so striking – his father or grandfather could never have pulled off the same trick. When Cupid's arrow strikes, and Trueman meets his second wife, Veronica, he could be writing a Mills and Boon novel, having studied O-level psychology at night school: 'There was something inside her that sparked something inside me. As we talked, I could feel an indefinable chemistry between us... My stomach was doing cartwheels and my heart was racing... She was beautiful, easy-going, fun to be with... I was comforted by her understanding, her sensitivity and her emotional empathy... We were not only supportive of one another's physical needs for security and survival, but also supportive of each other's intellectual and spiritual needs.'

Is this the Fred Trueman who terrorised batsmen from Sydney to Trinidad? Whose growls and curses rang across the cricket field? Who must have sat in every pub in Yorkshire, pint in hand, puffing at a pipe, surrounded by blokes called Ted and Barry? Whose no-nonsense, working-class humour, with its combative edge, spoke to a generation? Is this the son of a man's man who grew up to be a man's man himself, hung out with men's men and only respected other men who were men's men?

The answer, miraculously, is yes.

If the 1950s belonged to the anti-heroes, from the Angry Young Men to James Dean and Marlon Brando – not forgetting Fred Trueman himself, the rebel in cricket whites – there was still room for heroes of a more traditional stamp: the type every man wanted to be and every woman wanted to bed.

The archetypal fictional figure of the age, his influence still felt today, was Ian Fleming's James Bond. The first of the Bond novels, *Casino Royale*, appeared in 1953, the year after Trueman made his England debut, and the last of them, *The Man with the Golden Gun*, in 1965, the year he played his last Test, against New Zealand at Lord's. By that stage, of course, the Bond films were beginning to appear and a character from a series of niche English adventure stories was well on his way to becoming a global brand. But it is Fleming's Bond, not Sean Connery or Roger Moore or his other screen impersonators, who is the real McCoy – and who tells us quite a lot about perceptions of manliness in the 1950s and early 1960s. Forget the asinine props: the vodka martinis, the Aston Martin, the Morland's cigarettes. Fleming set out to create a character who would speak to a generation – and achieved his goal with panache.

Bond is physically tough. That goes without saying. He is not quite in the Brian Close league. When the villains torture him – flaying his genitals with a carpet-beater, as Le Chiffre does in *Casino Royale*, or breaking his little finger, as Mr Big does in *Live and Let Die* – he shows that he is hurting. On more than one occasion, he passes out with pain. Brian Close would have hung grimly in there. Or he would have chuckled, asked for another martini and started holding forth about the evils of one-day cricket. But Bond is certainly virile, and brave with it. He is also handsome, albeit in an unconventional way, with a comma of black hair flopping over his forehead – shades of Fiery Fred running in to bowl – a scar on his cheek and blue-grey eyes, with a hint of cruelty in them. But looks and physical toughness, although they are part of the identikit male hero, are only half the story. James Bond's enduring appeal – to both sexes, if not necessarily to the same extent – has more complex roots.

'I would remember him forever as my image of a man,' says Vivienne, the heroine of *The Spy Who Loved Me* – an execrable film, but an interesting book, if only because Fleming uses a female narrator for the first and last time. Vivienne is an American motel-owner who is rescued from the clutches of a pair of vicious hoodlums by a handsome British secret agent who happens to be passing. After killing the hoods,

Bond has his way with a grateful Vivienne and drives off. It is a silly plot, even by James Bond standards, but there is no mistaking the mythical qualities with which 007 is imbued. Vivienne is certainly not blind to them: 'Apart from the excitement of his looks, his authority, his maleness, he had come from nowhere, like the prince in the fairy tales, and he had saved me from the dragon.'

In the films, Bond is serially promiscuous, and flippant with it. But Fleming's Bond is a more interesting character altogether, a throwback to the age of chivalry. He saves a lot of women from a lot of dragons, not because he wants to get them into bed, but because he sees dragon-slaying, and the rescuing of damsels in distress, as part of his natural function as a man – one could almost say part of his *duty* as a man. Where women are concerned, it is vulnerability, not looks per se, that attracts Bond. He likes finding birds with broken wings and taking them under his own wing. Honeychile Rider, the heroine in *Dr No*, played by Ursula Andress in the film, has a broken nose – a detail the cinema airbrushed out. Tiffany Case in *Diamonds Are Forever* was gang-raped as a girl. The same pattern is repeated again and again, with Bond not just a sex symbol, but a man of compassion.

There is no point in pretending the character has stood the test of time. Nowadays damsels are expected to slay the dragons for themselves, or at least have a degree in dragon-slaying from a reputable university. Even if a knight in shining armour does slay a dragon, the most he can expect from the damsel he has rescued is a short text message with an X at the end. The sexual quid pro quo which Bond regards as his right, and which the women in the novels accord him as his right, is a thing of the past. Reading one of the Bond books today can be a surreal experience: one minute you are swept away by the vigour and economy and sheer virtuosity of the storytelling – which none of the films has come close to replicating – the next you are wincing at sentiments which belong to the Stone Age, never mind the 1950s.

In *Casino Royale*, Ian Fleming has hardly taken guard before he is essaying this inelegant slog over cow corner: 'These blithering women who thought they could do a man's work. Why the hell couldn't they stay at home and mind their pots and pans and stick to their frocks and gossip and leave man's work to the men?'

Feminists scouring the Ian Fleming oeuvre for evidence of male chauvinism have found such easy pickings that most of them have abandoned the task as tediously simple. Here is 007 in *Thunderball*, plugging a commercial product so shamelessly that you wonder if Fleming owned shares in the company: 'Any more ticking-off from you, Moneypenny, and when I get out of this place, I'll give you such a spanking you'll have to do your typing off a block of Dunlopillo.'

The principle of sexual equality might have been conceded in the 1920s, when women were granted the vote, but the practical application of the principle was proving problematic. In the home, the balance of power was shifting. The war had empowered women in all kinds of ways. Between 1931 and 1951, the proportion of married women with jobs – and the greater independence that went with them – rose from 16 per cent to 40 per cent. It was a big increase and, in time, would have revolutionary implications. But the playing field was not yet level – or the marital home a place of harmony and peace.

The gulf in understanding between the sexes was as deep as ever. 'The women, and the lives they lead, and what they talk about and think about, are an impenetrable mystery,' wrote Clancy Sigal after his 1961 visit to a Yorkshire mining village. Many men were still more comfortable in the company of their own sex than in the bosom of their families.

Running through the Bond novels is a strong scepticism about the institution of marriage. 'Most marriages don't add two people together,' says Bond in *Diamonds Are Forever*. 'They subtract one from the other.' Bond is a lone wolf, partly because he works in such a dangerous profession; and although he does briefly get hitched, in *On Her Majesty's Secret Service*, his appeal as a fictional hero resides in the fact that his life is not dominated by dreams of wedding bells. The rituals associated with courtship bore Bond, as this typically sardonic passage from *Casino Royale* illustrates: 'The conventional parabola – sentiment, touch of the hand, the kiss, the passionate kiss, the feel of the body, the climax in the bed, then more bed, then less bed, then the boredom, the tears and the final bitterness – was to him shameful and hypocritical.'

Fred Trueman would have heartily despised such sentiments and dismissed them as fashionable twaddle. Fleming was an Old Etonian, always a red rag to a bull with Trueman, and had a frivolous streak later replicated in his nephew Matthew Fleming, who played cricket for Kent in a manner that would have caused a riot at Headingley – his first two scoring shots in first-class cricket were sixes. In matters matrimonial, as we have seen, Trueman was pretty conservative, marrying young, feeling miserable and guilty when that marriage failed, then re-marrying in a late flush of romantic fervour. Marriage, for men of his generation, was the unassailable norm. In 1956, the statistical probability of a man marrying before he was 50 was 94 per cent – it had never been so high before and it would never be so high again.

'They fitted together with the comfortableness of two people who knew each other's strengths and weaknesses,' remembers Alan Titchmarsh of his parents, an Ilkley plumber and his wife, who married in the late 1940s. Mrs T did most of the talking. Mr T hid behind his newspaper, poring over the small ads in the *Daily Express* as a pretext for not making conversation. It was a cocoa-and-slippers relationship, with its own precise rituals. Mrs T would send Mr T off to work with a packed lunch and, on parting, they would exchange three kisses, two short, one long, like a message in Morse code. But the marriage worked. It was solidly built. Both partners to the relationship knew their place.

Monogamy did not preclude infidelity. Clancy Sigal captures the gossipy, hard-nosed world of a Yorkshire mining village of the era, when the sight of a pregnant woman in a pub would start a 'Who's the father?' guessing game. But as an institution, marriage remained the bedrock of society.

Fred Trueman may have been less cynical about marriage than Ian Fleming, but in one important respect, his views about the relationship between the sexes chimed with those of Fleming and other men of the time, or the great majority of them. Men and women were *different*, and had different roles in life. A man's man encapsulated those differences. He did not strive to bring out his feminine side, as the men of today feel enjoined to do. He strove to bring out his masculine side, to do everything in his power to conform to age-old ideals of strength and vigour and self-sufficiency. Life was simpler that way.

The clearest statement of James Bond's views on the subject can be found in *Goldfinger*, after he has drawn a blank with a woman who turns out to be lesbian. He is sulking furiously, like a boy who has lost the chocolate bar on which he has spent his pocket money. The passage flies so much in the face of political correctness that one feels embarrassed quoting it, but it also captures, with brutal precision, the mindset of a certain kind of man at a certain point in history: 'As a result of 50 years of emancipation, feminine qualities were dying out or being transferred to the males. Pansies of both sexes were everywhere, not yet completely homosexual, but confused, not knowing what they were. The result was a herd of unhappy sexual misfits – barren and full of frustration, the women wanting to dominate and the men to be nannied. Bond was sorry for them, but he had no time for them.'

Fred Trueman lived long enough to benefit from changing social attitudes and to recognise some of the deficiencies of the hard, unsentimental men of his father's generation. But in the 1950s, that more nuanced way of looking at the world was quite rare. Men saw themselves as so fundamentally different from women that it was futile to try to bridge the gulf: better to act the hard man and play the virility card; better to dissemble than to admit to doubts or weakness.

Whether they were angry or just irritated, the young men of the period had a long way to go. They were still wearing a mask, playing up to cartoon stereotypes. There was a revolution just around the corner, but they never saw it coming – or foresaw that, after the Swinging Sixties, life for the male of the species would never be the same again.

CHAPTER 5
GEOFFREY BOYCOTT: MANLINESS ON THE BACK FOOT

*Does coming from Yorkshire make this relic believe that
he can say what he likes about everything? He trades off his
sham of a Yorkshire stereotype and doesn't have the brains to
know what he's talking about half the time. I don't understand
why this loud-mouthed old twit is still employed by anyone.*

'Barry', in a post on the Eurosport website in March 2011,
after Boycott had criticised Michael Yardy for returning
home early from the Cricket World Cup, citing depression.

*Boycott is dead right. Modern sportsmen are soporific drips.
To be selected to play for your country is the highest honour
you can have. Saying that you are going home because of
depression or your wife is having a baby or your big toe hurts
is a flabby, gutless attitude. God Save the Queen.*

'Ebrington Oik', in a post on the same site.

'*Boycott?*' said a bemused friend, when I explained about this book.
'What's he got to do with manliness?' I could see what he was thinking.
   Geoffrey Boycott's worst enemy never questioned his proficiency
as a batsman. He had a famously flawless technique: feet, hands and

head moving in perfect concert. It was not pretty, but it was a thing of beauty if you were an England supporter desperate not to see a wicket fall in the last over of the day. He raised the forward defensive shot to an art form. Ditto the backward defensive shot. Ditto the tuck into the leg side for a single to keep the strike/get off the strike.

'He was a genius,' conceded my friend. 'There was a touch of the mad scientist about him. If he hadn't been a cricketer, he might have invented the internet.' To his fans, he was a working-class hero, someone they could relate to: not super-gifted, but with the determination and the work ethic to make a little go a long way. He was the geek's geek, accumulating an improbable number of runs with the air of a bank clerk counting out £20 notes.

He might not have had the charisma of a Botham, or the elegance of a Gower, but that was not necessarily fatal. He made the humdrum heroic. He was the quiet boy at the back of the class, the one nobody took seriously, who ended up a millionaire. Boycott has many admirers – more than the equally self-absorbed golfer Nick Faldo, for instance – but even they have never regarded him as a virility symbol. He is just too weird: as unorthodox as a man as he was orthodox as a batsman. If you had a son with a picture of Geoffrey Boycott pinned to his bedroom wall, you would worry for him. If you had a daughter, you would worry even more.

An England batsman capable of scoring a century against Australia – and Boycott scored seven – should by rights be a romantic figure, a white knight in pads, acting out a million schoolboy fantasies. But there was something unromantic, even anti-romantic, about Boycott at the wicket. His determination to occupy the crease, often regardless of the state of the game, had an intense, fetishistic quality. Wasn't cricket, even at Test level, supposed to be *fun*? There was not much fun in a Boycott innings: even when he played a sweetly struck four, his face would pucker up as he contemplated the next ball. It was like a Tiger Woods round of golf: ferocious concentration made ugly by its joylessness. You instinctively knew that, if Boycott lost his wicket, he would treat it like a Greek tragedy, with himself as hero, the victim of malign Fate.

And you could sense, even while he was still batting, that he would not be a bundle of laughs in the bar afterwards; that he would still be brooding, replaying shots in his mind, defending with a straight bat, leaving balls outside the off stump. In a nutshell, he took the game too damn seriously. It was bad for his health. It was bad for everyone's health.

Perhaps the most frustrating thing about Boycott the batsman was that inside the tenacious, keep-the-bastards-at bay opener, there was a much freer spirit screaming to be let out. Very early in his career, in the 1965 Gillette Cup final, he scored 146 in such sparkling style, scoring freely all around the wicket, that it was like watching the ghost of Victor Trumper, a throwback to the Golden Age. But that more impish, more playful batsman was rarely seen again. The Roundhead in Boycott strangled the Cavalier.

He could talk a good game. He could talk a wonderful game. On retiring as a player, he became, by a distance, the outstanding commentator of his generation, elucidating the finer points of the game with the same skill he brought to his batting. If he had been a cautious batsman, as a pundit he gave full rein to his views: he had a bumptious energy, a relish in his own prejudices, that was instantly engaging; it made a splendid antidote to the blandness of his fellow commentators.

His early days in the commentary box were a revelation. In a nice re-working of the fable of the hare and the tortoise, Boycott at the microphone revealed a flair, a nimbleness, a vitality, an expressive range, which he had rarely shown at the wicket – while those great entertainers, Botham and Gower, churned out cliché after cliché.

He palpably enjoyed the work, in a way he had never enjoyed batting – or not that the spectator could see. But even talking about cricket, with his knowledge and enthusiasm shining through, his intensity could be off-putting, his intolerance of fools grating. He had been a mad scientist at the crease. Now he was the mad scientist at the lectern, too wrapped up in his subject to notice if anyone was listening – or the fact that he had overshot his time allocation and was keeping the next lecturer waiting.

Boycott was as immodest as Fred Trueman, as cocky, as sure of his own abilities, but in a less engaging way. Confidence was warped by arrogance. Of the self-deprecating charm that wins friends, he had not a thimbleful. His talents lay in the opposite direction – making people gasp at his sheer preening chutzpah.

Yorkshire in the latter half of the Boycott era became a soap opera: a club at permanent war with himself, with the committee room as the battleground. There was a time when you could hardly open a newspaper without reading about a bust-up between Boycott and Close, or between Boycott and Illingworth, or between Boycott and Close and Illingworth with additional material from Trueman. It was sad, sad stuff and it would be tedious to reprise the details here. Hard men from Yorkshire? More like babies throwing their toys out of the pram.

The ferocity of their rows certainly showed how much they cared about Yorkshire cricket. But there is caring and then there is *caring*. As feelings boiled over, and ego clashed with ego, good manners went out of the window. Even the diehard Yorkshire supporter Roy Hattersley, who had served in Harold Wilson's cabinet and knew everything worth knowing about the dark arts of political spinning, found the posturing of the principals demeaning. 'Each time there is a little dispute at Yorkshire, everybody attacks each other in public,' he wrote, more in sorrow than in anger.

The 1960s, the decade in which Boycott made his debut, was one of the most successful in Yorkshire's history, with the club notching up six county championships. The 1970s, mostly with Boycott captaining the side, were correspondingly disastrous. Were there just fewer good players in the team? Or had Yorkshire cricketers suddenly gone soft? And was the right man in charge? The arguments swirled around Boycott's head, season in, season out.

The great run-getter – and he was not the first batsman of whom this could be said – was not a great leader of men. In fact, judging by the number of fellow players he rubbed up the wrong way, he was an absolutely terrible leader of men: ten out of ten for being able to contribute his share of runs and demonstrate a correct forward defensive stroke; nought out of ten for tact, psychological acumen, consideration for others and the ability to foster loyalty and team spirit.

To his acolytes, who were well organised and split the club down the middle, he was a Coriolanus figure, a giant among pygmies. Yorkshire might have won nothing, but it was not his fault. Look at the runs he scored! Look at his batting average! To his detractors, he was at the root of Yorkshire's decline, eroding morale among his team-mates. Or he was something monosyllabic and unprintable.

Stories of Boycott's rudeness are legion. If Trueman was a lovable stage Yorkshireman, the plain man who speaks his mind, Boycott was the stage Yorkshireman gone haywire: the bluntness no longer charming, but abrasive. He scored over 8,000 runs for England, but must have upset far more than that number of people with the way he treated them. Mark Nicholas, who would commentate alongside Boycott at Channel 4, recalls a county match at Southampton in the 1980s when the elderly lady serving lunch put potatoes on Boycott's plate which he had not asked for. 'I don't bloody want your bastard potatoes,' said Boycott, before sweeping the potatoes off his plate and storming out of the room. Imagine George Hirst or Hedley Verity behaving like that. It was as if Yorkshire cricket had curdled: all that hard graft and steely competitiveness turned sour.

Always controversial at the best of times, Boycott found himself in much deeper water in 1998, when a French court convicted him of assaulting a former lover, Margaret Moore. The conviction, upheld on appeal, albeit in disputed circumstances, dealt a hammer blow to his career in the media – Boycott was fast making a name for himself in the commentary box – and did lasting damage to his reputation with the public. Was he guilty as charged? Only he and Margaret Moore know. But there is a painstaking account of the case in Leo McKinstry's excellent biography, *Boycs*, which casts doubt on the verdict, and my gut instinct is to follow McKinstry. In any event, the episode cast a spotlight on Boycott's private life, which he had previously – and laudably, many would say – defended as doggedly as his wicket.

There was a time when a Boycott-ologist, pondering what he was like off the field, could have been forgiven for concluding that he was gay. The evidence was patchy, circumstantial, rooted in crude stereotyping, but it was there:

1. He was unmarried, devoted to his mother and lived with her till he was nearly 40.
2. He preferred Cinzano to beer.
3. He was a fastidious, even dandyish dresser, with a trademark Panama hat.
4. He was pernickety about his diet, worked out and watched his weight like a hawk.
5. He was ultra-sensitive to slights, with a penchant for making himself the centre of attention.

Gay? Nothing could have been further from the truth. As the Margaret Moore case dragged on, and girlfriends and ex-girlfriends came forward to defend him, it became clear that Boycott had racked up women almost as voraciously as he racked up runs. His private life was so crowded that, if you had tried to represent it in graphic form, it would have looked like a century against Australia, with strokes all around the wicket: sweeps, pulls, off drives, square cuts, nurdles into the leg side, even the odd hooked six. Oozing self-confidence, and master of the bold chat-up line, Boycott wooed and won, but on his own terms – none of his conquests was going to get him to the altar.

Margaret Moore may have been the first woman to bring an assault charge against Boycott, but she was not the first of his lovers to discover that he was not the marrying type. Lovers came and went. Some overlapped with others. Some stayed with him for years. But if they dreamed of wedding bells, they were dating the wrong man. Boycott was dead set against the whole institution. He was a loner on the field – congenitally selfish, according to his critics, particularly fellow batsmen he had run out – and a loner off it. If Fred Trueman was soulmate to the Angry Young Men of the 1950s, Geoffrey Boycott represented a new type of man, a type that became increasingly familiar in the 1970s and 1980s, as the dust settled after the Beatles and Vietnam and the CND marches.

No rushing into marriage for *Homo Boycottensius*. No pram in the front hall or patter of tiny feet. No pipe-smoking paterfamilias with a dutiful wife to fetch his slippers. Let his girlfriends grumble that he was scared of commitment. He didn't care. He was his own man, entire unto himself, an island in the shifting sea. Boycott was well into his sixties before he finally tied the knot.

Time – and a brush with cancer – may have mellowed the one-time bachelor. Depending who you talk to, he seems to be slightly less rude slightly less often to slightly fewer people – although there are Boycott-watchers who would want that verdict reviewed by the third umpire. The nasal-voiced curmudgeon, the cocky Tyke whose mam could play modern fast bowling with a stick of rhubarb, will probably end his days dandling grandchildren on his knee, grinning at strangers and admitting to a sneaking affection for Twenty20 cricket. But when his obituaries are written, the word 'selfish' is sure to feature.

Rightly or wrongly, the label, so damning in a team sport, has stuck to him for half a century. In fact, it looms larger than all those batting records that seemed so important at the time. People forget statistics, eventually. They never forget the qualities that make and unmake human beings.

There are a lot of Geoffrey Boycotts dotted around England, wrapped up in their private worlds, obsessed with their hobbies, ploughing lonely furrows, interacting only gingerly with their fellow men – and women. Boycott may not represent anybody's ideal of manliness. But, warts and all, he is a man of his times, reflecting the confusions and uncertainties of the age.

Born in the mining village of Fitzwilliam, near Wakefield, on 21 October 1940, Boycott's autobiography talks almost as lyrically about his childhood as Fred Trueman's did about his. They were very different men, but came from very similar worlds, rooted in traditional family values.

The man was the breadwinner, the woman was the homemaker and the children did as they were told or they got a clip around the ear. At school, they did their lessons or their teachers clipped them around the ear. Then they grew up, married, had their own children and clipped *them* around the ear. Compared with the rules of cricket, life in a Yorkshire mining village in the mid-20th century had the simplicity of a

Punch and Judy show. The spirit of Dotheboys Hall – Charles Dickens' savage Yorkshire boarding school, presided over by Mr Wackford Squeers with his cane – lived on.

Michael Parkinson remembers one of his teachers at Barnsley Grammar School – a refugee from Nazi Germany who, of all people, should have known better – stomping around the class bashing children on the head, practically at random. 'I still feel angry when I think about him,' says Parkinson. It was hardly a child-centred world – many children suffered neglect and abuse – but at least there were clear and understood boundaries. 'If a teacher clipped your ear, the assumption was that you had earned it, and that assumption was usually right,' Boycott remembers. With discipline, however rough and ready, came structure.

A national poll of teachers in 1952, when Boycott was 12 years old, found that 89 per cent wanted corporal punishment to be maintained. In Yorkshire, the figure would probably have been even higher. It was at least ten years before attitudes started to change. But if children got hit a lot, they were nurtured in other ways. Boycott – piquantly, for a man later so seemingly bereft of team spirit – lays particular stress on the sense of community in his village. 'It seems hopelessly outmoded and old-fashioned now, but it was in many ways better than the society which is overtaking and replacing it,' according to his autobiography. He has moved a long way from his roots, but he has not forgotten them. His father was a colliery worker, and he grew up in a terraced house, but if he was poor or underprivileged, that was not how it felt at the time: 'All we knew was that we had clothes on our backs, enough food to eat and a rugged affection for our parents which was no less warm – and probably more lasting – for being laced with discipline. We led a knockabout, simple existence bordered by breakfast at one end of the day and an unwilling bedtime at the other.'

If playing cricket and football in the streets offered an escape from the daily grind of school and homework, the same was true of trainspotting, a hobby so exquisitely apt it can only be called Boycott-esque. The thought of the future England cricketer peering through the Yorkshire fog for a glimpse of the 6.43 from Wakefield, notebook in hand, almost makes you love the man. Boycott was also an enthusiastic patron of the local cinema, the Plaza, rushing to get a seat in one of the front three rows, within touching distance of the screen. He developed a particular passion for Westerns starring John Wayne: 'They were the sort of pictures that modern-day intellectuals would probably dismiss as superficial. True enough, the good guys always won, the cavalry always arrived in the nick of time and nobody who died actually looked hurt. But that was what we wanted… I was an absolute sucker for it all, unashamedly and without reservation.'

Anatomise any complex human being – and Geoffrey Boycott is as complex as they get – and you often find disarmingly simple components. If the child is father to the man, that bug-eyed boy at the Fitzwilliam Plaza, fixated by Westerns starring John Wayne, neatly anticipates the dogged England opener, standing fast against a marauding enemy. For arrows, bouncers. For whooping Apaches, Australian slip fielders. It is a strong human narrative, of mythic resonance.

One person to see that link was the poet Irene Murrell, who watched Boycott batting in the West Indies in 1980 and was immediately reminded of a Hollywood Western:

Five hours and more
Stalwart Boycott batted
Against the scathing bullets
Coming fast and furious
From the most savage bowlers
In this, or any other town:
Like the matured Gary Cooper
In High Noon
He played the hand
From where he stood, solo.

If John Wayne and his ilk embodied physical courage, they also had a bloody-minded, stubborn streak which would have appealed to Boycott. 'Never apologise,' says Captain Nathan Brittles, the character played by Wayne in the 1949 classic *She Wore a Yellow Ribbon*.

'It's a sign of weakness.' Did that line seep into the Boycott cerebellum? Apologising has never been his strong suit.

Outside the cinema, a harsher reality was beginning to intrude. When he was eight years old, Boycott nearly died after falling off an iron railing and impaling himself on the handle of an old mangle in the next-door garden. He spent two weeks in hospital and had to have his spleen removed. Two years later, his father had a serious accident at the colliery, damaged his spine and never fully recovered. A stable home became an anxiety-ridden home, with money worries never far away. If Boycott had come from a middle-class family, he would probably have gone to university – he had the brains. As it was, he left school at 17 and, before making the grade at Yorkshire, worked at the Ministry of Pensions.

The biggest hurdle to his ambition to play cricket for his county was the fact that, from the age of 16, he had to wear glasses. 'Nobody, but nobody, in top sport needed glasses,' Boycott remembers. 'Specs were for intellectuals and weeds, not sportsmen.' For a time, he was inconsolable, consumed by a sense of failure. It was a letter from M. J. K. Smith of Warwickshire, later captain of England, which alerted him to the possibility of wearing rimless glasses with special shatterproof lenses. 'I probably looked like Himmler, but the psychological effect was amazing,' says Boycott. His self-confidence restored, he was soon scoring a stack of runs, first for Barnsley – where his contemporaries included Michael Parkinson and umpire Dickie Bird – then for Yorkshire, then for England.

Spectacles were still not the ideal accessories for a professional sportsman. When Boycott made his Test debut against Australia in 1964, according to Leo McKinstry in *Boycs*, he was greeted by Aussie sledging at its most unsubtle. 'Hey, Garth, look at this four-eyed fucker,' yelled the Australian captain Bobby Simpson at his fast bowler Graham MacKenzie. 'He can't fucking bat. Knock those fucking glasses off him right away.' Boycott, thick-skinned, ignored the insults and scored a creditable 48.

He later changed to contact lenses, with no adverse effect on his batting, and the glasses, perversely, have done his reputation more harm than good. If courage is one of the manly virtues, and is embodied by a batsman standing his ground against a fast bowler, then a bespectacled batsman facing the same fast bowler – and far more vulnerable in the eyes of the spectator – embodies that courage even more. He may not be a Byronic figure, but he inspires admiration. He is like a diminutive rugby full-back waiting beneath an up-and-under with the opposition scrum bearing down on him. The spectators are on his side, anticipating his pain, admiring his pluck and determination.

Boycott's short-sightedness, and the owlish associations that went with it, probably helped him in other ways. As memories of the war receded, action men were losing ground to intellectuals. It no longer mattered whether you could strangle a German paratrooper with your bare hands: the ability to get a well-paid job was more important. The age of John Wayne was drawing to a close. If Arthur Miller, who looked as if he could hardly hold a gun, never mind kill 30 Apache horsemen with his arm in a sling, could marry Marilyn Monroe, the sex symbol to end all sex symbols, there was hope for everyone.

Boycott, with his slight physical frame and receding hair, could never out-Trueman Trueman, but he offered something a little bit different, for which there was a growing market, among men and women alike. A star in glasses could be likeable, intriguing, even cool: he chimed with the values of a prosaic age. In the cinema, Michael Caine's laconic Cold War spy Harry Palmer, who made his debut in *The Ipcress File* in 1965, enjoyed a cult following – his glasses were just so deliciously incongruous. James Bond suddenly had a rival, a hero who ticked very different boxes but was still a charismatic figure.

On the cricket field, one of the most popular players of the Boycott era, if briefly, was the bespectacled Northamptonshire batsman David Steele. His heroics in the 1975 Ashes series, when he was dubbed 'the bank clerk who went to war' after standing up stoutly to Lillee and Thomson, so endeared him to the public that he was voted BBC Sports Personality of the Year.

Boycott himself never got a sniff of the award, despite the massive contribution he made to the England cause. His 22 centuries for his country put him equal top of the all-time list, alongside Hammond and Cowdrey. None of them were easy on the eye. Some of them were positively painful on the eye. But they were testimony to a conscientious, hard-working professional who won the respect, if not always the affection, of his contemporaries.

At the wicket, Boycott grafted, as Sutcliffe had grafted. There were no grace notes, no histrionics, no flashy cover drives. That sort of thing had been drummed out of him when he was young. His apprenticeship as a cricketer followed a trajectory familiar to generations of Yorkshire players: a begrudging recognition that he had talent, followed by years pouring cold water on his achievements. 'Nothing was given easily at Yorkshire, which is precisely as it should be,' Boycott wrote in his autobiography. From his coach, the famously hard-bitten Arthur 'Ticker' Mitchell, the highest praise he could expect was 'Not bad, not bad'. His faults were dissected so pitilessly that it would have broken a lesser player. But Boycott toughed it out, like a persevering novice in a particularly strict religious order.

By his mid-twenties, he was opening the batting for England and, technically, the best player in the country. With time on his side, he could look forward to reeling off centuries as effortlessly as Herbert Sutcliffe in the 1920s and 1930s. That it did not quite work out like that, that Boycott endured setback after setback – dips in form, rows over the England captaincy, rows over the Yorkshire captaincy, the humiliation of being dropped for slow play after scoring a Test double century – owed as much to his idiosyncratic personality as to the vicissitudes of fate.

He was not a monster, but he seemed an awkward bugger, however you sliced him. He could be quite affable one minute, impossibly surly the next. People never knew where they stood with him. Again and again, he would get into an argument, then make the argument worse by digging in his heels when the situation called for a graceful retreat. Feuds swirled around him.

An armchair psychologist, surveying Boycott from afar at the start of the 1970s, when he was about to turn 30, would probably have come up with a simple diagnosis: 'Still a few rough edges there. Bit of a chip on his shoulder. Not fully house-trained yet. But nothing that the love of a good woman can't put right.' The trouble was that, as Leo McKinstry relates, Boycott enjoyed the love of so many good women that, in some ways, it compounded his problems.

He was devoted to his widowed mother Jane and lived with her till her death in 1978. He had a relationship for over 40 years with Ann Wyatt, a colleague from his days at the Ministry of Pensions. He also had a ten-year affair with Shirley Western, a blonde singer whom he met in 1963. After that, there was Rachael Swinglehurst, the mother of his daughter, Emma, whom he eventually married. Throw in the many women who were around more fleetingly and it was a crowded canvas, with a strangely muted hero at the centre. 'I don't know,' he told a newspaper interviewer in 1999, when asked if he had ever been in love. 'I don't know,' he repeated, when asked what the lovers with whom he had been in long-term relationships had given him. He was as reticent about his emotions as he was forthright about the evils of reverse sweeps and slow over rates.

There is a rather poignant passage in his autobiography – poignant because it is so matter-of-fact – dealing with the death of his father in 1967: 'He had been ill in the Gateforth hospital near Selby for some time and I was at the Oval with Yorkshire when the secretary John Nash rang with the news. Close suggested I stayed and played the match. There was, after all, very little I could do until the funeral. He was probably right.' Very little he could do until the funeral? Given his known closeness to his mother, it is an extraordinary statement, certainly read from a modern perspective. But the episode sheds light both on the tight-lipped culture in the Yorkshire dressing room – where little had changed since the 1930s – and on Boycott's own reticence.

It is commonplace for women to rail at the way men are able to decouple sex from long-term commitment. Boycott seems, on the surface, to have offered a textbook case. At least, if he was non-committal, anti-marriage, resolutely single, he was honestly non-committal. 'It's no use guessing what other people bloody think,' he told the same interviewer. 'I just give them what I am. There are no hidden agendas. I'm open and frank. If they misunderstand my intentions, they can't be listening.'

The contrast with Herbert Sutcliffe, his fellow England opener, is quite revealing. Both were consummate professionals. Both were dour players, grafters not showmen. Both were physically vain, pernickety about their appearance. Both were ladies' men, happier exerting their charms on the opposite sex than bonding with their male team-mates. But there the comparison comes to a grinding halt. Sutcliffe, being a man of his times, married in his twenties, settled down, had children, played the paterfamilias. Boycott, born into a different world, pursued a diametrically opposite course: chasing women, but resisting getting married to them. Was he just luckier than Sutcliffe, less constrained by social convention, the beneficiary of new sexual freedoms, a red-blooded, bedpost-notching male able to have his cake and eat it? Or was all that a mirage?

One of the central ironies of Geoffrey Boycott's career was that, while he was scoring runs at a tempo that ranged from funereal to glacier-like, the wider society of which he was part was changing so rapidly that some people found it hard to keep up. It was like watching two parallel universes.

That was never truer than in the summer of 1967. On the morning of 8 June, Boycott went out to bat for England against India at Headingley. Struggling for form before the match, he began cautiously and continued in the same vein, as if batting on a minefield. It was turgid stuff, even by Boycott standards. By lunch, he had scored just 25, including eight in an hour at one point. Time seemed to be standing still. By tea, even the long-suffering Yorkshire fans were fidgeting, taking a nap or drowning their sorrows in the bar. By close of play, he had reached a buttock-numbing 106 not out. And he was not done yet. Resuming the following morning, he continued to play conservatively and, by the time England declared after tea, was undefeated on 246, scored off 555 balls in 573 minutes. Overall, the statistics do not seem too shabby – there have been slower innings, including some by Boycott himself – but against a toothless Indian attack on an innocuous wicket, the lack of urgency in Boycott's play, particularly on the first day, was widely condemned. The press were scathing, the selectors unforgiving. Boycott, ignominiously, found himself dropped for the next match, accused of slow and selfish batting – a slur he resents to this day.

Whatever the merits of dropping him, it was certainly a snail-like innings, remembered like a bad dream by those unlucky enough to watch it. The contrast with events taking place at Westminster at the same time – where Parliament was passing the Sexual Offences (No. 2) Bill at a cracking pace, sweeping away centuries of discrimination against homosexuals as if swatting long-hops over square leg for six – could not have been starker. The bill, which decriminalised homosexual acts between consenting adult males, was passed by the Commons in June, had its second reading in the Lords on 13 July and received the Royal Assent on 28 July, after an all-night sitting. It was the parliamentary equivalent of a Twenty20 match.

Backed by a reforming Home Secretary, Roy Jenkins, the private member's bill was co-sponsored by the backbench Labour MP Leo Abse, a practising psychiatrist, and Lord Arran, an eccentric Tory peer who had also tried – without success – to introduce legislation protecting badgers. Asked why he had failed in his campaign to protect badgers, but had better luck with homosexuals, he replied: 'There are not many badgers in the House of Lords.'

Dipping into *Hansard* reports of the debates on the bill, it is clear that its passage by Parliament was by no means a foregone conclusion. The 9th Baron Auckland, one of the Tory backwoodsmen in the Lords opposing the bill, evinced social attitudes that were not unrepresentative: 'My Lords, whatever happens to this Bill, will the full stretches of medical research be put to the limit to try to help these unfortunate people, the homosexuals, and to try, at least in part, to cure them of these habits? With medical research as it is at present, I believe this can be done, even if it takes a long time…

'In one of the more popular Sunday newspapers last week, there appeared an account of a homosexual wedding in a Continental country. I think the newspaper concerned is to be congratulated on highlighting this very nasty happening. I do not think these things could ever happen in this country, but it is possible…'

In the event, the opponents of the bill were routed, the reformers carried the field and, in Parliament at least, the momentum for change had become unstoppable. Just three months later, in October 1967, another landmark piece of legislation reached the statute book – David Steel's Abortion Act, which licensed the carrying out of abortions by registered practitioners.

In the same month, Desmond Morris, a zoologist at London Zoo, published *The Naked Ape*, serialised in the *Daily Mirror*. It was a runaway bestseller – sales were so substantial that Morris briefly had to flee the country to escape the taxman – and one of the most influential books of the decade. Noting that *Homo sapiens* did not just have a bigger brain than any other species of primate, but a bigger penis as well, Morris declared him 'the sexiest primate alive' – giving yet another green light to any male members of the *Homo sapiens* club who might have been backward in coming forward. Morris also pointed out that the earlobes were an erogenous zone, which would have been news in Yorkshire, but news not without interest. It was like discovering a new way to bowl an off-break.

With the contraceptive pill now in common use – its availability on the NHS had been announced in December 1961 by Enoch Powell, of all people, then Minister of Health – the last bricks of the sexual revolution had been put in place. Philip Larkin's wry poem 'Annus Mirabilis' (*Sexual intercourse began/In nineteen sixty-three*) perfectly caught the spirit of the age.

The sexual revolution might have come too late for the lecherous Larkin, as determined and bloody-minded a bachelor as Boycott, but born half a generation earlier; for Boycott, who won his county cap in 1963, the year sexual intercourse began, it was as perfectly timed as a crisply struck cover drive. He was young, he was fit, he was highly sexed and he was about to take the field in what Larkin, in the same poem, called the 'quite unlosable game'. Bliss was it in that dawn to be alive, but to be a rising star of English cricket, free to sow his wild oats all over the world, from Sydney to Barbados via Cape Town, must have been very heaven.

The Yorkshire in which Boycott had grown up was still pretty conservative. One of his jobs at the Ministry of Pensions in the early 1960s was to vet claims for maternity benefits, which required applicants to state whether they were married, divorced, separated and so on. Boycott hated every minute: 'There was an enormous social stigma associated with unmarried mothers and even divorcees. People would leave that part of the form blank on purpose. I had to press them for answers – it seemed very hurtful and personal.' Post-1963, attitudes changed at breakneck speed. A survey that year found that three-quarters of people still thought that sex before marriage was wrong. By 1973, the figure had fallen to just ten per cent – an astonishing turnaround.

There were still pockets of resistance, some in Yorkshire. When the *Sun* introduced page three girls in 1970, the library at Sowerby Bridge – 'a grim pimple on the face of the Pennines', as the *Sun* described it – refused to stock the paper. But there was no doubt which way the wind was blowing. The family, the bedrock of society for so long, was wobbling. Fred Trueman, married in 1955, divorced in 1972, admitted to feeling ashamed and embarrassed about the break-up of his marriage. If he had lived just ten years later, his experience would have been different. In 1950, for every 1,000 married men, there were just 2.2 divorces a year; by 1980, the figure had climbed to 11.4. The scandalous was fast becoming commonplace.

Fathers were coming under the microscope as much as husbands. The old-style domestic autocrat no longer ruled unchallenged. In fact, if he was seen as stuffy, he courted ridicule. One of the most influential films of the decade was *The Sound of Music*, released in 1965. Change the scenery, the accents, the costumes and the weather, and the Christopher Plummer character could have been a tyrannical father in a suburb of Leeds. He needed Julie Andrews to soften and humanise him.

Historians will argue for years who were the real winners and losers in the Swinging Sixties, but it was certainly a decade in which being a man was problematic as well as pleasurable. Trends that seemed to betoken progress with a capital P had hidden downsides. After the greyness of the 1950s, there was suddenly an embarrassment of choice: any number of paths a man could follow without making himself a social pariah. If some men were cheerfully promiscuous, wallowing in the new hedonism, others went the other way, embracing the ascetic lifestyle advocated by Indian mystics, some of whom achieved guru status.

'He keeps himself in superb physical trim,' wrote the *Daily Express*'s Herbert Kretzner, in a 1969 profile of the actor Terence Stamp. 'He does not smoke or drink or take stimulants of any kind. He is a vegetarian and fasts for a whole day every week, usually on Thursdays… He recently sent back his rented television and sold his Rolls-Royce.' While most men did not go as far as Stamp – who probably needed a bit of detox, after years in the fast lane – they were certainly prepared to ditch some of the old macho posturing. The habits of sexual equality were becoming ingrained.

Martin Peters, one of England's 1966 World Cup heroes, admitted that he helped with the washing-up, put his baby to bed and changed nappies. Ten years earlier, he might have been committing professional suicide. But the new-look Britain could embrace a nappy-changing footballer – so long as men's men like Nobby Stiles and Ron 'Chopper' Harris and Norman 'Bite Yer Legs' Hunter did not jump on the bandwagon. Healthy trends were healthy trends, but there were limits.

'A man who doesn't spend time with his family can never be a real man,' declared Don Corleone in *The Godfather*, one of the most influential movies of the period. It is hard to imagine exactly the same line in a film of the 1930s. But lovey-dovey domestication had disadvantages as well as benefits. Research published in 1970 suggested that a typical married man in his thirties or forties spent just five hours a week relaxing with his mates, whether in the pub or on the sports field; the rest of his spare time was spent in the bosom of his family. Men of a liberal disposition started out doing the washing-up and changing nappies and, in no time at all, they were vacuuming the spare bedroom, cooking coq au vin and going on shopping expeditions to Marks and Spencer. The traditional dividing lines between the sexes had become blurred. No bad thing, said some. Emasculating, said others.

Many men found sexual equality threatening. It robbed them of a role. It challenged their traditional hegemony. Some of them started to harbour dark misogynistic impulses, like batsmen sulking because they had got a bad lbw decision. At its aggressive worst, such misogyny could be lethal. Boycott's most infamous contemporary, born in Bingley in 1946, was the Yorkshire Ripper, Peter Sutcliffe, who killed 13 women, mainly prostitutes, and terrorised a whole community. But even in much smaller doses, it could wreck marriages and sour relationships.

Men whose own parents had enjoyed stable, if often dull, marriages found themselves in a bewildering free-for-all, where more and more people were having sex with more and more partners, but there was no guessing who would end up in bed together at the final curtain. It was a great time to be a writer of bedroom farces and, in Scarborough, beloved of Yorkshire cricket fans, a master farceur was starting to make a name for himself. The 1970s produced more eminent writers than Alan Ayckbourn, but none whose work so perfectly caught the confusions of the time.

On 8 July 1971, as Boycott was scoring 112 against India at Headingley, one of Ayckbourn's early successes, *Time and Time Again*, had its premiere at the Library Theatre, Scarborough. It is one of very few stage plays to feature cricket – Ayckbourn was tickled pink when the Chappell brothers, Greg and Ian, went to see the play the following year – and makes satirical hay with the sort of men who excel at sport, but are correspondingly inept in their relationships with women. The action takes place beside a sports field, variously used for cricket and football. A farcical plot features sexual shenanigans, misunderstandings and petty jealousies, and ends on a bleak note, with a woman who has juggled two men deciding that neither is good enough for her. 'There's more to life than winning trophies,' reflects the rueful sports buff, Peter, who has been left on the discard pile.

Ayckbourn was as prolific in his field as Boycott in his. In the 1970s, his plays were hugely popular, not just because they were so skilfully crafted, but because they struck a chord with contemporary audiences. In the chaos of flaky marriages and grimly unsatisfactory affairs, often born as much out of desperation as love, people recognised the shifting quicksands of their own lives. They had thought they were better off than their parents, freer, less hidebound. Now, suddenly, they were not so sure.

Greater sexual freedom, perforce, meant greater diversity – and the embarrassment of choice that went with it. With fewer and fewer rules, men had to make up their own rules, and different men responded to the challenge in different ways. The largely homogenous world of pre-war Yorkshire, where every family unit looked pretty much identical, was just a memory.

Of Boycott's celebrity contemporaries at Barnsley Cricket Club, Michael Parkinson got married at the age of 24, had three children and has lived happily ever after, while Dickie Bird has never been married at all, except to cricket. Boycott himself, though shy of commitment, as we have seen, has steered an intriguing middle course between domesticity and blokeishness. Not for Boycs, the lads' night out at the pub with the beer flowing. The Boycott portrayed by Leo McKinstry in his biography seems happier chatting up a pretty brunette over a cocktail, telling her he is a Libra, asking what star sign she is, and taking it from there. You don't have to dig too deep to find his feminine side: a lot of the time, he wears it on his sleeve.

Chinese horoscopes – he was born in the Year of the Dragon ('strong, self-confident, assertive… do not suffer fools gladly… speak their mind, even when it is not appropriate') – are another of Boycott's areas of expertise. Inside the hard-boiled Yorkshireman, the instinctive Thatcherite, the über-rationalist, analysing the finer points of cricket in forensic detail, is a screaming New Ager, fascinated by alternative faiths. He has even visited a medium, he explained to Anthony Clare during his interview for the radio series *In the Psychiatrist's Chair*, and been impressed with what she told him.

At the greatest crisis of his life, when he was diagnosed with cancer in 2002, Boycott was not afraid to trust his feminine side. He gritted his teeth and toughed it out, the way John Wayne might have done in the Westerns he devoured as a boy. But he also sought advice from a feng shui teacher, and slept in a separate room to his partner Rachael, with his body facing in a certain direction to assist the healing process. He never learnt *that* trick from John Wayne.

Whatever Boycott's other faults, his receptiveness to new ideas has helped him to develop and mature in unexpected ways. He may come across as prosaic but, in many ways, he has the soul of a poet. One of his most engaging qualities – for which he is rarely given credit – is his unstinting admiration for cricketers with more natural gifts than him. His boyhood idol was not a fellow Roundhead, but that graceful Cavalier, Tom Graveney. Commenting on the 2005 Ashes series, Boycott could hardly keep the boyish enthusiasm out of his voice as Flintoff and Pietersen struck extravagant sixes of the kind he would never have dared attempt himself.

'Mediocrity knows nothing higher than itself, but talent instantly recognises genius,' wrote Conan Doyle in one of the Sherlock Holmes stories. By that yardstick, Boycott has talent in heaping profusion. But if he seems comfortable in his own skin – and it helps that the skin, or much of it, is rhinoceros-thick, impervious to criticism – the same has not been true of many of his contemporaries – even if, in some respects, they had never had it so good.

The world of the Hollywood Western, from which Boycott took such inspiration as a boy, was changing quicker than a sheriff reloading his gun. *How the West Was Won*, released in 1962, was the last hurrah for a traditional fictional genre which had male nobility at its core. By the mid-1960s, spaghetti Westerns were all the rage, with the amoral anti-hero Clint Eastwood superseding John Wayne in public affection. The decade ended with John Schlesinger's masterpiece *Midnight Cowboy*, in which the would be cowboy, trading off past glories, has become a pathetic figure. 'I may not be much of a cowboy, but I sure am one hell of a stud,' says Jon Voight, as he is reduced to selling his body for sex. A whole male mythology lay in ruins. Was it surprising that so many men felt vaguely confused about their sexuality?

Those of a homosexual disposition – or at least tempted to act in edgy, counter-cultural ways that might be construed as homosexual – had theoretically been given the green light by the 1967 legislation. But most were still too timid to embrace their new freedoms – particularly if they were professional sportsmen, subject to relentlessly macho peer pressure.

The short, sad life of figure skater John Curry, who won gold for Britain at the 1976 Winter Olympics and was voted BBC Sports

Personality of the Year, was emblematic of the residual furtiveness of the age. Birmingham-born Curry was gay but, until outed by a German tabloid newspaper, chose to conceal the fact, fearing that it would sabotage his career. He later contracted AIDS and died at the age of 44. Only after his death did the fact that he had conducted a two-year affair with the actor Alan Bates become public.

Parliament could pass all the laws it wanted, but it could not shift attitudes overnight, even in its own backyard. The Liberal Party leader Jeremy Thorpe was only one of a number of politicians whose careers were blighted by their homosexuality – or, more accurately, by the fear of exposure – years after the 1967 legislation was passed. Even in 2010 a cabinet minister, David Laws, was forced to resign because of an expenses fraud designed primarily to conceal his homosexuality.

In the arts, attitudes were more liberal, although it depended where you lived. Yorkshire was just not ready for full-on homosexuals. The painter David Hockney, born in Bradford in 1937, found his natural milieu in California, thousands of miles from home. But in the metropolitan south of the country, it was a rather different story. There was not quite a stampede to come out of the closet, but there was a greater tolerance of alternative lifestyles. There was also, in consequence, a greater willingness to experiment.

One of Boycott's most fascinating contemporaries, born in the same decade, was the singer David Bowie, a man who sedulously cultivated an androgynous look and whose shilly-shallying about his sexuality was reminiscent of Boycott trying to pinch a single off the last ball of the over, with a skittish partner. 'Yes!... No... Wait!... Come on!... Get back!... Sorry!'

Bowie, previously assumed to be straight because he was married, outed himself as bisexual in an interview with *Melody Maker* in January 1972. An admission of engaging frankness? Or a cynical attempt to drum up interest in his new album, *Ziggy Stardust*? Opinion in the music industry was divided. Bowie repeated his assertion that he was bisexual in an interview with *Playboy* in 1976, but then added cryptically: 'I can't deny that I have used that fact very well.' Curiouser and curiouser.

Talking of his relationship with his first wife Angie, Bowie used to joke that 'we met while fucking the same bloke'. It was a good line, and conceivably true, but most Bowie-watchers remained sceptical. The riddle of his sexuality remained – which was probably just what he wanted. David Buckley, one of his biographers, concludes that Bowie was 'a taboo-breaker and dabbler who… mined sexuality for its ability to shock'. While he was probably never gay or 'consistently actively bisexual', he did from time to time 'experiment, even if only out of a sense of curiosity and a genuine allegiance with the transgressional'.

Whatever the truth about Bowie, his willingness to play the bisexual card – at a time when John Curry, Jeremy Thorpe and thousands of other gay men were still frantically trying to conceal their sexual orientation – was symptomatic of some of the confusions which surfaced during the period of consolidation and retrenchment that followed the Swinging Sixties.

Men who had rebelled against what they perceived as the stuffiness of the wartime generation were not quite sure what they wanted to put in its place. They were tired of the tough-guy posturing, the hard-as-nails, never-give-an-inch mentality epitomised, for example, by the Leeds United team managed by Don Revie – and widely hated outside Yorkshire. They wanted to project a softer, gentler image. But how much softer? How much gentler? Overdo it and they risked making fools of themselves.

The most obvious manifestation of changing attitudes to masculinity was hair. Even in the late 1950s, a man who had let his hair grow so much as a millimetre over his collar would have been ridiculed as a sissy and deemed de facto homosexual. In fact, it would have been very hard to find such a man outside a gypsy encampment. Even if a rebellious teenager had managed to defy his parents, siblings and friends, and grown his hair long, he would have been chucked out of school by an incandescent headmaster, then frogmarched off to the barber by an even more incandescent regimental sergeant major – National Service was in force until 1960.

By the early 1970s, such is the power of peer pressure, long or longish hair had become not just acceptable, but pretty much compulsory. Even bishops and cabinet ministers went with the flow, visiting the barber less and less frequently and, in some cases, looking positively raffish. A short-back-and-sides haircut was tantamount to an admission that one was a fuddy-duddy. Even the bachelor and evidently celibate Prime Minister Ted Heath grew his hair longer and longer, millimetre by cautious millimetre, until he could have played a fop in a Restoration comedy.

In cricket team photographs of the period, hair extending over the collar is almost as ubiquitous as moustaches had been in photographs taken before the Great War. The trend for long hair was tough on those, Boycott included, who were not naturally hirsute; and in time, the tide would turn the other way, with skinheads in the vanguard of the counter-revolution. But what was so interesting about the trend was the way it blurred traditional gender boundaries.

A teenage boy growing a moustache or beard is saying, proudly and unambiguously: 'Look at me! I'm a man!' Whether he is short or tall, weedy or muscular, the one thing he is not, by iron biological logic, is a girl. The same boy growing long hair is making a very different statement. In fact, in the half-light of a cinema or nightclub, he is at serious risk of being *mistaken* for a girl. He could hardly put a bigger question mark over his sexuality if he wore high heels and make-up and called himself Wendy.

Young men who overdid the long hair, to the point where you could hardly see their faces through the forest of winsome curls, could expect a ribbing from men of an older generation. One of the best-loved sitcoms of the period was *Rising Damp*, which ran from 1974 to 1978, and featured a seedy northern landlord, Rigsby, played by Leonard Rossiter at his inimitable best. The clash of generations was intrinsic to the comedy, and no episode was complete without sarcastic comments from Rigsby at the expense of his long-haired student lodger, Alan, played by Richard Beckinsale. For Alan, as for many young men of the period, long hair was a mask for diffidence as much as a deliberate fashion statement – the character had even less success with women than the goatish, blundering Rigsby. But others turned hairstyles that looked vaguely girlish to positive advantage – which infuriated men of a more conservative stamp.

Fawlty Towers fans will need no reminding of the blissfully funny episode in which Basil locks horns with a cocky playboy-type guest, Mr Johnson, played by Nicky Henson. Johnson not only has shoulder-length hair, but wears a gold bracelet, an Egyptian fertility charm around his neck and a white cheesecloth shirt unbuttoned to his waist, to reveal a forest of dark hair. To Basil, the man is little better than an ape, and he makes no effort to hide his scorn. Sybil disagrees. 'You think we girls should be aroused by people like Gladstone and Earl Haig and Baden-Powell,' she taunts Basil, after flirting with Johnson. The gulf in perceptions of what constitutes manliness yawns between husband and wife like the Grand Canyon.

To the original audience, or 99 per cent of them, it was Basil, not Sybil, who was the absurd figure in the scene. He thought he was further along the evolutionary scale than the ape-like Johnson but, of course, and hence the comedy, the reverse was true: it was his own attitudes that belonged to the Neanderthal era. Later in the same episode, Basil works himself into a frenzy of outrage as the unmarried Johnson tries to smuggle a woman into his room, in breach of hotel rules.

History does not relate whether Geoffrey Boycott watched the *Fawlty Towers* episode when it was first screened, on 26 February 1979. Probably not. He had just returned from a frustrating tour of Australia and would still have been miserably analysing how he only managed to score 263 runs at 21.91 against a second-string Australian attack, weakened by defections to the TV tycoon Kerry Packer's rival series. His top score was 77 at Perth, which did not include a single boundary. He was at a very low emotional ebb, having lost his mother and the Yorkshire captaincy the previous year. But, even in the doldrums, brooding, his sympathies would have been with Johnson, not Basil. If unmarried men were to be debarred from entertaining female visitors in their hotel rooms, his own social life would have disintegrated. The permissive society, certainly so far as it extended to non-marital sex, was here to stay.

The professional sportsmen of the 1970s did not grow their hair as long as some of the pop stars of the period – Boycott himself never indulged, although he did let his sideburns go for a time – but with

143

more disposable income than they had ever imagined possible, they were regulars at trendy unisex hairdressing salons, paying silly money for hair-dos that would have made their fathers blush.

To Englishmen of the old school, the biggest blot on the sporting landscape in the 1970s was the succession of perms adorning the head of footballer Kevin Keegan, each more over-the-top than the last. The England centre-forward looked presentable at kick-off, but by half-time, when he had headed the ball a few times, resembled Michael Palin in drag in a *Monty Python* sketch: it only needed a headscarf, a pinny and a falsetto voice to complete the transformation. Men in their thousands imitated the Keegan perm. He was a sexy footballer, like David Beckham later, ergo male perms had to be sexy – the logic of the madhouse. But the fashion was short-lived and, like bell-bottoms and mullets, the Keegan perm died an ignominious death, mourned by few.

Keegan, like Boycott, had been born in a Yorkshire mining village, Armthorpe, but if one thing was certain during the 1970s, it was that where you had come from was no guide to where you would end up. Social mobility was increasing exponentially. There was an almost vertiginous sense of new freedoms waiting to be grasped. If only the choices facing people, men in particular, had been *simpler*.

George Hirst's finest hour came at the Oval in 1902, Herbert Sutcliffe's on the same ground in 1926, Hedley Verity's at Lord's in 1934. Fred Trueman didn't really have one finest hour – he had so many. But Geoffrey Boycott was the luckiest of the lot. The zenith of his career, the moment when the nation came closest to taking him to their hearts, occurred at his home ground, Headingley, in 1977, in a Test against Australia.

As he clipped Greg Chappell through mid-on to reach three figures, becoming the first player to score his hundredth first-class century in a Test match, the statisticians purred, the Yorkshire faithful went wild and Boycott himself looked happier than anyone could remember. It felt like an epiphany, a liberation from the straitjacket of caution that he had worn for so long.

The century itself – Boycott went on to score 191 – was unremarkable. A single here, a scampered two there, the odd punched four through the off side, the usual plethora of dot-balls and maiden overs. By his standards, it was a serene, stately innings, not the usual *angst*-ridden affair. But as always when he was at the crease, the spectator would have had ample time to think about other things. If Botham and Gower emptied bars, Boycott had a genius for sending people into a post prandial reverie.

And if such a spectator – say one of the Boycott-worshipping anoraks from the suburbs of Leeds – had chosen to spend the afternoon pondering the issue of masculinity, weighing the pros and cons of being a man in 1977, his ruminations would have been quite revealing.

On the plus side:

1. He did not have to worry unduly about getting his girlfriend(s) pregnant.
2. He was under no obligation to marry a woman just because he had slept with her. He could live with her for years without outraging the neighbours.
3. If he played his cards right, he could expect to have more sexual partners than his father, grandfather and great-grandfather put together.
4. He could take a woman out to dinner with a sporting chance that she would insist on paying her share of the bill.
5. He could date women who had interesting careers of their own and had interests that extended far beyond the home.
6. Provided he was discreet, he could have sex with a man, if he was so minded, without ending up in jail.
7. If he got married and was miserable, he could extricate himself from the marriage far more easily than had been possible before the war.
8. He no longer had to sport a stiff upper lip at all times, like his father and grandfather. Expressing emotion, within reason, was acceptable. He could even cry, in an emergency, without losing face.

9. He might have to wear a suit at work, depending on his job, but away from work, he could wear pretty much what he liked. He was free to follow fashions, or not follow fashions, in a way his father had never been. If he wanted to spend Saturday afternoon clothes-shopping, he could get away with it, so long as it did not become a habit.

10. He could wear his hair short, medium or long or splash out on a Keegan perm.

11. He could attend the birth of his children without attracting comment. In fact, he would attract comment if he *didn't* attend their birth.

12. He could drop his children off at school, if he wanted to, and flirt with the mothers of his children's friends.

13. He could wear aftershave to his heart's content. Or not wear aftershave. Or only shave every other day. Or not at all.

14. He could cook his own food, if he felt like it, and not be forced to eat the vegetarian fare served up by his wife/girlfriend.

15. He could spend the evening with his mates in the pub and, if he did not fancy beer, drink wine or vodka with impunity.

16. He could go to French films, the opera or even the ballet, provided he kept quiet about it.

On the debit side:

1. He was still expected to be faithful to his wife/girlfriend. The new sexual freedoms were not a licence for promiscuity.

2. He might be able to look forward to an action-packed love life, freed from the spectre of unwanted pregnancies, but so could women. Where their mothers, or most of them, had been staidly monogamous, women born post-1950 were far more adventurous in their relationships – and far more demanding, particularly if they read *Cosmopolitan*. A man had to know his G-spot from his G-string.

3. He was still expected to be physically robust and an efficient hunter-gatherer.

4. He had to be a high-achiever at work, rising effortlessly up the career ladder, and an all-rounder in the home. He had to be good at DIY, mow the lawn, cook the odd omelette, fill in income tax forms, kill spiders, read children bedtime stories, sew buttons back on shirts, and be a sensitive and expert lover, the sort who could make post-coital conversation about art and literature, not just fall asleep.

5. He had to listen patiently while his wife/girlfriend complained that women were expected to do everything these days.

6. Having attended the birth of his children, he was also expected to change their nappies and bottle-feed them at two in the morning.

7. He had to know the location of the vacuum cleaner, the toilet-cleaner, the washing-up liquid and other household items with which his father would have been unfamiliar.

8. He had to iron his own shirts, unless he asked very, very nicely – and offered something in return.

9. He was expected to talk about his feelings.

10. He was expected to listen to women talk about their feelings.

11. He had to endure unflattering comparisons with Clint Eastwood, Steve McQueen and Robert Redford – but not lust publicly after Raquel Welch or Barbara Windsor.

12. He had to mothball his best mother-in-law jokes. Ditto his jokes about women drivers.

13. He had to treat women as equals at all times and not patronise them or hold doors open for them – except when they wanted doors held open for them.

14. He had to spend more time at Sainsbury's than sanity could bear.

15. He was expected, on occasions, and as proof that he was not uptight, to hug other men in public – but without the benefit of guidelines as to what those occasions were.

16. On becoming a father, he would be expected to give his family priority 95 per cent of the time. If he wanted to play golf on Sunday afternoons, or join a judo club, he would have to get special dispensation.

17. He had to put up with his father telling him how lucky he was, and

how the kids of today were spoiled, and how tough life was in the 1930s, when there was no television, and families did not have two pennies to rub together, and when one loaf of bread had to last…

Did the pluses outweigh the minuses? It depended who was doing the counting. Certainly there were men for whom the 1970s were a golden age: a time when they could be far more true to themselves than their fathers or grandfathers had been. But what proportion of men of Boycott's generation felt fully secure in their manhood – sure what was expected of them and confident that they could deliver it? Twenty per cent? Ten per cent? Probably not even that. There were just too many conflicting pressures, too many overlapping roles a man was expected to perform if he was to be regarded as a man.

The pressure to do a man's job on the cricket field certainly got to Boycott. At the height of his powers, he was expected to be a cricketing Superman: someone who could not only score runs consistently at the top of the order, against some of the most fearsome fast bowlers in the history of the game, but shrug off dips in form, unsympathetic team-mates, civil war at Yorkshire and the slings and arrows of Fleet Street.

He wasn't Superman, he was Everyman, with ordinary human frailties; and he buckled under the pressure, withdrawing altogether from Test cricket in the mid-1970s. Years later, when Marcus Trescothick also buckled under the pressures of Test cricket, Boycott was conspicuously sympathetic. He had been there himself.

What he has never done, at any stage, is embrace the softer, gentler model of manliness which has attracted so many of his contemporaries. He may dabble privately in feng shui and Chinese horoscopes and New Age philosophies but, in public, the carapace of toughness is as impregnable as ever.

As a commentator, the persona Boycott has adopted – the no-nonsense Yorkshireman who tells it like it is – has quite a lot in common with the Fred Trueman persona or, for that matter, the Ray Illingworth persona. Away from the cricket field, it has been adopted by figures as diverse as Bernard Ingham, Mrs Thatcher's bushy-eyebrowed press secretary, the football manager Mick McCarthy and

David Blunkett, Home Secretary under Tony Blair. It is so unvarying that the plain-talking Yorkshireman now resembles a stock comic character in *commedia dell'arte*. He is not afraid of turning into a parody of himself; indeed, a touch of sly self-parody is intrinsic to his performance, which is rooted in masculinity at its most rudimentary, without nuances or complications.

A man, as the stage Yorkshireman sees it, should be tough, stoical, businesslike, undemonstrative, rock-solid in a crisis. Whatever he is like in private, he should not do anything in public which undermines his authority, makes him look weak or lays him open to the charge of effeminacy.

This last point is critical. Boycott's impatience with the touchy-feely cricketers of today is no secret and, whenever he gives vent to it, he implicitly calls their masculinity into question. 'The modern back-slapping and hugging is a bad thing,' he opined in 2008. 'I know some people feel that such congratulations help team spirit – but not love and kissing.' He has been equally outspoken about the start-of-session huddle which, under Michael Vaughan's captaincy, became an established bonding ritual: 'They should get rid of the huddle on the field of play. It's cosmetic and done for the cameras. It's like big girls before a hockey match.'

Batsmen punching gloves with their partners ('nancy-boys') are another Boycott bugbear. He is nothing if not consistent. And if he comes across as a reactionary, and a male chauvinist to boot, a surprising number of cricket fans, perhaps even a majority, share his views. He has put his finger on something that instinctively bothers the man in the street – and for that matter, the woman in the street.

Cricket is a hard game, played with a hard ball. The artists of the game – like the Indian batsman, V. V. S. Laxman – exhibit a balletic grace. They always have done. But a Test match is not *Swan Lake* or *Les Sylphides*: it is a war of attrition, and cricket fans expect the combatants to behave accordingly. The glove-punching batsman – or, for that matter, the mid-off who pats extra cover on the bottom when he stops the ball and prevents a single – belongs in a different script. He would be better off playing football, in bright yellow boots, wearing woollen mittens in winter and writhing about in agony after getting a tap on the shoulder.

Geoffrey Boycott will remain controversial until the day he dies. He wouldn't be Geoffrey Boycott if he didn't rub people up the wrong way. In March 2011, when Michael Yardy of Sussex returned home early from the World Cup in India, blaming depression, Boycott showed far less sympathy than he had shown to Trescothick, suggesting that Yardy was only depressed because he knew he was not good enough to play for England. Boycott respected Trescothick as a worthy fellow-practitioner; a lesser cricketer did not merit the same sympathy. His comments caused an outcry. But there were plenty who agreed with their substance, if not their tone.

In his clumsy way, he had gone in to bat for old-fashioned stoicism – a quality so quintessentially English that it will never become redundant. For as long as roast beef is served with Yorkshire pudding, the strong silent man will be a revered figure in this country – and not just in Yorkshire. The spirit of *Brief Encounter* – heartbreak suffered without fuss – lives on.

Some who know him are convinced that, inside the Boycott who alienates people with his abrasiveness, there is a Boycott who desperately wants to be loved, has many of the qualities for which people are loved, but has never found the right language to express those qualities. He remains a loner, an outsider. But like other outsiders, his detachment from the tribe has made him an acute, acerbic observer of it. He has certainly done the game – and perhaps men in general – a service by challenging the cosseted Test cricketers of 2012 to look at themselves in the mirror.

The trouble is that most of them are doing that anyway.

CHAPTER 6
DARREN GOUGH: THE TWINKLE-TOED RHINOCEROS

*I prefer it when the woman is in charge. I think
that's the way it should be in life. Women are more
intelligent. They know what they're doing.
So I'm happy to let them be the boss.*

Darren Gough, *Dazzler on the Dance Floor*.

Should we have been surprised as we were?

When Darren Gough signed up for the 2005 series of *Strictly Come Dancing*, waltzed and tangoed through the early rounds, wowed the judges, captivated the public, disarmed the cynics, then went on to win the show with a jaw-dropping final routine, it felt like the last fairytale in a year of fairytales, an *annus mirabilis*. In that year of years, as the Ashes were so gloriously regained, a man in an England cricket shirt was no longer a loser: he was a knight in shining armour; or he was a Greek god, come down from Olympus to bless mortals with his presence. Superlatives rained down like confetti on Michael Vaughan and his men.

Darren Gough was not one of them, to his lasting regret. He was still part of the England one-day squad, but had retired from Test cricket in 2003. Still, a little of the fairy dust of the Ashes series glittered around that ruddy Yorkshire face. After a decade of sterling service to the England cause, Gough was one of the most instantly recognisable sportsmen in the country – and one of the most popular.

Even so, for a no-nonsense cricketer from Barnsley to share the stage with the rabble of gay prima donnas, weeping women, superannuated comedians and B-list celebrities who comprise the cast list of *Strictly Come Dancing* – a reality TV show, improbably resurrecting a format from a bygone age – was a joke too far for many England cricket fans. We tuned in, but we feared the worst. Gough had already upset the Yorkshire faithful by transferring his allegiances to Essex in 2004. Had the southern air turned him soft in the head?

He was not exactly venturing into the unknown. In the Barnsley of the 1930s, Michael Parkinson's cricket-mad father took lessons at Madame Woodcock's Emporium of Dance, perfected some show-stopping routines, involving dancing cheek-to-cheek with his partner, and foxtrotted his way into the affections of the future Mrs Parkinson. But he was straying a long way from his comfort zone.

Cricketers may be light entertainers, but they mingle with other light entertainers at their peril. In the 1960s, two of the stars of the Yorkshire team, Phil Sharpe and Don Wilson, inveterate stage door Johnnies, made a foray into show business that would have had them sacked on the spot in the Lord Hawke era. They were loitering outside the Alhambra Theatre in Bradford, where the Black and White Minstrels were performing, when they were asked if they wanted to work backstage for a week. 'One look at the girls, one whiff of the greasepaint and one nod between us was enough,' Sharpe remembered. 'Sadly the job didn't turn out to be quite as exotic as we had hoped. In fact, we turned out to be more like odd-job men.'

Sharpe, best remembered as an outstanding slip fielder, remained hopelessly star-struck, and was almost happier mingling with showbiz celebrities ('…I met Jimmy Tarbuck at a health farm, of all places… Ian Carmichael… Donald Sinden… David Frost, now Sir David…') than with his fellow professional cricketers. But his luvvie tendencies put him at odds with the hard-man culture in the Yorkshire dressing room.

In Darren Gough's case, it was the fact that he was a Yorkshire fast bowler – of all the many subspecies of cricketers, the most uncompromisingly virile – that made his appearance on *Strictly* so incongruous. A Yorkshire batsman, maybe. Len Hutton was keen on ballroom dancing. Even Geoffrey Boycott had a twinkle-toed side to his character. 'Like Fred Astaire, I never stopped dancing,' he said in 1987. 'It is fatal to become flat-footed.' But a fast bowler? A 90mph speed merchant? One of the heirs to Fiery Fred?

In a sense, the sceptics, and I confess I was one, were fighting yesterday's war. Since the Millennium, it had been perfectly acceptable for an Englishman to express himself through dance, and do vaguely girlish things with his body. Dancing was OK, kosher. We knew that because of the hit movie *Billy Elliott*, released in 2000, in which the son of a Durham miner becomes a ballet dancer in the teeth of fierce objections from his father, who tells him he will look a poof. The trouble was that most of us – the dance sceptics, that is – had not actually seen the film. We made our excuses when our wives/girlfriends tried to drag us to the cinema.

Darren Gough had to run the gauntlet of the same blokeish scoffing as Billy Elliott. In fact, to begin with, he was a scoffer himself. 'Being a tough lad from Barnsley, I thought dancing was for softies,' he said in his memoir, *Dazzler on the Dance Floor*. 'You're taking the mickey,' he told his manager, when he heard he had been invited to appear on *Strictly*. It was only the coaxing of his mother, a fan of the programme, that tipped him over the edge. As he was put through his paces in rehearsal by his professional dance partner Lilia Kopylova – who really should be in a cricket limerick, rhyming with 'Tufnell over' or 'Strauss in clover' – Gough found himself catapulted into a world far, far removed from the Yorkshire dressing room.

'But my mates, my mates,' he yelped, as he was told to stand, Travolta-like, with one arm pointing upwards, the other on his hips. Anxieties of the kind he had never experienced on the cricket field gnawed away at him. 'I'm going to get some serious stick for this… Suppose I come across as a big ponce on national TV… My mates are going to kill me…' Gough was all right with the paso doble. 'It's a proud matador's dance, full of aggression… I liked all the theatrics of puffing out my chest, stamping and looking angry.' But the cha-cha-cha was purgatory, while the Viennese waltz was 'a bit of a fairy-pot dance'. And he hadn't even paid a visit to the costume and make-up department…

Still, like a good Yorkshireman, he toughed it out, blossoming in confidence as he realised that, if he applied himself, he could dance not just competently, but with panache. When Freddie Flintoff, the most macho of his England team-mates, came to watch one of the early rounds of *Strictly*, and gave his tango the thumbs-up, he knew he could stop worrying about his mates, and just be himself, warts, sequins and all.

Gough had already dipped his toes into the same counter-cultural world as some of his male contemporaries, wearing an ear-stud and having the initials of his children tattooed on his arm in Gothic print. But ballroom dancing represented near-total immersion in that world. It was like walking through the centre of Leeds in a T-shirt which read I AM NOT WILFRED RHODES or RAY ILLINGWORTH CAN TAKE A RUNNING JUMP. It took balls, and it was a gamble – suppose he had been eliminated in one of the early rounds, after a botched rumba or a mincing quickstep? – but it paid off. His fast-fading celebrity was miraculously resurrected.

As a fast bowler, Darren Gough was Trueman-lite. He would hate the 'lite', being every bit as cocky and self-assured and truculent and generally opinionated as Trueman; but in truth, he fell short of the very highest level. He might have been, for a time, the best fast bowler in England, but he never terrorised and demoralised batsmen like the great West Indies quickies of the 1980s. He was broad of beam and shoulder, but slightly shorter than ideal for a fast bowler: a master of the late away swinger, not the brutal, eviscerating bouncer. All the same, he led the attack with gusto, tried his heart out, was a superlative team man – 'the heartbeat of the England side', David Lloyd called him – and played the game with a Hirst-like smile on his face, which nobody ever accused Boycott of doing.

The fans adored Gough and, after his triumph on *Strictly*, he had a whole new constituency, running into millions. The ranks of the beer-swilling Barmy Army hearties who had chanted his name from Melbourne to Karachi were suddenly swelled by vegetarians, Liberal

Democrats, readers of *Hello!* magazine, New Age therapists, aesthetes from the suburbs, sippers of Pinot grigio, gay civil servants called Tarquin and Crispin, and whole coachloads of those most cricket-averse of specimens – women.

The truth is that, with Gough, as with Boycott and Trueman, the image of the hard-as-nails Yorkshireman, blunt to a fault, telling it like it was, without fannying about, had only ever been part of the story. It was a role he played, and played well, blustering like a gale on the Yorkshire moors; but when push came to shove, he had the skill, and the courage, to make a bold departure from type. 'When I first saw the dancers together at the beginning of the series, I thought they were a bunch of weirdos,' he admitted. 'I couldn't stop staring at them… hugging and grabbing each other, dancing all closey-closey and playing around… I'd never seen 'owt like it. But by the end of the series I was totally comfortable with it… I'm very comfortable with my sexuality. I consider myself to be "metro" – that's metrosexual, lads – which means I'm in touch with my feminine side. I can wear pink shoes or a pink shirt, confident that I am a man's man.'

It is easy to smile. The passage reads like a manifesto by a candidate to be best man at Kevin Pietersen's wedding – a plum metrosexual role, which Gough duly landed in 2007. But there is substance behind the posturing. If Gough is in touch with his feminine side, it is not because he has located his inner sequin-wearer, but because he appears to hold women in high respect and, unlike many men of the Trueman and Boycott generation, does not knowingly patronise them. 'I prefer it when the woman is in charge,' he said of his experience of being bossed about by Lilia Kopylova. 'I think that's the way it should be in life. Women are more intelligent. They know what they're doing. So I'm happy to let them be the boss.'

Did he mean it? Or was he just being gallant? Either way, it is hard, if not impossible, to imagine a Yorkshireman born before the war talking like that. If Boycott as a boy idolised John Wayne, the young Darren Gough seems to have had a sneaking crush on Margaret Thatcher, who became prime minister when he was eight years old. Her name was mud in the Yorkshire mining community is which he grew up – both his grandfathers worked in the pits – but he was impressed enough by her stewardship of the country to become a staunch Conservative.

He is now such a true-blue Tory that David Cameron tried to get him to stand as Conservative candidate in the 2011 Barnsley by-election. Gough put the phone down, thinking it was a wind-up from one of his friends. The prime minister had to try again. Panic at the Downing Street switchboard. Thank you, but no thank you, said Gough, when he realised the call was genuine. Fred Trueman would have loved that story. Yorkshire fast bowlers don't put themselves at the beck and call of Old Etonians. It goes against everything they hold most dear.

You can glean a lot about cricketers from the nicknames they are given by their fellow players. Gough has two main nicknames, Rhino and Dazzler, which testifies to the two contrasting sides of his personality: the fast bowler and the show pony. Dazzler would probably talk about the yin and yang of Darren Gough. Rhino would think that was twaddle. But the duality is key to understanding Gough. He may have been a fast bowler but, as a man, he qualifies as a hard-hitting all-rounder.

Born on 18 September 1970 in Monk Bretton, near Barnsley, Darren Gough grew up in a world so different from Trueman and Boycott that, in some respects, it was unrecognisable. Simply the fact that, unlike the other two, he was brought up in a home with a television made him part of a new generation, with changed horizons. Boys still played cricket in the streets, with dustbins for wickets, but when they got home, the world beyond dustbins was spread out before them on an 18-inch screen.

Gough describes himself in his autobiography as 'good Yorkshire stock, working-class'. His father's father was a miner. His father was a milkman for a time, then worked in pest control – a gift to the tabloids, who dubbed Gough 'the son of a Barnsley rat-catcher', which infuriated the Gough household.

The bog-standard secondary school he attended, the Priory Comprehensive, already had an interesting claim to fame: it had been used as the backdrop for the classic film *Kes*, released in 1969. Ken

Loach's heart-warming tale of a fatherless boy who is neglected, bullied at home, caned at school, but finds emotional release through falconry, captures the Yorkshire of the period: a grey, harsh world, but with latent possibilities for tenderness.

At least the greyness was lifting, certainly at Priory Comprehensive, where there was no school uniform, resulting in a fashion free-for-all that Gough remembers fondly: 'We had our own group – the Farrah boys. Most of us were Jam fans. Our desire to look the part cost our folks a fortune. Trainers, like Thedora Gold and Adidas Los Angeles, meant no change from £50. The Farrah trousers we thought so trendy are worn mainly by old men now. Our tops would have to show the Pringle or Lyle & Scott logos. And, of course, we would wear the corduroy jackets with hoods… There were lots of guys with Mohican haircuts, but we were the cool group.'

Out of little acorns… The Darren Gough of *Strictly Come Dancing*, whose spangled sausage-skin tops made ex-Yorkshire miners weep into their beers, was already no stranger to the bathroom mirror. In fact, he seems to have had an intense love–hate relationship with it. 'What did concern me most when I was growing up were my ears: they were rather pointed.' One could build a whole PhD thesis about teenagers on the 'most' in that sentence. Famine in Africa, the IRA, mass unemployment, the Falklands, the miners' strike, the sexual revolution… and a boy in Barnsley is miserable because he thinks his ears are pointed. Shades of Adrian Mole, aged 13¾, who made his fictional debut in 1982, became a cult character, and hated his spots almost as much as Gough hated his ears. Men change, a little, over time. Teenage boys have been the same since Cain and Abel.

Fashion-consciousness aside, Gough could not yet be said to have engaged with his feminine side. It was lurking there somewhere. His favourite footballer when he was growing up was not one of the hard men of the game but the delicate Glenn Hoddle, a man so incapable of a crunching tackle that he acquired the nickname Glenda. But in other respects, Gough was predictably laddish. If the archetypal Yorkshireman is brusque, thick-skinned, undemonstrative, he played to type, certainly when he was young.

157

'It's hard for people who don't come from Yorkshire to know what that means,' according to his autobiography. 'I can walk into my folks' house and sit down and watch TV without saying a word. We are not ones for the big greetings... We Yorkies don't show our feelings. In a way, that's sad... I think the world of my brother and sister, but I've found it hard to be close to them. I don't think I've ever kissed my sister or hugged my brother and told him I love him.'

After a happy, largely uncomplicated childhood, Gough made the grade at Yorkshire and, for a time, was the epitome of the testosterone-fuelled professional sportsman, happiest with a pint in his hand and prone to get into brawls, if provoked. He turned up at Headingley Cricket School one Boxing Day with eight stitches in his lip after a difference of opinion with a bouncer. 'It's just the way we are in Barnsley,' says Gough. 'I'm still aggressive.' Luckily, redemption was at hand in the pulchritudinous shape of Anna Kratovil, a woman from the south of England, whom Gough wooed and wed in a style that suggests his Rhino nickname was well earned.

The two first met on a winter break in Spain. Gough and a mate of his walked into a bar with only about eight people in it, including Anna, who was drinking with a woman friend. 'I am going to marry her,' Gough told his mate, after giving Anna the once-over. In an attempt to chat her up, he asked her to guess what he did for a living. 'Builder,' said Anna. Ouch! Gough persisted but, when he and his mate invited Anna and her friend out to dinner, realised he was running short of cash. The women ended up paying for themselves.

It was a wretched start, like a cricket team losing three wickets in the first over, but Gough is nothing if not persistent. He extracted Anna's phone number, drove down from Yorkshire to Hertfordshire, where she lived, and took her out on a date in London. They hit it off, went on a few more dates and, eight weeks later, Gough proposed – by telephone. Bad move. Schoolboy error. Another clatter of wickets. Anna told him to get in his car and drive down and propose in person. He got in his car.

As love stories go, this one has a cartoonish quality, with the blundering Rhino making a hopelessly unromantic hero. But it is to

Gough's credit that he is able to tell the story against himself. What a contrast with the dense veil of secrecy with which Geoffrey Boycott has surrounded his love life! And it is also to his credit that, having wooed his wife like a man downing a last pint of lager before closing time, he was canny enough to realise that, if wanted to keep her, he would have to raise his game.

At the time he met Anna, in 1992, Gough was, in his own words, 'a pushy, chubby toyboy' – she was two years older than him. He had battled his way into the Yorkshire team, and taken a few wickets, but his diet was poor, he drank too much and he was overweight – not attributes conducive to becoming a top fast bowler, representing his country as well as his county.

'When your girlfriend tells you to get fit, you want to get fit for her,' he remembers. 'Yorkshire never gave me the kick up the arse I needed. Anna did that.' Within two years – fitter, leaner and far more focused – he was making his England debut. Anna also educated him in other ways. Her father was American, she had spent five years working in California, so she used an emotional language – and a body language – very different from anything Gough had experienced in Barnsley. 'Anna could not believe my family,' he says. 'She was used to the full works. hugs, kisses, the lot.' On his own admission, it took him years to adapt to a different way of doing things.

If learning when and how to give family members a quick peck on the cheek was an uphill struggle, it probably helped that, for all Gough's outward laddishness, he had been raised in a family that was more a matriarchy than a patriarchy. 'Dad's softer than Mum,' he wrote in his autobiography. 'I've always been able to do what I wanted with my dad – not the case with my mum… My dad used to give me a belt when I was younger, but my mum was the one who had to tell him to do it. He hated having to do it… He's got a heart of gold.'

Belting children who played up – almost as time-honoured a Yorkshire tradition as brass bands and bacon butties – was still a knee-jerk parental instinct. Attitudes were slowly changing. Corporal punishment in state schools was abolished in 1986, when Gough was 16. The cartoon character Dennis the Menace, the archetypal naughty schoolboy, who had been slippered every week since 1951, was henceforth spared such indignities. Not before time, said some. Political correctness gone mad, said others. But in the home, there was no such fastidiousness, just a bewildering number of local rules, with every family doing its own thing.

With the Truemans, the father was belter-in-chief. With the Boycotts, it was the mother – Boycott's father hit his son only once and was immediately told off by his wife. With the Goughs, it was the father acting under instructions from the mother. He might have been executioner, but she was judge, jury and court of last appeal – in a word, the boss.

In the Britain in which Gough grew up, the balance of power in the household varied from family to family. It always has done and it always will. Mrs Gough may have worn the trousers chez Gough but, in the next-door house, Mr Hinchcliffe might have called the shots, while Mrs Hinchcliffe played the dutiful wife, subservient in kitchen and bedroom alike. But, after the sexual revolution of the 1960s, there had also been a generational shift. Families were getting significantly smaller, post-Pill, more women were going out to work, and more of them were doing serious, demanding jobs. By 1980, there was a woman in Downing Street, for heaven's sake. To have treated the sexes as anything other than equal would have been preposterous.

And it was no longer just middle-class London intellectuals beating the drum for feminism. The 1975 movie *The Stepford Wives*, a sci-fi satire on robotically submissive housewives brainwashed by their husbands, helped bring disquiet about the evils of sexual stereotyping into the cultural mainstream. The winds of change might have blown more slowly in the north than the south, but blow they did.

Viewed as a clash of ideas, the battle of the sexes had become embarrassingly one-sided, with women winning the argument hands down. The men didn't really have ideas, beyond parroting stale old prejudices, throwing their weight about in the office and making jokes about women drivers. Most men did not concede defeat as graciously as Darren Gough, when he said, as if stating a fact of life, 'Women are more intelligent than men'. But in the face of a new generation of women who were bright, self-confident, sure of their rights and determined to give as good as they got, they were bereft of a counter-strategy.

One of the most successful TV series of the period – indeed, for people who had never visited Yorkshire, one of the prisms through which they viewed the county – was *Last of the Summer Wine*, which was first screened in 1973 and ran for nearly 40 years, watched by millions. Written by Roy Clarke, who was born in Austerfield in 1930, the sitcom featured a trio of dysfunctional pensioners who had never really grown up: they were perpetual schoolboys, frozen in time. None of them was capable of having a grown-up relationship with a woman. Any manliness they might have had in their youth had long since withered and they were now pathetically emasculated, playing childish pranks and living in terror of Nora Batty and her rolling pin.

It was a caricature, and a crude one, but it had a significant grain of truth. Across large swathes of Britain, a seismic shift was taking place. More and more women were taking control of their lives, while more and more men had been reduced to second-class powers: ineffective in the workplace, impotent at home. Roy Clarke would later tinker with the same stereotypes in another hit sitcom, *Keeping Up Appearances*, aired in the early 1990s. Next to the larger-than-life figure of Hyacinth Bucket, running her suburban home like a multinational corporation, the henpecked husband was a cipher.

One of the signature TV dramas of the 1980s – capturing the sense of demoralisation by which so many men were gripped – was *Auf Wiedersehen, Pet*. The basic storyline should have been upbeat, even heartwarming: a group of Geordie builders travelling to Germany to get work. Fun, foreign travel and Fräuleins – perfect. But most of the characters were so lacking in oomph, such miserable advertisements for the British working class, that the overall effect was more depressing than entertaining.

From the slobbish Oz (Jimmy Nail) to the drippy Neville (Kevin Whateley) to the boring Barry (Timothy Spall) to the stammering Moxey (Christopher Fairbank) to the self-styled Jack the Lad Wayne (Gary Holton), every variant on the inadequate male was played out in cringe-making detail. We warmed to the characters: they had very human frailties. But we certainly did not admire them, still less associate them with manliness.

Straight and gay men alike found themselves in the grip of an ongoing identity crisis. Stephen Fry, having come out as gay at the start of the decade, remembers hanging around outside the Colherne Arms in Earls Court in the early 1980s, surrounded by 'squadrons of tight-jeaned, heavy-booted individuals' with whom he realised he had next to nothing in common: 'I was not even faintly drawn to these preposterous Tom of Finland caricatures with their muscle vests, leather caps and joyless stares. My dream partner was a friendly, dreamy, funny young man with whom I could walk, talk, laugh, cuddle and play.'

With so much diffidence in the air, the times were crying out for certainty, clear guidelines, a new framework of values – although when certainty did come, it came from an unexpected source. The dominant figure of the 1980s, ruling Boadicea-like over her troubled tribe, was Margaret Thatcher. She could never have become prime minister in the 1960s, for all the lip service paid to women. Even in 1979, her arrival in Downing Street was greeted with widespread scepticism. What had we done? Were we ready for a woman in charge? But she did not take long to silence the doubters.

In no time at all, she was lording it over her male-dominated cabinet, reducing alpha males from Eton – or, more accurately, men who *thought* they were alpha males because they had been to Eton – to the level of messenger boys. She treated the Tory wets with a contempt she never directed at the Labour Party. It was every Etonian's worst nightmare: the nanny who had spanked him with a hairbrush when he was a boy turning up again after 30 years and insisting on taking charge of his chequebook. Political satirists had never had it so good. *Spitting Image* got particularly good mileage out of the Thatcher cabinet, with its handbag-wielding figurehead and supporting cast of wimps, yes-men and oddballs – from Michael Heseltine, raving like a long-haired evangelist, to John Major, the grey politician par excellence.

Whatever you thought of her politics, Margaret Thatcher challenged men – inside and outside the Westminster village – in ways that many of them had never been challenged before. If she could play the Iron Lady, why couldn't they play the Iron Man? What was wrong with them? Didn't they have the balls?

Her battle cry, distilled in one of her most famous aphorisms, was shrill but clear: 'If you want something said, ask a man. If you want something done, ask a woman.' There were women who had never voted Conservative in their lives who heard those words and nodded knowingly. This was not the feminism of the newspaper column, the debating chamber: it had a hard practical edge.

For the male of the species, it was a particularly unsettling period. Some men took up the Thatcherite challenge, displayed entrepreneurial flair, set up their own companies or made silly money in the City. But they were in the minority. Most men, particularly those in public sector jobs, felt a vague mixture of inadequacy and resentment, as if they had been asked to perform tasks for which they were not equipped. As for those forced to join the dole queue, many of them Yorkshire miners, their sense of self-worth had never been lower. They felt not just undervalued, but castrated. *Boys from the Blackstuff*, Alan Bleasdale's gritty Liverpudlian drama, spoke to a generation. 'Gissa job,' the catchphrase of the unemployed, desperate Yosser Hughes, was like the howl of a trapped animal, ringing across the frozen wastes.

On the cricket field, at least, the 1980s began in style, with the Ian Botham-led Ashes triumph in 1981. But it was too good to last. Botham and Co. did not look so tough when confronted by the West Indies pace attack of the mid-1980s, who really were tough, battle-hardened warriors. In the last Ashes series of the decade, 1989, a spineless England, playing cricket of which Sutcliffe and Verity would have been ashamed, were thrashed 4-0 by a resurgent Australia. The heroes had fled the field with their tails between their legs.

That same year, the Hillsborough tragedy marked a sporting low of another kind, a reminder of the grubby underbelly of what had once been seen as a wholesome, manly pastime. Football was in far more trouble than cricket.

In the 1950s, when Ken Taylor played cricket for Yorkshire in the summer and football for Huddersfield Town in the winter, his manager, the legendary Bill Shankly, told him cricket was 'a lassies' game'. It was a harsh verdict, but it contained a germ of truth. Compared with elegant amateur cricketers like Colin Cowdrey, the professional footballers of the day were tough, knobbly-kneed types who left lumps in their opponents, never shirked a tackle and never complained. Fast-forward to 1990 and the footballing landscape had changed beyond recognition. Not only was writhing in agony now part of the choreography of the game but, post-Gazza at the 1990 World Cup, the weeping footballer enjoyed folk hero status. It all felt very odd.

Even in the *Roy of the Rovers* cartoon strip, the last redoubt of male escapism, all was not well. Since it first appeared in 1954, the strip had prided itself on moving with the times, with topical references and storylines. Melchester Rovers aped sporting England. Geoffrey Boycott was installed as chairman of the club for a time, while Roy's hairstyle followed the fashions of the day, embracing quiffs, glam-rock bouffant and mullets. But if the hero carried on scoring winning goals in Cup Finals, as if nothing had changed, his home life had gone pear-shaped. In the 1970s, Roy had taken time off to marry Penny, the daughter of the Melchester Rovers manager. In the 1980s, Penny walked out on Roy, complaining that he was devoting too much time to football – a fact gleefully reported on the BBC evening news. It was as if the tides of feminism were lapping at the dressing room door.

At least, if men were in retreat, demoralised, in the grip of a full-blown identity crisis, the fightback was about to start.

Just as the history of cricket is littered with tales of the unexpected, the battle of the sexes has been fought in some deliciously improbable arenas. Who would have guessed that one of the first books to try to rally the beleaguered male sex, exhorting men to be true to their traditional strengths, would focus on an egg-and-bacon tart associated with Alsace-Lorraine?

Real Mean Don't Eat Quiche, by the American writer Bruce Feirstein, was published in 1982, enjoyed cult status in America, where it was on the *New York Times* bestsellers list for more than a year, then brought its message across the Atlantic. At the height of its popularity, it must have been in the window of half the bookshops in Britain. Even people who had not read a word of the book had heard of it, and there were umpteen imitations and parodies, including *Real Women Send Flowers*,

Real Kids Don't Say Please, Real Women Never Pump Iron and that seminal work of scholarship, *Real Dogs Don't Eat Left-Overs.*

In content and style, the book was light, flimsy, tongue-in-cheek. Feirstein was no intellectual, but a writer of ruggedly uncomplicated views, who later wrote screenplays for the Bond movies. Quiche-eaters, in his knockabout thesis, were men who had lost sight of old-fashioned masculine virtues and become dilettantes and trend-chasers, conforming to every latest fad and desperate not to give offence. They empathised with women, cooked their partners quiche and did the washing-up afterwards. A Real Man, by contrast, preferred the simple life. His role models were Gary Cooper and Spencer Tracy. He didn't have his hair styled, didn't floss his teeth, didn't worry about the ozone layer, didn't sniff the cork in restaurants, didn't do brunch and didn't meditate or do t'ai chi.

Thick and fast the prejudices flew, and there was no nonsense about constructing a coherent thesis. Margaret Thatcher, despite having her hair styled, was a Real Man. François Mitterand, a hero of the French Resistance, was a quiche-eater, purely by being French. But the prejudices achieved an unstoppable momentum – millions shared them. The real genius of the book lay in its title. *Real Men Don't Do the Ironing* or *Real Men Don't Hold Hands* would have been all wrong, sending out sexist or homophobic messages. The humble, harmless quiche was the clincher. It just seemed such a footling peg on which to hang a thesis about virility. It hit quiche-eaters where it hurt, causing them nagging doubts in areas of their lives where they had previously felt secure, happy in their own skin. If eating quiche was a no-no, what *else* were they doing wrong?

Well, for one thing, they were cooking the quiches they were eating. On both sides of the Atlantic, there was a new generation of men who did not just concede that domestic duties should be shared, but cottoned on to the fact that, if they were going to cook, they might as well enjoy it. In fact, they might as well try to be good at it. Master the necessary skills and, if that soufflé rose and that jelly set, they could beat women at their own game – a small victory, but a morale-boosting one.

The 1980s saw an almost Gadarene rush of men to the kitchen, spurred on by TV cookery shows. In the 1950s and 1960s, when Fanny

165

Cradock was the face of cooking in Britain, her husband Johnnie was a largely ornamental figure, lolling in the background in a blazer, uncorking the wine occasionally. Now, increasingly, the man took centre stage. One of the TV chefs in the vanguard of the revolution was the late, great Keith Floyd, who pre-empted any suggestion that cooking was effeminate by taking man-sized gulps of full-bodied red wine while he was at the stove. Spiky-haired Gary Rhodes – who would later appear on *Strictly Come Dancing*, like Darren Gough – also made his TV debut in the 1980s. Men doing the cooking was not just a middle-class fad: the working classes had been conscripted, too.

It seemed a healthy enough social trend, certainly one which satisfied the high priestesses of sexual equality. But was it that simple? Weren't there hidden dangers in men donning aprons and making lime-and-coriander marinades for halibut? Shouldn't they, at least figuratively, be out on the high seas, in force-nine gales, catching the halibut themselves? Bruce Feirstein, for one, thought the question was worth asking.

If he gave quiche-eaters a glimpse of their own ridiculousness, it was the men who did not eat quiche who were his real constituency. Even Stone Age types who never read books, had no interest in gender politics, and could not have boiled an egg without logistical assistance from Delia Smith, saw that catchy title, winking at them from a bookshop window, and felt an instinctive kinship with the author. Real men? Yes, they were real men. Or they had *thought* they were real men, before women started bossing them about, taking their jobs and undermining their authority. Had they finally found an ally?

If Darren Gough had tasted quiche by the time the book was published – or even knew what a quiche was – he has kept quiet about it. In fact, his diet as a boy and young man was embarrassingly unsophisticated, not to mention unhealthy. Dietary highlights from the 1970s and 1980s, as Gough ruefully admits in his autobiography, included:

Full-fat cheddar cheese
Crisps
Tizer

Bacon sandwiches
Sugar Puffs
Yorkshire pudding
50p boxes of mixed biscuits
Burgers and chips
Half the beer in Barnsley

Not even Keith Floyd at his most inventive could have taken those ingredients and turned them into a meal you could serve in a respectable restaurant. But, quiche-eater or not, Gough was certainly one of the real men Feirstein was trying to conscript. If a tearaway Yorkshire fast bowler couldn't bang the drum for old-fashioned virility, who could?

By the time Gough became a Yorkshire regular, in the early 1990s, the male counter-revolution, such as it was, was gathering steam. Another influential book, targeting a more highbrow readership than Feirstein, was *Iron John: A Book About Men* by the American poet Robert Bly, first published in 1990. Taking his inspiration from an old German fairytale, Bly used the mythic figure of Iron John – a hairy, iron-clad man who acts as a mentor to a boy prince – to argue that the reason so many male adolescents of the late 20th century were a mess was the absence of an Iron John father-figure in their lives. Some came from broken homes. Others were brought up in matriarchies and encouraged to develop feminine attributes such as sensitivity. Either way, they lacked a strong male guide who could help them negotiate the peril-strewn journey from boyhood. In layman's terms, they were wimps waiting to happen.

Bly's book became an international bestseller and a bible to the so-called Men's Movement of the early 1990s, a very loose coalition indeed, with a bewildering number of agendas, often in conflict with each other. In Britain, its notional members ranged from middle-class intellectuals, groping for a synthesis between their yin and their yang, to divorced plumbers from Billericay angry at the amount of their alimony and demanding better access to their children. All they really had in common was a vague sense that, as men in the late 20th century, they were playing for a losing team. They had to raise their game, and soon, or they would be relegated.

There was nothing new in men trying to rebut the arguments in favour of sexual equality – or at least re-define the terms of the debate. As early as 1913, a peppery British socialist, Ernest Belfort Bax, published a pamphlet entitled *The Fraud of Feminism*, damning the suffragettes and all their works. But, for most of the 20th century, men of a revisionist tendency lacked ammunition. 'Masculism' was coined, but struggled to gain admission to the dictionary. The same applied to 'misandry', an impeccably formed antithesis to 'misogny' which fell at the first fence – nobody took the word seriously. It might have been bandied about by writers like Warren Farrell, another American gender-studies guru, whose counter-feminist works included *Why Men Are the Way They Are* and *The Myth of Male Power*, but it had no resonance in the pub.

At least, in the irreducibly male figure of Iron John, men now had something solid they could cling on to. The name had a good ring. It was as if the Iron Lady had finally met her match. And if Iron John never acquired cult status in Britain, he could be said to have subliminally shaped attitudes. Butch was good again. Macho was all right. The kind of men who might have formed book groups in the 1970s and 1980s now went on all-male bonding expeditions in the woods.

Or they took up martial arts instead of jogging.

Or they went to films starring Bruce Willis and didn't care who knew it.

Or they joined the Barmy Army and cheered on Darren Gough.

By the time Gough made his England debut in 1994, the national game was in such a sorry state that the last place anyone would have gone looking for manly role models was the home dressing room at Trent Bridge or Headingley. They would have found Alec Stewart arranging his kit, Mike Atherton eating a tub of coleslaw, Angus Fraser deep in a newspaper and Phil Tufnell having a shifty cigarette.

The away dressing room was another matter. If the West Indies were in decline, the Australians were well on their way to becoming one of the most formidable outfits in the history of team sport. Shane Warne, who had toured England for the first time in 1993, might have looked a bit iffy, with his peroxide-dyed blonde hair, but the hard men of that side, like Merv Hughes and David Boon – both sporting moustaches of Edwardian splendour – sent a chill down the spine of England fans. Never mind their technical skills. They just looked so much tougher than our lot.

'That toughness was the key,' says Michael Parkinson. 'I recognised it from the great Yorkshire teams I watched as a boy. When I played league cricket for Barnsley, no quarter was given. You didn't get out to a loose shot because you were in a hurry to get to the pub – or you'd have got a rollicking from your team-mates if you had. The Australians of the 1990s were the same. In fact, I often tell my Australian friends that Yorkshire and Australia are part of the same big tribe.'

The fact that these Aussie supermen were able to thrash England on the field and – certainly in Boon's case – drink prodigious amounts of beer afterwards only enhanced their aura of impregnability. At least, as England prepared for the 1994–95 tour of Australia, they had a new weapon at their disposal in the 24-year-old Darren Gough: fast, furious, intermittently accurate and with the attitude to back up his bowling.

His first Ashes tour turned into a soap opera: all the highs and lows of being a professional sportsman crammed into a few months. On the eve of the first Test in Brisbane, his wife Anna gave birth to his first-born son, Liam, 12,000 miles away. England lost, then lost again in Melbourne. In the third Test in Sydney, Gough was named man of the match, following a lusty fifty with the bat with a blistering spell of six for 49 – earning praise from Harold Larwood and Ray Lindwall, no less.

England should have won by a distance, but were thwarted by rain. They *did* win the fourth Test, in Adelaide, but there was no Darren Gough in the side – he was already on the plane home, having broken his foot. When he got back to Yorkshire, to be reunited with his wife and see his son for the first time, his house was surrounded by TV cameras. Who would be an England cricketer?

At least Gough had won the lasting affection of the Barmy Army, the ragbag of England supporters who first came to prominence on the 1994–95 tour and have been a fixture ever since. The mighty, mighty Army divide opinion in the cricket world: their songs are witty before lunch, repetitive by tea, loutishly incoherent by stumps. But they love a trier, they love a fast bowler who can stick it up 'em, they love a fellow beer-drinker and, most of all, they love a no-nonsense working-class hero, preferably from the north – in a word, Gough. Of recent England cricketers, probably only Freddie Flintoff has enjoyed higher standing with the Army. They respect Andrew Strauss. They admire Kevin Pietersen. They have a soft spot for Paul Collingwood and Monty Panesar. But Darren Gough is one of them.

The nine years in which he was in the England side saw a bewildering mixture of triumphs and disasters. The former included an Ashes hat-trick in Sydney in the 1998–99 series and a famous victory against the West Indies at Lord's in 2000. The latter tended to involve revoltingly confident Australian batsmen scoring unfeasible amounts of runs in humiliatingly quick time. A bowler with figures of nought for 100 against his name cuts a sorry figure, however fast he bowls.

Questions about Gough's fitness were a recurring riff in his stop-start career. People wondered, as they wondered with Flintoff, whether his lifestyle contributed to the spate of injuries he suffered, curtailing the number of Tests he played. 'I'm not fat, I'm broad,' he snapped at one interviewer. Fred Trueman would have enjoyed that one.

Overweight or not, taking wickets or being carted around the field, Gough kept his equilibrium. Even trudging back to his mark in 100-degree heat in Perth or Peshawar, with no help in the wicket, he never sunk into the kind of Dostoyevskian gloom that enveloped other England fast bowlers of the period. His natural joviality, a quality so absent in Boycott, was a throwback to George Hirst. Gough rejoiced in the good times, and we rejoiced with him. But he didn't wallow in self-pity in the bad times. He was sanguine in defeat. 'If you can look on triumph and disaster/And treat those two impostors just the same…' Kipling's England, land of the level-headed, had a new recruit.

On that 1994–95 tour of Australia, when the Barmy Army was born, with Gough as one of their idols, the locals were mystified. What did these drunken poms have to be so *happy* about? Their team was losing, wasn't it? Why weren't they jeering and throwing bottles on to the field? But that, in a way, was the point.

One of the uglier aspects of the Thatcherite 1980s, against which people were starting to rebel, was the apotheosis of winning – in all walks of life – and as its corollary, the disdain for losing. 'Greed is good,' proclaimed Gordon Gekko, the predatory banker played by Michael Douglas in the 1987 movie *Wall Street*. And if greed was good, and was to be allowed to reap its rewards, it had to be accompanied by ruthlessness. The cold-eyed sharks of banking had their counterparts on the sports field – intense, unsmiling men who trained harder than the others, competed harder than the others and did not head for the bar after play – they were in bed by ten, reading motivational manuals, or they were working out in the hotel gym, preparing for the next morning.

The golfer Nick Faldo was the prototype of the breed, but cricket had its fair share. No player of the 1990s was more ruthless, more uncompromising, more cold and intense in his body language, than the Australian captain Steve Waugh. If the Australian team he led seemed like an unstoppable juggernaut, it was not just because it contained players of genius, but because it embodied a tough, competitive ethos which Waugh epitomised. In the main, the toughness was admirable. But it was not totally admirable. The Barmy Army would have loved to see Steve Waugh in an England shirt. He was just so tenacious, a born scrapper. They would have swapped him for Graeme Hick or Mark Ramprakash. In fact, they would have swapped him for Graeme Hick *and* Mark Ramprakash, and thrown in Robert Croft and Alan Mullally for good measure. But would they have swapped him for Darren Gough? Probably not.

The fact is that, as a man, in the fullest sense of the word, Waugh did not tick quite as many boxes as Gough. The Barmy Army instinctively sensed, even if they were too drunk to put it into words, that ruthlessness, winning at all costs, is not quite the same as manliness. Make yourself hard, eliminate all your softer feelings, and you are in danger of losing touch with your essential humanity. Your compassion – and this was the great charge levelled at the Thatcherites – goes missing.

Appeals to the spirit of Iron John were all very well, and it was good that men were allowed to be real men again, not surrogate women, but there had to be some sensible middle way – between the faddishness of

171

the New Age and the brutal pursuit of self-interest that had been such a feature of the 1980s.

Even in Australia, where Steve Waugh was idolised, there was a sense that, if he lightened up, people would like him even more. Cricket fans of an older generation harked back to the Corinthian values of Keith Miller, the *preux chevalier* of the 1940s and 1950s, the ex-fighter pilot who nailed his colours to the mast when he said, 'Pressure's having a Messerschmidt up your arse.' Miller was a man's man, by any yardstick. But he played the game for fun.

Which was better? A dour, remorseless winner? Or a player who sometimes won and sometimes lost but, whatever happened, walked off the field with a smile on his face? The Barmy Army knew what they thought – which is why they loved Darren Gough.

If Darren Gough had an up-and-down England career, dogged by injury, his life off the field has been equally volatile. In 2002, eight years after he had married her, he split up with his wife Anna. The two remained on reasonably good terms and shared the parenting of their two sons, Liam and Brennan. By 2008, they were back together again. Beyond hinting at the pressures of living apart so much of the time as a consequence of his job, Gough has not talked about either the break-up or the reunion. But his devotion to his children, like his brusque wooing of his wife, bears out something J. B. Priestley wrote nearly a century ago: 'As a lover, the Yorkshireman cuts no great figure, but he shapes well as a husband and, best of all, as a father.'

Gough was lucky to get a second chance to make his marriage work. The marriage with wobbles – some short, some long, some terminal – was characteristic of the times. The whole institution was wobbling. Couples who might have been reasonably content in the 1950s fell prey to the illusion – and, as often as not, it *was* an illusion – that the grass was greener on the other side of the fence. When they found it was not greener, they cast longing looks back over the fence to the garden they had left behind. Or they started looking over another fence into the *next* garden and thought the grass looked greener there…

Married life was an obstacle course, even for those with successful careers. One Yorkshireman whose life reflected the turbulence of the times was actor Sean Bean, born in Sheffield in 1959. After getting his kit off in the BBC adaptation of *Lady Chatterley's Lover*, and enjoying further success in the ITV drama series *Sharpe*, playing a bluff English soldier in the Napoleonic Wars, Bean became the fantasy 'bit of rough' for millions of women. But his private life was a mess, he was divorced four times and, despite impeccable working-class credentials – supporting Sheffield United from the terraces etc – seemed happiest sketching, gardening and playing the piano. A man's man? Or a man in the grip of a mid-life crisis? It was hard to be sure.

Men whose fathers would have emerged from newsagents with copies of *Playboy* or *Penthouse*, wrapped up in brown paper bags, now proudly took out subscriptions to *Loaded* or *FHM*, both launched in the mid-1990s. The new wave of men's magazines still gave their readers plenty of female flesh to ogle, but they also encouraged neurotic introspection, even self-loathing, of the kind in which women's magazines had once enjoyed a monopoly. The *FHM* cover in February 1998 was not untypical: 'Fat? Boring? Crap in Bed? Does This Sound Familiar to Anyone?' No wonder so many relationships were on the critical list.

One of the signature TV sitcoms of the period, making capital out of relationships that were on one minute, off the next, was *Men Behaving Badly*. Simon Nye's warm, clever comedy was first screened on ITV in 1992, the year Darren Gough met Anna, then migrated to the BBC in 1994, the year they married. Gary, the central character, deliciously played by Martin Clunes, was a blundering foot soldier in the male counter-revolution of the early 1990s. Along with his flatmate Tony (Neil Morrissey), he was determined to defend every last redoubt of traditional masculinity, however petty. The right to burp, fart, go unshaven, talk about football, keep a fridge stuffed with cans of lager, was sacrosanct. There were to be no concessions to the female enemy – or only such concessions as were needed to get her into bed. No kowtowing to feminism for Gary. In fact, he took on the shibboleths of feminism with gusto, gleefully re-asserting the innate superiority of the male of the species: 'I mean, look at the fuss women make about childbirth.

173

Now I'm not saying it doesn't smart a bit, but if blokes did it, I reckon you'd be looking at, what, give birth, have a couple of paracetamols, maybe a bit of a nap, and then back to work within an hour.'

Gary's long-suffering girlfriend Dorothy – Caroline Quentin at her acerbic best – was pushed to explain why she put up with him. 'I'm condemned to perpetual misery by the god of crap boyfriends,' she sniped, as Gary, for the umpteenth time, preferred quality time in the pub to quality time with her. 'But, darling, we each bring our own strengths to the relationship,' said Gary, trying to wheedle his way back into her affections. 'Mine seems to be cooking,' said Dorothy. 'What's yours?' 'I'll have a pint of lager please,' said Gary – followed by his trademark braying laugh, a gloat of male triumph which seemed to go back to the dawn of time.

If Dorothy had been Germaine Greer, she would have thrown the lager back in his face. But, of course, she wasn't. She was just a normal young woman of her times, with limited expectations of men, jockeying for temporary advantage, content with small tactical gains, not even daring to dream of outright victory. The fact that she was a nurse, used to babying men, used to mopping up after them, seemed entirely apt. Her sparring with Gary was a constant delight:

Dorothy: You really are a yob, aren't you, Gary?
Gary: On the contrary, I think I am remarkably sensitive.
Dorothy: Oh, that must be why you refer to Luciano Pavarotti as
    'that fat git'.

They muddled through, of course. They had to, or there would have been no scripts for Simon Nye to write. But as they bickered, fell out, cheated on each other, got back together again, fell out again, moved in together, bickered some more, got drunk, tumbled into bed, it seemed to sum up the age: men trying to re-assert their authority; women clinging on to their gains; and an uneasy accommodation being reached.

A fly on the wall of the Gough household in the 1990s – or so it seems safe to assume – would have heard caustic, Dorothy-like comments from Anna about Gough's predilection for boozing with his mates. But Gough, like Gary, was a decent soul. He wanted to hang on to his ancient male rights. But he was not, and never had been, an unreconstructed caveman. There was more in his fridge than cans of lager – literally.

Soon after getting back with Anna in 2008, Gough got involved with a new website-based campaign to encourage men to do more cooking. It was called 'Give the Bird a Break', and Gough threw himself into his new role with the same gusto he had brought to his cricket, chivvying other men to follow his example: 'We're the ones who are lazy and make excuses not to be in the kitchen. What I've done is show men how easy it is to cook meat and give the other half a break. While they're out shopping, we should be in the kitchen with a pinny.'

It's jaw-dropping stuff. That pinny… Surreal images of Lord Hawke basting a chicken flutter into the head and flutter out again. But as he had done when he signed up for *Strictly*, Gough had history on his side. He knew that some men would scoff at him, but not most men, even in the back streets of working-class Yorkshire.

If *Men Behaving Badly* captured the half-hearted shadow-boxing in which the men of 1990s indulged, the defining movie of the decade, certainly in South Yorkshire, was *The Full Monty*. Set in Sheffield and released in August 1997 – when Darren Gough was licking his wounds after being sidelined from the Ashes series with an inflamed knee – Peter Cattaneo's elegiac comedy featured a group of unemployed ex-steel workers reduced to earning a few quid as strippers.

The prospect of 'doing the full monty' in front of an audience of 200 drunken women, shrieking their heads off, reduced the men to gibbering wrecks. What more humiliating ordeal could any man be asked to endure? There had been women strippers for years – they were part of the furniture – but this was a role-reversal too far. For overweight Dave, who nearly bottles out at the last minute, it is a living hell. For middle-class Gerald, clinging to the last remnants of bourgeois respectability, it is a nightmare of unimaginable proportions. But it is Gaz – divorced, struggling to meet his child maintenance payments, terrified of losing face in front of his son – who really feels the heat. He digs in his heels, and refuses to go ahead with the performance. Only when he realises that he will win the respect of his son, not forfeit it, does he finally get his kit off. Even his ex-wife, improbably, thinks more of him.

It is a bold, quirky storyline, and it is doubtful if the same movie could have been made in the USA, or even be made there today. Nudity apart, the themes are just so confusing. What is the moral of the story, the simple back-of-an-envelope message beloved of Hollywood movie moguls? That more men should work as strippers? Hardly. That men should be proud of their bodies, good, bad or indifferent? Up to a point. That men are the breadwinners, the hunter-gatherers, and that, however low they have to stoop, they are better off earning money than sitting on their backsides doing nothing? Again, only up to a point. When Margaret Thatcher lit the fires of entrepreneurialism, and Norman Tebbitt told the unemployed to get on their bikes, it wasn't *this* they had in mind. They envisaged something a bit more respectable, like setting up a computer software business or opening a tea-shop in Leamington Spa.

Ultimately, it is as a fable of manly courage, if an eccentric one, that *The Full Monty* is best appreciated. The male strippers confronting their demons stand in the same tradition as John Wayne circling the wagons and James Bond abseiling down mountains to save the world from nuclear annihilation. They would love it if they could display their courage in some more dignified arena, but they have no choice – which only magnifies that courage. There will be no VCs for them, no invitations to Buckingham Palace, just a grudging acknowledgement from their peers that, even bollock-naked, they have exhibited grace under pressure.

When Darren Gough put on the sequins of *Strictly Come Dancing*, laced up his high-heeled dancing shoes, then strutted his stuff before a TV audience of millions, he did not have to risk as much as the Sheffield strippers in *The Full Monty*. But he risked something. It took bottle to do what he did. He showed the same wholehearted courage as he had shown on the cricket field, steaming in to bowl against Matthew Hayden or Adam Gilchrist, knowing there was a fair chance he would be carted for six and the Australian fans would jeer him when he went down to third man at the end of the over.

Like the movie, Gough's victory in *Strictly* offered a parable of manliness in straitened times. Men of his generation knew they were not in charge any more, that they had to share power with women. They also knew that, if they gritted their teeth and kept their nerve, they could still give a good account of themselves. In cricketing terms, they could save the follow-on.

CHAPTER 7
MICHAEL VAUGHAN:
CAPTAIN SUSHI

Jonathan Agnew: *Real men eat pies.*
Michael Vaughan: *Real men eat everything these days.*

Test Match Special, 1 August 2010, after Vaughan
had confessed to liking sushi

One of the glories of cricket, perhaps *the* glory of cricket, is the way in which a team sport, pulsing with the joy of collective endeavour, also places the individual centre stage.

A rugby team surging up the field is a stirring spectacle but, in the blur of testosterone, one beefcake in muddy shorts fades into another. Only when a penalty is awarded, and all eyes are on the kicker, does the spotlight fall on the individual, as his skill and character are tested. In cricket, by contrast, an individual player – whether it is the batsman or the bowler he has to face – is in the spotlight the whole time. How will he do? Will he let the side down or keep his nerve under pressure? Is he a scrapper or a paper tiger? Does he have the strength of character to go with his abilities? What sort of man is he?

In the England cricket team that regained the Ashes at the Oval in 2005, and wrote their names in the book of their country, there was a bewildering human variety – far more so than in the England football team that won the 1966 World Cup. Heroes all – or so they seemed, lit by the Oval sun – but what very different heroes, no two remotely the same. It was a stirring reminder of how many contrasting forms manliness could take in 21st-century Britain.

There was the he-man, the warrior, the gorilla in trousers, the tower of strength on which the whole structure rested. Iron John was a spotty schoolboy compared with the human colossus that was Freddie Flintoff. There was Kevin Pietersen, genius and clothes horse, the compulsive bling-wearer who seemed to spend longer at the hairdresser than in the nets. There was the ruddy-faced countryman, Marcus Trescothick, with his sanguine outlook on life, spanking the ball through the covers as if cricket was the simplest game in the world. (How little we knew *him*.)

There was Andrew Strauss, the gent, the safe pair of hands, the one you would want your daughter to marry. There was Ian Bell, the boy next door, who looked as if he should be in short trousers, with those spindly legs and that apology for a moustache. You wouldn't let your daughter marry *him* – or not yet – but you would let him take her to the cinema and know he would deliver her back safely by 10.30.

There was the grafter, Paul Collingwood, not a man to set the Thames on fire, but a battler, a team player and an excellent man in a crisis. There was the diminutive wicketkeeper Geraint Jones, the quiet one, who looked as if he might have hidden depths. He had spent his childhood in Australia. We liked that. The Australians didn't like that. We liked that even more. There was Ashley Giles, the honest journeyman, Mr Steady, epitome of decency and imperturbability. What was he doing playing cricket for England? He should have been mowing a lawn in a suburb of Birmingham.

There was Matthew Hoggard, the gap-toothed Yorkshireman, man of t'people and proud of it, openly contemptuous of slick metropolitan ways. While Pietersen was at the hairdresser, Hoggy was walking his dogs on the moors in muddy wellies. There was big Steve Harmison, the archetypal fast bowler from the north, born within spitting distance of a coalmine, a figure wreathed in sporting myth, heir to the mantle of Trueman and Larwood. And there was Simon Jones – injured at the Oval, but a key player in the earlier Tests – who looked like a squaddie in the Welsh Guards, with his lean physique, close-cropped hair and uncomplicated virility.

All male life was there, and what made the human tapestry so rich was the fact that even the players who seemed to conform most neatly to stereotypes of masculinity had qualities that contradicted those stereotypes. The earringed Pietersen exuded raw physical strength, hitting the ball stupendous distances, while the most ferocious of the England fast bowlers, Harmison, was the biggest softie in the side. Simon Jones might have looked like a squaddie, but he was a snappy enough dresser to be signed up as a fashion model after the series. The gorilla-like Flintoff was a gentle soul, chivalrous in victory. No member of the side was quite what he seemed.

Manliness, once such a simple concept, had become a pick 'n' mix bazaar, a winding river with many tributaries. The year the Ashes was regained, fittingly, was also the year of *Brokeback Mountain*, a Western so boldly counter-cultural that it could never have been made before the Millennium. John Wayne suddenly had a boyfriend – and audiences rather warmed to the idea.

It took a captain of authority to weld such a disparate group of individuals into an effective fighting force and, in Yorkshire's Michael Vaughan, England had such a captain. In a team of strong personalities, he was the natural leader. Strauss would later make a fine captain himself, but Flintoff failed in the role, while Pietersen fell by the wayside. It was Vaughan   soft-spoken, mild-mannered, unprepossessing in appearance, but with a ruthless streak that caught his opponents on the hop – who wore the crown as if it was his birthright.

In the ranks of the manly, the captain of a team, like the CEO of a business, enjoys a special place. Even now that, in Test cricket, his role has been diminished by the rise of the coach, he is not just one alpha male among many, but the leader of the pack, the top banana, the one who gives the orders.

In George Hirst's class-ridden England, it would have been pretty much unthinkable for a professional cricketer to captain either his county or his country. The jobs went, as of right, to amateurs, usually ex-public schoolboys, and it was 50 years before another Yorkshireman, Len Hutton, became the first professional to be appointed England captain. Michael Vaughan was born into a more egalitarian world, but was confident enough to assert his authority, when required, not let the England team become rudderless, run by a committee. He might not have been as eye-catching a personality as Flintoff or Pietersen, but he was not afraid to lead from the front.

I met Michael Vaughan once. It was in the bar of the Royal Westmoreland in Barbados, where I had just been chatting about cricket, golf and life to Sir Gary Sobers. (And if a writer who can use a line like *that* does not seize the moment, he should be in a different profession.) Vaughan was at a frustrating point in his career, still in rehab after the knee surgery that kept him out of the 2006–07 Ashes tour, but what most struck me about him was how relaxed he was: calm, easy-going, affable; comfortable in his own skin.

I now realise, looking back, that I was conned: that the affability was a facade. Beneath the smiling, laid-back cricketer was a man who worried himself sick, almost literally. Worried about his fitness. Worried about his form. Worried about the captaincy. Worried when England were doing badly. Worried, worried, worried.

Worried so much that, a year later, he consulted a homeopath, fiddled about with his diet, and started keeping a diary into which he poured his neuroses like an adult Adrian Mole: 'It's almost as if I am scared of anyone getting to know me… Maybe I am more of a loner than I think I am… Feel as if I always want to sleep, always tired… I have lost confidence… My best days are behind me… Am I good enough? Why should I continue?… I'm finished. I don't need this any more… Very stressed, head feels tight, agitated… Can hear people criticising… Struggling to focus… Boredom creeping in… Must stop being irritable about little things I cannot control… Head constantly aching… Keep smiling, stop feeling sorry for myself… Must stay relaxed, be what I am… Not too serious, focused but not anal…'

What a performance! Lord Hawke would have taken one look at the diary and told Vaughan to pull himself together or he would be on the next train home. No wonder Vaughan's batting average fell the longer he stayed captain. But, unintentional humour aside, the diary is a touching document, raw with unprocessed feeling.

Inside every successful man, the fear of failure – as visceral as the fear of impotence, to which it is intimately linked – gnaws away like a cancer. And Test cricketers, particularly batsmen, get it worse than anybody. The first-ball duck – the ultimate failure – is a real possibility. It can happen. It does happen. Then suppose you get *another* first-ball duck, in the next innings…

When Vaughan resigned the England captaincy in 2008, the neurosis-riddled Pepys behind the suave professional sportsman came bursting from the closet. 'I've got to be *me*,' Vaughan said to himself, as he prepared for the press conference at Loughborough at which he was to make the announcement. 'I haven't been me for such a long time, so now is the time to be me again, after all those years of putting on the mask of positivity… No more bloody diplomacy.'

Minutes later, in front of the TV cameras, the floodgates burst and most un-Yorkshire-like tears were cascading down his face. It was a poignant moment, such a contrast with the unbridled joy of 2005, as he held the replica Ashes aloft at the Oval. But nobody in the cricket world breathed a word of criticism. People rallied round. All that 'bloody diplomacy', as Vaughan put it, had paid dividends. Why make enemies if you can avoid making enemies? Why not go on the front foot and try to make a few friends? If you are nice to other people, polite, courteous, pleasant – as Vaughan was to me and thousands of others – they don't kick you when you are down.

I still have a photograph of Vaughan and me in Barbados. It is out of focus – the rum punch was flowing – but I treasure it. I just look gormless and adoring. Vaughan, who is young enough to be my son, looks effortlessly regal. He is wearing a pale pink polo shirt, and it has struck me since that I have nothing that colour in my entire wardrobe – nor am ever likely to have. I missed the metrosexual boat. Vaughan is a paid-up passenger but – like Darren Gough, in this respect – knows where to draw the line. He is a dapper dresser, but not a poseur or attention-seeker. He can throw himself into a night out with the lads, eat in a Japanese restaurant or have a quiet meal at home with his wife and kids.

Moderation is his byword. In the Ashes-winning side of 2005, he was in the middle of the metrosexual spectrum: not as frequent a visitor to the mirror/hairdresser/toiletries cabinet as Pietersen, not as infrequent as Hoggard, a happy medium. He is a man of his times, in that respect, not afraid to take a tad more trouble over his appearance than his father before him.

When Brian Close started to go bald, he did not give a damn. If the ball bounced off his head with a loud clunk, so much the better: it suited his hard-man image. When Boycott went bald, it seemed to embarrass him. He was rarely seen in public without his trademark Panama. He even wore the hat indoors, on occasion, as if covering his shame. When the same thing happened to Vaughan, there was no sense of mid-life crisis. Like Shane Warne, he spotted a nice little earner and started doing hair transplant ads. So what if he was a few follicles short of a Fiery Fred? He fertilised his thatch with as little hesitation as an actor from Manhattan or Los Angeles undergoing plastic surgery.

His relaxed attitude to such matters threw some of his more butch opponents. When Graeme Smith, the South African captain, first locked horns with Michael Vaughan, he taunted him that he was 'queer'. South of the Limpopo, the metrosexual is still a theoretical construct, at the development stage. But Vaughan shrugged off the jibes. He wasn't playing *that* game.

In the flesh, Vaughan comes across as self-confident but not bullish, sensitive in his dealings with others without being over-sensitive. His critics, and he has had his share, find him smooth, even smarmy; they wish he had more of the bluntness of the honest-to-God Yorkshireman. At one point, he started referring to himself in the third person ('Michael Vaughan needs to stand up and be counted'), which got him the bird in Barnsley and Bradford, where they don't talk like *that*, thank you very much. But he seems level-headed enough, his yin and yang in near-perfect balance. He shares with George Hirst the knack of being simultaneously modest and assertive.

As a batsman, he was a stroke-maker, not a grafter – although, again, there was a pleasing sense of balance, a fusion of opposites. His two signature shots were the cover drive, effortlessly graceful, and played with the straightest of bats, and the pull over midwicket, lusty and purposeful. Connoisseurs of classical batting drooled when Vaughan was at the crease.

Yorkshire fans with long memories likened him to the young Len Hutton, but even Hutton at his most carefree never expressed himself as exuberantly as Vaughan. He wanted to take on the bowlers, even if they were great bowlers, *particularly* if they were great bowlers. On the 2002–03 tour of Australia, he treated Warne and McGrath as ordinary mortals, scoring a stack of runs in handsome style, while others wilted under the pressure. Soon afterwards, he was made England captain, and was never the same batsman again. The cares of captaincy weighed on his shoulders. Some of the spontaneity went. But he never lost his attacking instincts.

Taking a leaf out of the Australian book, Vaughan's England scored their runs at helter-skelter speed, demoralising the opposition. Batsmen occasionally got out to rash shots, but the fast-and-furious approach paid handsome dividends, particularly in the golden years of 2004 and 2005. It also made for five-star sporting entertainment. Sir Matt Busby, the great Manchester United manager, used to tell his players to go out and express themselves: they might let in three goals but, if they played without fear, they would score four at the other end. Vaughan had a similar philosophy. Cutting out mistakes – a hallmark of Yorkshire cricket for more than 100 years – was not enough. Attack with conviction, whether with bat or ball, and you would carry the day.

If Vaughan had been merely an elegant player, a right-handed David Gower, he would never have had the success he did. He had a streak of steely competitiveness – he read that bit of the Yorkshire coaching manual – that was largely absent from Gower. Under his captaincy, the body language of the England team was the most combative, determined, in world cricket. There was no point in sledging them, or trying to pick on the weaker players: they stuck up for each other, through thick and thin.

Even the celebrated start-of-session huddle – perhaps the single abiding image of the Vaughan years – was a masterstroke. Until it descended into self-parody, the huddle *worked*. It was the outward and visible sign of a team that was bigger than the sum of its parts. Cricket traditionalists, particularly those from Yorkshire, were suspicious of all the hugging and kissing. Every wicket sparked a mass love-in. The stump microphone picked up girlish squeals as well as the customary expletives. But they were forced to acknowledge that Vaughan was an accomplished leader of men.

He was not doing anything novel or revolutionary. He was just putting into practice precepts propounded by Lord Hawke when Queen Victoria was on the throne – cricket is a team game and teamwork starts with a strong captain.

Michael Paul Vaughan was born in Manchester on 29 October 1974. Talk to Yorkshire diehards and they will tell you that, from the day Vaughan came into the world, he has been an impostor. By 'eck! What's a lad from Manchester, of all places, doing wearing the white rose of Yorkshire?

Until 1992, Vaughan would have been ineligible, full stop. There was the odd exception, including Lord Hawke himself, but generally you needed to have been born within the county boundaries to qualify for Yorkshire – a proud tradition, with a whole folklore attached to it. Many is the tale, usually apocryphal, of ambulances driving pregnant mothers-to-be helter-skelter along the M1, so that their sons could be born in Yorkshire, not a mile outside. 'Personally, I feel sad that they relaxed the rule,' says Michael Parkinson. 'It helped shape the identity of Yorkshire cricket. This is a big county and there is a wealth of Yorkshire-born talent, particularly in some of the Asian communities, which has not been fully tapped. We should be nurturing local players, not bringing in overseas players on the cheap.'

Vaughan's parents had moved to Sheffield when he was nine, so he was able to benefit from the 1992 rule change, under which boys educated in the county, even if they had been born outside, became eligible. Tyke or no Tyke, he was a welcome addition to a weak Yorkshire squad.

A once proud institution was in decline. Under-investment, poor management, lack of facilities, the Boycott wars, the rise of other counties, studded with overseas stars… the causes were many and various. By the time Vaughan made his county debut in 1993, it was a quarter of a century since Yorkshire had last won the county championship. He could not rely on pipe-puffing old-stagers to induct him into the mysteries of Yorkshire cricket, the way Trueman and Boycott had been inducted. He had to learn on the hoof – which perhaps enabled him to express himself more freely than he would otherwise have done.

Some of the old values and attitudes lingered. 'At Yorkshire nobody seemed to mind you getting out as long as you were playing a defensive stroke when dismissed,' Vaughan wrote in his autobiography, *Time to Declare*. 'But if you were out playing an attacking shot, there was the allegation that you were playing like a millionaire.' It was an austere creed and, little by little, Vaughan became an unabashed heretic. To put his cricket career in a nutshell, he played like a millionaire, became a millionaire, and sod Yorkshire tradition.

Like Darren Gough, he showed promise when he was young, made the grade at Yorkshire, but had to wait a few years before winning his first England cap. The laddish delights of being a young professional cricketer were intoxicating, and Vaughan drank deep from the well. At the Yorkshire Academy, which Vaughan joined in his late teens, players repaired to the bar within minutes of stumps being drawn. 'Between 7.30 and 11 p.m., it was one long Happy Hour,' he remembers. There were karaoke nights, toga parties, silly drinking games, banter a-plenty and – the icing on the cake – women. 'A lot of the chat was about who had pulled which girl, and about who could come back with the best story from the night before... It was more like Freshers' Week than serious professional sport.'

Like Gough, Vaughan met his future wife, Nichola, in a bar. His account of their wooing is terse: 'She was not that interested in me at first because I had a bit of a reputation as a lad about town at the time, but I brought her round to my way of thinking in the end.' The passage would make a good set text in an examination paper for students reading gender studies at Cambridge:

What does this sentence tell us about the relations between the sexes in early 21st-century Yorkshire? Discuss in particular the significance of the phrase 'my way of thinking'.

Is old-fashioned romance dead?

Where does the real power reside in the relationship?

And what clues are there that, five years after meeting in a sports bar in Sheffield, the couple will be married at Chatsworth House, as guests of the Duke and Duchess of Devonshire?

If Vaughan was a lad's lad before he graduated into a man's man, he was also honing the diplomatic skills that would stand him in good stead as England captain. Fred Trueman was an argument waiting to happen. So, to a degree, were Geoffrey Boycott and Darren Gough. But Vaughan's instincts were very different. One of the films that influenced him as a teenager – light years from the John Wayne Westerns that made such an impact on Boycott – was *Road House*, released in 1989. The film starred Patrick Swayze as a bouncer working in a bar where fights were always breaking out and furniture being thrown. 'You've got to be nice,' the bouncer would plead, in an effort to calm things down. Vaughan adopted the phrase as his mantra, biting his tongue rather than let himself be riled when someone tried to provoke him – a lesson he took with him on to the cricket field.

It was a significant departure from type. How many Yorkshire cricketers of the past had told themselves to be *nice* when they woke up in the morning? They were too busy grinding down the opposition and wearing regulation Pennine scowls. If they had a mantra, it was 'You've got to be tough' or 'You don't give away owt to t'buggers from Lancashire'. But niceness – an insipid but nonetheless resonant word – went with the times. The economy was booming. People had enough disposable income to enjoy themselves. Optimism was in the air. Why wouldn't people be nice to each other? Life was too short to get into punch-ups.

The dominant British figure of the age – prime minister for virtually the whole duration of Vaughan's England career – was Tony Blair. Until we discovered he wasn't at all nice, Tony Blair was very nice indeed: a folksy politician who sweet-talked his way up the greasy pole, then made a virtue of his affability. He took his cue from that other master schmoozer, Bill Clinton. Blair had a relaxed manner, a good sense of humour and the knack of putting people of all classes at their ease. His nickname, Bambi, was as apt as the Iron Lady had been apt for Margaret Thatcher. One was a Cold War battleaxe; the other was a smile on wobbly legs. Both won three general elections.

'I spent a bit of time with Tony Blair and found him very likeable,' Vaughan notes in his autobiography. The two men were such a perfect mirror image of each other that they bought suits made by the same Indian tailor. The only time they had a serious ideological difference was in September 2005, when Blair welcomed Vaughan and his team to Downing Street after their open-top bus tour to Trafalgar Square and offered them *pineapple* juice. Shocking. Schoolboy error. Denis Thatcher would have had his guts for garters. Otherwise, the two men had much in common, indeed their careers at the helm of their respective ships could be said to have followed a not dissimilar trajectory: a period of winning hearts and minds, trying to be all things to all men, followed by a rude awakening.

But they were not wrong in their instinctive niceness. It fitted the zeitgeist. Cool Britannia, as the Britain of New Labour became known, was so determinedly laid-back that the shrill confrontations of the Thatcher years seemed like a bad memory. There was sofa government in Downing Street, recreational drugs in Notting Hill and happy hours in Leeds and Bradford. If you didn't know how to chill, there was something wrong with you.

When Bruce Feirstein had made fun of quiche-eaters in the 1980s, and again when the word 'metrosexual' surfaced – it made its debut in the *Independent* in 1994, in an article by Mark Simpson, although it was some years before it entered the mainstream – a lot of attention focused on the props. Skincare products, scented candles, aromatherapy sessions, That Sarong worn by David Beckham… How the real men tittered! But it was the simple niceness of this new breed of men – none grinning more winsomely than Beckham himself – that was their most striking feature. They didn't want to conquer, or not by old-fashioned rutting-stag methods. They wanted to *charm*.

In their dealings with other people, men of the metrosexual type did what women had been doing for centuries: sought consensus, not confrontation; displayed consideration for others; listened politely, rather than hogging the limelight; discovered the power of a simple smile.

No Hollywood star of the golden age had more influence in shaping attitudes to manliness than Tom Hanks in the 1990s: Mr Nice in person, a man of such palpable small-town decency, allied to gentleness and sensitivity, that he made the hard men of Hollywood – Bruce Willis, Arnold Schwarzenegger, Sylvester Stallone – look very flat-footed. A romantic comedy starring Tom Hanks – *Sleepless in Seattle* was the prototype – had a feel-good schmaltziness not seen since the days of Frank Capra. To women who didn't give a damn what a man earned, but just wanted a mate who would treat them well, share the chores and be kind to their children, Hanks offered a vision of manliness that was no less attractive for being down-to-earth. He made niceness heroic.

Others followed Hanks' lead. The characters they played were kind first and virile second. They took their parenting responsibilities very, very seriously. In *Mrs Doubtfire*, released in 1993, the same year as *Sleepless in Seattle*, Robin Williams played an estranged husband so desperate to see more of his children that he was prepared to dress up as a woman to get his way. Imagine Spencer Tracy or Gary Cooper doing the same.

If Michael Vaughan, like Hanks and Williams, made niceness his trump card, he also had backbone, more than people realised. He might have looked fragile at the crease, and even more so in the field, where he minced about like an extra in *Les Miserables* and was the last man you would expect to make a diving stop or a blinding catch. But the fragility was deceptive.

Vaughan's England debut, on the 1999–2000 tour of South Africa, would have tested the backbone of any player. If there was Yorkshire grit beneath the elegance, he had the perfect stage on which to show it. Batting at number four, he came in with Allan Donald running amok, two runs on the scoreboard and two men out – it would soon be two for four. Panic stations! Vaughan scored a calm 33, revealing a temperament to go with his natural gifts as a batsman. It was not quite Jessop or Botham, more like a Muriel Spark novel, but he had arrived.

After that, he became a fixture in the England side, moved up to open the innings and, by early 2003, was officially ranked No. 1 batsman in the world. At which point he was given the England captaincy – and the kudos that went with it. He had achieved his dream. Or he thought he had. He did not realise what a mixed blessing the captaincy would prove.

Beyond the boundary, the debate about masculinity had moved on. If *Real Men Don't Eat Quiche* had set the tone for the 1980s, and *Iron John* had got the 1990s off to an impressively butch start, one of the books to be seen with in the mid-1990s, and well into the new century, was *Men Are from Mars, Women Are from Venus: The Definitive Guide to Relationships*.

Published in 1992, the book was written by Texas-born relationships counsellor John Gray PhD, who went on to write a string of follow-up books developing his Mars–Venus thesis. His works have sold over fifty million copies, and been translated into 45 languages, although the man himself remains an enigma, his qualifications as a relationships guru disputed.

Born in 1951, the son of a Texas oilman and a woman who ran a spiritual bookstore in Houston, Gray attended two universities in Texas without receiving a degree. He later got degrees in creative intelligence. But who cares what qualifications a man has if he can put his finger on the nub of an issue as unerringly as Gray? No Texas oilman ever struck such a rich well as Gray with his innovative Mars–Venus thesis. It was hooey, unless you happened to believe in New Age astrology, but it was superior hooey, thought-provoking hooey, the right hooey for the times. As with *Real Men Don't Eat Quiche*, the very title of the book was enough to make people stop outside a bookshop window and think, 'I've never heard of John Gray PhD But he could be on to something there. Tell me more, Doc.'

There was nothing new, obviously, in his notion that men and women were fundamentally different, so far apart, not just biologically, but in their attitudes, that they could indeed have come from different planets. No poem in the history of the English language says as much in as few words – half of them not even words at all – as the doggerel attributed to the 19th-century American philosopher William James, brother of Henry:

191

Hogamus, higamus
Man is polygamous
Higamus, hogamus
Women monogamous.

But the exact nature of those differences was still disputed.

The more men's and women's lives overlapped, the leveller the playing field, the harder it was to pinpoint what exactly differentiated the sexes, beyond the obvious biological markers. During the period when the battle of the sexes was essentially a power struggle – women fighting for equality, men regrouping and trying to re-define their role – the issue of communication between the sexes was secondary. Everyone knew that men and women regularly got their wires crossed. 'It was like talking to a brick wall – stupid bastard.' 'She just wasn't listening – silly cow.' Such grumbles were the small change of domestic life the world over. But Gray was one of the first authors to attempt to codify the differences between man-speak and woman-speak and how those differences affected couples in relationships.

It was a quixotic enterprise. For every Martian who bought his book, there must have been a dozen Venusians. Analysing relationships is a quintessentially feminine pastime. Most men are just not interested in picking over the bones of that misunderstanding in the kitchen last night: who said what, who meant what, who asked the wrong question, who changed the subject, who used aggressive body language, blah blah blah. They are more interested in analysing why the FTSE is up or why Manchester United lost to Arsenal.

Gray did his best to spell out his theory in terms men would understand. One of his central contentions – endearing to cricket-lovers – is that men and women keep running scorecards, awarding each other points, but according to different principles. Thus a man would award himself 20 points for giving a woman an expensive present, but only 1 point for helping her lift a heavy bag – whereas the woman would award the man the same number of points for each action.

Duckworth-Lewis eat your heart out. But a lot of Gray's theorising passed over men's heads. You did see a few men on Greek beaches reading *Men Are from Mars*, brows furrowed; but it only took a pretty woman in a bikini, or the glint of a lager can from a neighbouring taverna, to distract them from their studies.

Still, at least they tried, or some of them did. What the huge popularity of the Mars–Venus books did demonstrate was a renewed interest in the idea that there were certain inalienable differences between the sexes. Men liked that idea. They liked that idea a lot. Without necessarily being sexist – although, in the way of things, many *were* sexist – they wanted to keep areas of their lives totally free from female interference, whether it was the no-holds-barred stag night in Leeds or the all-male Pall Mall club, fiercely resisting moves to admit women.

There had been times in the 1990s when the rise of the feminised man – not just cheerfully accepting sexual equality, but systematically plagiarising all that was best and most enjoyable about being a woman – had seemed like one of those unstoppable historical forces that would never be reversed. John Gray PhD, whoever he was, had other ideas. His books helped re-define the terms of the argument. Among the chattering classes, on both sides of the Atlantic, there was now a rush to find counterweights to metrosexuality, standards around which men of old-school values could rally.

The word 'retrosexual' had a good innings, and you still hear it occasionally today. It denoted the type of robustly uncomplicated man – step forward, Matthew Hoggard – who didn't own a sarong, wasn't going to be seen dead in the wrong sort of hairdresser, and would kick a scented candle a hundred yards, if anyone had the temerity to light one in his presence. Did Hoggy even own a comb? The evidence was ambiguous.

Another word to surface fleetingly was 'über-sexual'. In *The Future of Men*, published in 2005, three American authors – Marian Salzman, Ira Matathia and Ann O'Reilly – tried to move the debate on to the next stage. The future of men, they proclaimed, was 'not to be found in the primped and waxed boy who wowed the world with his nuanced knowledge of tweezers and exfoliating creams. Men, at the end of the day, will have to rely on their intellect and their passion, their erudition and professional success, to be acknowledged and idealised in contemporary society.' An über-sexual, as they defined the term, which they had coined themselves, citing Bill Clinton and George Clooney as examples, evinced 'a degree of greatness and perfection… so perfect as to leave little margin for error and fallacy.' He sounds suspiciously like one of those Aryan supermen Hitler was so fond of. Matthew Hoggard would have kicked the book even further than the scented candles. In any event, the idea never caught on.

In *The Times*, the novelist Tim Lott outed himself as 'stray', a neat hybrid of 'straight' and 'gay'. He was a heterosexual father of four, he explained, but so many of the things he did, such as leafing through Boden catalogues and listening to *Women's Hour*, were so irredeemably girly that it was a moot point whether he was the same sex as Jeremy Clarkson, Sir Alex Ferguson and other members of the Fraternity of Blokes. It was a nice conceit but like über-sexual – and for that matter, 'heteropolitan', another hybrid word, denoting a man who dressed stylishly while remaining masculine in other respects – it never entered the cultural mainstream.

In the real world, as opposed to the world of gender-studies gurus and lifestyle columnists, there were more pressing concerns. A lot of people, pondering why quite so many men were quite such unsatisfactory specimens of manliness, started to focus on boys rather than men. Were they being raised right? Or had the nanny state, in collusion with over-protective parents, produced a generation of male adolescents with thinner-than-thin skins and the backbone of a jellyfish? They *looked* good. They damn well should do. They spent enough on clothes. But had they been over-protected to the point that they no longer had the resources to cope with adversity?

The progression from boyhood to manhood is far harder than the progression from girlhood to womanhood – a point on which feminists and non-feminists agree. Camille Paglia ('A woman simply is, but a man must become') and Norman Mailer ('Masculinity is not something given to you, but something you gain') sing from the same hymn sheet. And it becomes harder still if the environment in which a boy grows up is unconducive to developing manly qualities.

A boy may play with toy soldiers while his sister plays with her dolls and, to a certain type of parent, that is a reassuring image, a confirmation of age-old differences. But if both children are playing in an environment in which their every move is anxiously supervised – whether by a parent or a teacher or a child-minder – those differences are largely meaningless. Until they are given the space to experiment, make mistakes, fail, their development will be arrested.

Darren Gough in his autobiography, published in 2001, bemoans the fact that the Britain in which he had grown up had changed beyond recognition: 'The street was our playground. I would come home from school, dump my stuff, grab a cheese sandwich and rush out again… occasionally Mum and Dad would look out of the window to check we were OK. But I would be out there till dark. Total freedom. Sadly, those days are gone forever. It hurts me that my kids can't walk out of the house and play with other kids.'

Millions of parents, even ones who were contributing to the problem, felt the same. They could see that, materially, their children had benefits of which they could only have dreamed; but they could also see that, for all sorts of reasons, childhood had become less fun, less adventure-filled. A whole generation was being infantilised.

From Middle England, its concerns vigorously voiced by the *Daily Mail*, there came a steady rumble of protest, rising to a roar at times, as once hallowed parts of childhood, like Bonfire Night and tobogganing and conker-fights, were sanitised, tied up in red tape or banned altogether. 'Health and safety' became the most reviled coupling of words in the language, a shorthand for everything that was wrong with modern Britain. The silent, sensible majority was being outflanked by a neurotic minority, spooked by non-existent terrors. And it was children – boys, in particular – who were the main victims.

What chance did they have of becoming tough, assertive men if Big Brother was watching every step of their childhood? How would they ever learn about the real world if they played computer games all day behind closed bedroom doors, or loafed about in shopping centres, pricing the latest trainers? Measures designed to protect them were stifling the life out of them. One-time breeding grounds of masculinity, like the school sports field, faced extinction. Rugby and boxing were out, aerobics and Pilates were in.

Many parents realised something was wrong, and raged against the nannying tendencies of the age, but they felt impotent to do anything. In Whitehall, Venus had beaten Mars. In Brussels, she had beaten him by an innings.

One of the books to tap into the frustrations festering in Middle England was *The Dangerous Book for Boys* by Conn and Hal Iggulden. Published in 2006, the book was a surprise bestseller, rocketing to the top of the non-fiction list, then taking the USA by storm the following year. Aimed at 'boys from eight to eighty', the book was a compendium of things which 'every boy should know', from the names of Kings and Queens of England to how to tie a reef knot. The 'dangerous' in the title was wildly misleading. Apart from the odd chapter, such as 'Hunting and Cooking a Rabbit', the content of the book was bland to a fault. Where was the danger in playing chess, using secret inks or making a paper boat? One got the whiff of a marketing ploy.

Cynics would say the most dangerous chapter in the book is the one explaining the rules of cricket, where the co-authors, two half-Irish brothers, are way out of their depth. They have England playing Australia for 'the ashes (*sic*)', assert that the umpire can 'send a player off' for misconduct, which would be news to Dickie Bird, and list 'the seven main shots in batting' as 'front-foot defence, back-foot defence, a drive, a square-cut, a pull, a sweep and a loft shot (*sic*)'. The loft is apparently 'similar to the lob in tennis', but not recommended against overpitched deliveries. Fascinating. Elsewhere they state, po-faced: 'A batsman's sole aim is to score runs' – a line that would have started a stand-up brawl if anyone had used it in a Yorkshire committee meeting, *c*.1975.

Still, there is no arguing with success, and the Igguldens, sons of a wartime fighter pilot, had their hearts in the right place. If the word 'dangerous' had not been in the title, would anyone have bought the book? The d-word struck a chord with parents who, however vaguely, *wanted* a little danger in their sons' lives. Not too much danger. Nothing reckless or life-threatening. They hedged their bets a bit. But they instinctively hated the new-look, safety-first Britain, where everyone brought into contact with children was viewed as a potential paedophile, and where experts could quantify the risk of every activity, but not the risk of a risk-free existence.

Whither masculinity in such a namby-pamby, emasculated world? The question refused to go away. Well-meaning parents enrolled their sons in Duke of Edinburgh Award schemes, and they went abseiling in the Peak District and came home and said they had had a wicked time, but that sort of thing in itself was not going to crack the problem. It was the material ease of the modern world, the dearth of harsh, rough-edged, character-building ingredients, that was turning boys soft.

One of the signature TV series of the age was of *Ray Mears' World of Survival*, which was first shown on the BBC in the late 1990s, then had a series of spin-offs. Couch potatoes in Bromsgrove and Hemel Hempstead watched hypnotised as the knobbly-kneed presenter, in his trademark shorts, explained how to light a fire in the bush – rubbing sticks together was recommended – where to find edible berries and mushrooms and how to make a canoe out of a hollowed-out tree trunk. All the TV scriptwriters on the planet would have been pushed to come up with a scenario in which the couch potatoes would have had to make a canoe for real, but the very fact that they were keen to see how it was done was indicative of unsatisfied yearnings, needs that the internet could not satisfy.

For all the theorising, and the prescriptions for re-connecting the men of today with their caveman ancestors, those simple hunter-gatherers, the male of the species remained an enigma. Some men, perhaps most, had moved with the times, albeit without much conviction, drifting on the tide of fashion, rather than marching with purpose towards an understood objective. Others were what men had always been: a chaotic mass of testosterone. In the cities, men might be loitering with intent in spas, stockpiling face creams or ordering cocktails with brand-name Cuban rums, but out in the sticks – and nowhere more so than in Yorkshire – life still had a raw, primitive quality.

In January 2002 – the start of a golden year for Michael Vaughan, who scored century after effortless century for England – a 23-year-old male chef was convicted by Hull Crown Court of having sex with a goat. Was it a comedy? Was it a tragedy? You could argue it either way.

But the episode dispelled any notion that post-millennium Britain had reached a point of happy no-return on the evolutionary scale.

Circumstances had conspired against the chef, who was doing what he was doing with the goat, female, on an allotment overlooked by a railway line, when a crowded Hull-to-Bridlington train came to a grinding halt at the signals. Within minutes, police switchboards were jammed by horrified commuters reporting what they had seen. Some of them took photos of the incident on their mobile phones. The chef was later arrested by Humberside Police. 'I don't normally do this sort of thing,' he told the court.

Detective Inspector Dave Crinnion of the British Transport Police – clearly one of those stolid common-sense coppers who are the glory of England – also investigated the incident. 'I saw the goat the next day,' he said in the witness box, choosing his words with care. 'It didn't seem too upset, but it's difficult to tell.' And they can put *that* in their pipe and smoke it.

A hundred years after Hirst and Rhodes got 'em in singles, Yorkshire phlegm was alive and well.

Like every England cricket supporter, I have wonderful memories of Michael Vaughan, both as player and captain. Not all of them involve things that happened on the field. I remember feeling a little twinge of pleasure in June 2004 when the TV cameras caught Vaughan – captaining England against New Zealand at the time – as he hurried out to the car park before close of play to drive to the hospital where his wife was expecting his child. It was a first for an England captain, but it felt right, somehow. And the fact that the only person to criticise him for leaving play early was his mother – who had given birth to Vaughan while her husband was playing cricket – made it even more satisfying. Priorities had changed, and for the better.

But I have one less happy memory of Vaughan. Not the tears at the final press conference. Those also felt right, in a Tom Hanks kind of way. It was the image – beamed into my living room 100 times – of the England captain sitting in the dressing room staring at a computer screen. The longer he was captain, the longer he seemed to spend staring at the screen. In 2004, in the good times, he had the odd peep, but that was all. By 2008, his last year as captain, he was totally hooked, like a teenager with a Nintendo DS.

What was on the bloody screen? We were never vouchsafed a look. But whatever it was – a slo-mo replay of his latest dismissal? Stats on Steve Harmison's economy rate? – it invariably reduced Vaughan to a nervous wreck. He would look at the screen, fiddle with the mouse, then plunge into an even deeper gloom, scratching his chin and running his hand through his fast-disappearing hair. If it was not obsessive-compulsive disorder, it came dangerously close to it. The worry-guts who kept a diary of his worries stood naked before us. Couldn't he just switch off his laptop and read a book? Or play cards with his team-mates?

Vaughan was hardly the first England captain to be a worrier – the job has proved a crown of thorns for many, if not most, of the men who have held it. What was new was the computer, and his apparent faith that the answers to his problems on the field were to be found on a computer screen.

An exaggerated trust in technology has long been a male trait – a trait that became more pronounced in the 20th century. To know how to change a plug, or mend a boiler, or set a video recorder, gave men the edge in their running battle with women. It showed that they were not just beasts of burden, valued for their strength alone. They could use their brains in practical ways. A man fiddling around under the bonnet of a car, watched by an admiring woman cooing words of encouragement, was a happy man. So long as he fiddled to good purpose, he was an authority figure, a hero with a spanner.

Every new gizmo was a chance to demonstrate his authority – and no gizmo in history offered the potential of the personal computer. Obviously women understood computers, too. At school IT lessons, girls were the equal of boys, if not superior. But it was men who embraced the computer age like religious zealots. They could glimpse the possibility of a new kind of virility, based on multi-tasking not raw strength.

In the Bond films, a clear distinction had always been maintained between the action man, licensed to kill, and the backroom boffin, Q. Brains and brawn occupied separate pigeonholes. Now a new type of warrior – epitomised by Jack Bauer in the long-running American TV drama *24* – was coming to the fore. Bauer could use hi-tech gizmos with the same effortless superiority as he could fire a gun or attach electrodes to the nipples of a terrorist suspect. To drive a car one-handed at 90mph, while simultaneously downloading the GPS coordinates of the warehouse where the villains where hiding, then texting his daughter to tell her he loved her, was all in a day's work. It was awe-inspiring stuff, and it set the pulse racing. It was also very, very silly.

Almost as silly was the preening competitiveness of this new breed of technocrats. After centuries of 'Mine's bigger than yours', it was suddenly 'Mine's smaller than yours', as dinkier and dinkier mobile phones came on the market, with each new model able to perform more functions than the last one, at double the speed.

Where women saw computers mainly as tools of communication, access roads to the information superhighway, men tended to view them as instruments of control. Master the new technology and they could micro-manage every aspect of their lives, from business to leisure. Better still, they could function in their own private space, without the hassle and the messiness of interacting face-to-face with other people. To a certain kind of man – intense, driven, solitary by temperament – that was the biggest prize of all. But there was a price to be paid.

In his book *Hamlet's BlackBerry*, the American author William Powers rails at what he calls 'the vanishing family trick': seemingly happy families gradually dissolving to screens in different corners of the house. 'What's lost in the process is so valuable it can't be quantified,' Powers writes. 'Isn't this what we live for – time spent with other people, those moments that can't be translated into ones and zeros and replicated on a screen?'

If computers have undermined family life, they have also dealt a body blow to manliness. One of the recurring images of our present age is men in suits in aeroplanes switching on their BlackBerries within nanoseconds of their planes landing. They have mistaken ergonomic efficiency for coolness. They can't see the uncoolness of clutching so pathetically at the umbilical cord separating them from their bosses/girlfriends/bookmakers.

They think they are self-sufficient, in control, but that sense of control is nine-tenths illusory. The more dependent men have become on technology, the harder they have found it to meet the kind of challenges that require the human touch. They can sit at their computers, masters of all they survey on their screens, but you know – and, deep inside, *they* know – that if you marooned them on a desert island, they would not know how to cope. The animal survival instincts of their ancestors have been bled from them.

What men do with their computers is neither here nor there. Some trawl porn sites or join Leeds United forums and crack off-colour jokes with other blokeish types. Others book tickets for the ballet or pore over online menswear catalogues. It is the very fact that their lives have been hijacked by machines that is significant. The technology has eroded something that was intangible, but nonetheless important. It is as if Frankenstein has finally triumphed over Tarzan.

No computer was going to help Michael Vaughan deal with a 90mph bouncer on a dodgy pitch. No computer was going to protect him from the sledging of the slip fieldsmen. No computer was going to give him the backbone – the bit Yorkshire gave to England, as Len Hutton put it – to lead his team to victory. The longer he stared at the computer screen, the more I feared for him.

The 2005 Ashes winners, Vaughan included, had a painfully short shelf life. Three months after their triumph at the Oval, they lost a series in Pakistan, after which things went from bad to worse. Vaughan crocked, Giles crocked, Simon Jones crocked, Trescothick torpedoed by depression, Flintoff reduced to a caricature, toppling off a pedalo in the Caribbean, Harmison losing it, Geraint Jones losing it, Collingwood wandering about in a fog of existential despair, Pietersen spending half his time modelling, Bell *still* looking as if he should be in short trousers… That manly-seeming group of men was revealed as a cruel mirage.

Less than 18 months after their open-top bus parade to Trafalgar Square, the tattered remnants of the team, minus the injured Vaughan, were pulverised 5-0 by an Australian side that held a pre-series boot camp, bonding around a billabong and probably eating raw platypus for breakfast. The MBEs with which the England players had been garlanded after the 2005 series were thrown back in their faces. If the initials stood for anything, it was Men Behaving Effetely. An entire narrative of masculinity – a thrilling synthesis of daintiness and toughness, a world in which a man could wear a diamond earring and still hit a cricket ball out of the park – had to be torn up.

Even Matthew Hoggard, robust, sanguine, commonsensical, the last man standing from Old Yorkshire, proved a man of straw. 'His lank hair, allied to a broad-beamed, stomping gait, encouraged so much farming imagery it would have been no surprise had he stopped midway through his run to close a gate or chase a sheep,' joked David Hopps in the 2006 *Wisden*. If any cricketer in England had his feet on the ground, it was Hoggy. Not so, apparently. On the tour of New Zealand in 2008, Hoggy's world disintegrated.

His first sin against the tutelary gods of Yorkshire cricket was to eat a tuna sandwich before a warm-up match in Dunedin. *Tuna?* What was wrong with cheese and chutney? The gods punished him for that one. He had to leave the field to throw up in an oil drum. But it was in his head, not his stomach, that the real demons were lurking. Back in England, his wife Sarah was suffering from postnatal depression, and there was ongoing friction between them. Hoggard tried to put a brave face on things, but found it harder and harder to cope. His performance on the field suffered, until things came to a head in the first Test at Hamilton: 'I was walking back to my mark when it all suddenly just hit me. As I got towards the end of my run-up, I felt as though I wanted to cry. I've always been a bit baffled about who controls the mysterious functioning of a man's waterworks. Well, now someone was trying to turn them on for me in the middle of a Test match.'

'I think I'm going cuckoo,' Hoggard said to Michael Vaughan, who was standing at mid-off. He held himself together, just, but his days as a Test cricketer were numbered, and he was dropped before the end of the series. A few months later, Vaughan also headed for the exit. The commentary box beckoned, the way the House of Lords beckons for an outgoing cabinet minister, and Vaughan has taken confidently to his new role.

He is not quite in the Boycott league as a commentator/sage/Tyke know-it-all, but he has got time on his side. He is relaxed, affable, intelligent, good at banter. You can still glimpse the diplomatic captain who thought that the best way to get on in life was to be nice to people.

Predictably, he remains a slave to technology, one of those obsessive-compulsive Twitter junkies who never know when to stop. In November 2010, he got into hot water after studying Carol Vorderman on television and speculating whether she had had her breasts artificially enhanced. 'She has definitely treated herself to a couple of new friends,' Vaughan tweeted. 'Big friends at that. Why not? That's what I say. Great viewing.' You can give a man a computer, but you can't stop him behaving like a prat.

The episode was simultaneously depressing and reassuring. Depressing because if seemingly house-trained men like Michael Vaughan still talk about women like that, the male of the species has a long way to go. Reassuring because without bucketfuls of pure testosterone, the kind that computers and citizenship classes and health-and-safety leaflets cannot dilute, the species itself would die out. Vaughan ogling the Vorderman mammary glands, tweeting on his BlackBerry, and probably forking himself a mouthful of sushi with his spare hand, is 21st-century man in dotty miniature.

If Vaughan has an unreconstructed laddish side, he is also branching out in other ways. You want a work of modern art by an Ashes-winning England captain? Yours for £300! Vaughan got the art bug after being taken around galleries in Shoreditch by Ashley Giles when play had been abandoned at Lord's or the Oval. Were the pubs closed? He now practises 'artballing', covering cricket balls in coloured paint, then hitting them, or throwing them, against a white canvas, until they form a pattern.

George Hirst would probably have told Vaughan he was bluidy daft, but if you had told George Hirst there was three hundred quid to be earned from half an hour of biffing cricket balls with no worries about being caught at extra cover, he would probably have concluded that it was other people that were bluidy daft, swallowed his pride and taken t'brass like a good Yorkshireman.

Vaughan is still in his thirties, a millionaire, a father of three, the owner of a substantial property portfolio, including a villa in Barbados, and may, who knows, end up winning the Turner Prize. By the time he is pushing up the daisies, he could have sent over a million tweets, none of them advancing the cause of civilisation one jot, and eaten so much sushi that his arteries are clogged with wasabi and yellow-fin tuna.

If there are new menswear fashions, he will follow them. If there are new gizmos, he will buy them. And if Twenty20 cricket supplants Test cricket, he will bow to the inevitable, not moan that things were better in his day, even if they were. He does not seem to have what it takes to be a curmudgeon.

The Yorkshireman in Michael Vaughan will probably fade with time, just as Yorkshire itself will eventually limp grumbling into the 21st century. The metrosexual will never fade. It will just be called something different. And even if the hair transplants go hideously wrong, and Vaughan ends up as bald as a snooker ball, with mottled skin, old gits will still stop him in the street, and ask to be photographed with him, and remind him of that summer of summers, when the Ashes came home. They will probably remind him of his cover drive, one of the loveliest sights in sport. And they will tell him what a good captain he was, a leader who was not a bully. A nice man.

For that, ultimately, will be Michael Vaughan's epitaph. The boy who went to the cinema and heard a movie character say 'You've got to be nice' became the very mirror of modern manliness – sushi, tweets and all.

CLOSE OF PLAY

Girls will be boys and boys will be girls,
It's a mixed-up, muddled-up, shook-up world.

The Kinks, *Lola*

If a man is feeling diffident in his masculinity, and wants to demonstrate that he is better than any woman – not just better, but effortlessly superior – his best remedy is to take a woman with limited knowledge of cricket to a Test match. I have tried it many times and it never fails to do the trick.

The script is invariably the same. The woman enters Lord's or the Oval or wherever in a respectful spirit – she has been forewarned that she is entering hallowed ground. She takes her seat, adjusts her dress, unpacks her M&S bag, feasts her eyes on the epicene Stuart Broad, fielding on the third man boundary, then looks long and earnestly at the scoreboard, which tells her that, say, Australia are 268 for seven. There is a brief, pregnant pause, then a hushed question: 'Are we winning?'

Oh dear, oh dear, oh dear.

Slowly, gravely, trying not to sound donnish, making allowances where necessary, I explain that cricket is not like football or rugby or basketball, one of those moronic games where the state of a match can be condensed into two simple numbers. It is more like chess, or quantum physics, or a Shakespeare history play. England *could* be said to be winning, I explain, but only if the Australian tail-enders are knocked over in reasonable time by the second new ball, if Strauss and Cook are in good nick, if Pietersen fires, if the pitch stays true and if there is no cloud cover in the evening session. After that, much will depend on such imponderables as rain delays, the rough outside the left-handers' off-stump, the amount of reverse swing, the third-umpire review system, the reliability of the technology – factors so many and various that the mind of woman is not large enough to contain them. I don't say that, of course. But, in the nicest possible way, I imply it.

I never feel manlier than when I am putting a woman straight about the 'Are we winning?' fallacy at cricket. But in the context of this book, perhaps the question is admissible. Are *we* winning?

By 'we', I mean the billions of beleaguered, rudderless, messed-up, gender-confused, testosterone-swamped, gym-haunting, mirror-gazing, lager-slurping, morally compromised, intellectually challenged, emotionally obtuse human beings who have been born with penises.

Every Saturday night of the year, at a karaoke bar somewhere in the world, a middle-aged man will put down his beer, totter to his feet, grab the microphone and belt out Frank Sinatra's *My Way*. When he gets to the line 'What is a man, what has he got?' his voice will wobble with emotion and he will probably make a little shrugging gesture, as if to say: 'These are questions to which there are no easy answers. Give me a break. Don't analyse me to death. I'm trying.' Then he will fill his lungs for the final, defiant '*My-y… wa-a-ay!*' He doesn't want the riddle of his maleness solved: he prefers to remain an enigma, a work in progress.

So much has changed in the 110 years since George Hirst and Wilfred Rhodes conferred at the Oval that it is hard to distinguish changes for the better from changes for the worse, progress from degeneration, the candyfloss of fashion from the hard rock of substance.

'Though much is taken, much abides,' wrote Tennyson. Sitting watching Yorkshire play Nottinghamshire at Headingley in April 2011, I was surrounded by a bewildering number of riffs on masculinity, from the retro to the contemporary.

Yorkshire past was represented by the white-haired patriarch in a Panama hat, his back straight as a cricket bat, studying the obituaries in the *Daily Telegraph*; by the middle-aged man drinking tea out of a Thermos; by the lantern-jawed curmudgeon in a Yorkshire sweater, gnarled and weather-beaten, muttering 'you looky booger' every time a Nottinghamshire batsman played and missed; and by what looked like a taxidermised corpse from the 1950s, slumped in a seat, eyes tight shut, mouth wide open.

Yorkshire present could be seen in the two chattering thirty-somethings in polo shirts and Calvin Klein sunglasses, their hair immaculate, their skins suspiciously bronzed, their mobile phones glistening in the sun. One of them had a copy of the *Independent* tucked under his arm. The other announced between overs, in a high, carrying voice, that he could kill a curry.

There was even a glimpse of Yorkshire future in the row in front of me: a boy of four or five, with a Foreign Legion sun-hat flopping over his shoulders, listening intently as his mother explained what a dot-ball was. He will have to watch a lot of dot-balls if he stays the distance, but from the earnest look on his face, he might just do it. Or, then again, perhaps not.

'Who's your favourite player?' I asked him.

'Rooney,' he said, screwing up his face.

'He's only young,' said his mother defensively. 'It's his first match.'

'Give t'lad a chance,' said a man with a hearing aid, whom I took to be the boy's grandfather. 'Cricket is a… *tricky* game. Rules take a while to master. Not like football.' With which he made a brusque gesture, indicating that the conversation was over, and leant forward to watch the next dot-ball.

Yorkshire lost the match — from a position of such overwhelming advantage that Herbert Sutcliffe's dogs could have knocked off the runs blindfold – and the fans grumbled their way home in time-honoured Tyke fashion. But not all is doom and gloom in Yorkshire cricket – even if they ended the 2011 season being relegated.

The week after they were humbled by Nottinghamshire, Yorkshire made history by picking wicketkeeper Barney Gibson of Pudsey – the epicentre of Yorkshire cricket, home to Herbert Sutcliffe, Len Hutton and Raymond Illingworth – for a county match against Durham. At just 15 years and 27 days, Gibson was England's youngest ever first-class cricketer and, ordinarily, would have been studying for his GCSEs at Crawshaw School. 'On a normal Wednesday, I would have science three times, maths and RE,' he told a reporter, in a voice that, if it had broken, had only just broken. 'The school set me work to do while I am here, so I will have to get cracking on some business studies tonight.'

Fifty years ago, Gibson would have been subjected to tough love, told not to get above himself, greeted with a 'not bad' when he took a blinding catch, expected to become a man before he was taken seriously. Now he will be encouraged and nurtured and protected from unfair criticism every inch of the way. Will New Yorkshire turn him into a better cricketer than Old Yorkshire? Time will tell.

At the national level, the future, in 2011, was looking pretty bright. The England team led by Andrew Strauss that retained the Ashes in Australia in 2010–11 did so with purpose and conviction, playing businesslike cricket. 'Lord Hawke would have been proud of them,' says Michael Parkinson, who had a grandstand view of proceedings at the last Test in Sydney. 'They looked the part. They dressed immaculately. Their body language was spot-on. They played as a unit.'

There was only one Yorkshireman in the side, Tim Bresnan, a journeyman bowler with the distinction of uttering one of the first f-words to find its way into the pages of *Wisden* – Lord Hawke would not have been proud of *that*. But he played his part in a well-drilled, well-led team.

Of more lasting significance than the Ashes victory was the announcement in February 2011 by Steven Davies – the Surrey and England wicketkeeper – that he was gay. He was joining a very small club indeed. Precedents for top professional sportsmen doing the same were few and far between, and Davies was widely praised for his courage. But the fact that you would have had to trawl the murkiest backwaters of the blogosphere to find anyone prepared to say publicly that they had a problem with a gay England wicketkeeper was salutary and heartening.

Davies would have been emboldened by the fact that, a few months earlier, his England team-mate James Anderson had posed naked in the gay magazine *Attitude*. Anderson is not gay, but a married man who flew home in the middle of the Ashes series, bless him, to attend the birth of his second daughter. But it was a sign of the times that an England fast bowler could simultaneously have men thinking '*phwoar*' and women thinking '*aaah*'. It was a stunning double, like getting five wickets in both innings.

As heartening as Steven Davies' emergence from the closet was the way almost everyone in the cricket world – Geoffrey Boycott was a dishonourable exception – rallied around England bowler Michael Yardy when he flew home from the 2011 World Cup in India, blaming depression. Mental illness, brushed under the carpet for so long, particularly in the macho world of professional sport, was no longer a taboo subject.

If the cricket world is less monolithic and hard-bitten than it was, it is only reflecting the generally more relaxed attitudes of the age. Who would have guessed that, 100 years after Baden-Powell launched the Scouts Movement, there would have been more girls than boys joining the Scouts? The fact that the *Daily Mail* only reported the news on page 26 showed how ingrained the habits of sexual equality have become.

Or that Freddie Flintoff, whom one had vaguely imagined living off raw meat and lager, would do a TV ad for a supermarket chain which led to a doubling in sales of quiche? 'We have sold 800,000 in one week alone,' announced high street giant Morrisons. Thirty years after Bruce Feirstein's diatribe, the real man and the quiche-eater had become indistinguishable.

Or that *Emmerdale*, rural Yorkshire's answer to *Coronation Street*, would be voted Britain's most gay-friendly soap in a 2010 poll, pipping *EastEnders* to the title? The sensitive treatment of a storyline involving an angry young teenager confused about his sexuality was widely praised.

People continued to rail at the excesses of political correctness, but if there was a new spirit of intolerance abroad, there was also a new spirit of tolerance. In September 2010, when foreign secretary William Hague – as proud a son of Yorkshire as ever whistled *Ilkley Moor Baht 'At* in the bath – was found to have shared a hotel room with a young male aide, he was not forced to resign, as he might once have been.

Men have more latitude, in all sorts of ways, than they have ever had before. There is no rigid pattern of masculinity into which they have to mould the attributes which nature has given them. They are freer to be themselves. Go to Headingley on the Saturday of a Test match and you will see a fancy dress party to match the Rio carnival. Crusaders, vicars, jailbirds in striped pyjamas, men in Homer Simpson masks, men dressed as policemen, men dressed as police*women*, men in *Monty Python* headscarves, men wearing lipstick, stockings, high heels... Everyone does their own thing and most people don't give a damn what anyone else does. To an incurable liberal like me, that is the clincher, the best possible reason for living in 2012, not 1912.

Painter David Hockney, who has returned to Yorkshire after years living in California, fades into the background in a way he would never have done 50 years ago. Visitors to his Bridlington home are likely to get roast beef and Yorkshire pudding cooked by his live-in partner Johnny, while Hockney plays the grouchy Tyke, grumbling about the excesses of the anti-smoking lobby in vowels as flat as his cap. Old Yorkshire and New Yorkshire have met in the middle.

If alternative lifestyles are tolerated as never before, there is still room for old-fashioned heroes. At the March 2011 by-election in Barnsley, stamping ground of Geoffrey Boycott and Darren Gough, the voters returned a Labour MP, Dan Jarvis, with a bracingly rugged CV. No computer games in the bedroom for Jarvis. At 14, thanks to a father determined to teach his sons self-reliance, he was camping with his brother on an uninhabited island off the Scottish coast. At 18, he joined an expedition to K2, the world's most feared mountain, wearing a fleece, a woolly hat and his grandfather's tweed jacket. He got a degree in international politics, went to Sandhurst, joined the Parachute Regiment and served in Afghanistan. Then life got *really* tough. Jarvis lost his wife Caroline to bowel cancer and was left with the challenge of raising two small children on his own while pursuing a political career at Westminster. He will no doubt hack it, the way he always has.

Other men's lives seem tepid in comparison. A shower, a shave, a bowl of muesli. A session in the gym. A latte in Starbucks reading the *Guardian*. A morning spent staring at a computer screen. A sandwich for lunch. More computer time, followed by a one-to-one with the boss, followed by a meeting to discuss advertising budgets or corporate branding. A quick foray to the pub. The latest Colin Firth movie, followed by Pizza Express. Vigorous sex with a nice girl called Emma. A quick text to confirm arrangements for golf on Saturday. And so to bed.

If the young men of today were called on to defend their country, as their grandfathers and great-grandfathers were, would they still have what it took? Would they find the steel in themselves that Hedley Verity found? Or would the steel not be there any more, after the soft years, the hair gel years, the health-and-safety years? Hypothetical question. Not relevant. Mass conscription is history.

Men certainly haven't conceded defeat. Old-fashioned, uncompli-cated machismo – the sort that gets feminists rolling their eyes in irritation – is more durable than it appears. Here is veteran Rhodesia-born novelist Wilbur Smith, a throwback to Rider Haggard, a churner-out of rugged adventure stories set on the African veldt, a man seemingly stuck in a Neanderthal time-warp, in an interview in the *Daily Telegraph* in April 2011: 'I'm a feminist. The women in my books in recent years have been powerful characters and I love to see a woman with a cute bottom walking past.'

'*Howzat!*' scream the feminists, outraged, convinced they have got the bastard caught at the wicket. But will Old Father Time, the arbiter of all these things, give Smith the benefit of the doubt? The more action-replays are shown of the incident, the more innocuous it looks. Men and women disagree about lots of things, but they have found common ground in their hatred of political correctness at its hair-trigger worst.

Outside the pages of a Wilbur Smith novel, or war zones like Iraq and Afghanistan, the battles men now have to fight are generally subtle, nuanced affairs. Most of them are no more than turf wars, in the workplace or the home: the staking out and defending of territory; modest advances followed by strategic retreats; bloodless engagements fought with the minimum of rhetoric. But, whether they win or lose those battles, they will never be able to duck that eternal question, thrown at them by men and women alike – 'Are you a man?'

They will have to tick far more boxes than George Hirst did 100 years ago. In the section of the questionnaire marked VIRILITY, they will have to field questions about their diet and exercise and

211

cholesterol levels as well as their physical strength. In the section marked INTELLIGENCE, they will need to demonstrate emotional intelligence as well as simple IQ. The section marked APPEARANCE AND GROOMING will run to seven pages. And the section marked RELATING TO WOMEN AND CHILDREN will have so many multiple choices that it will take a week to finish. But they will muddle through eventually. Men like ticking boxes. It is a boy thing.

Whether they will be as happy as George Hirst when they look at themselves in the mirror in the morning, or when they go to bed at night, is another matter. Of the cricketers I have featured in this book, three were batsmen – Sutcliffe, Boycott and Vaughan – and three were bowlers – Verity, Trueman and Gough. But it is the all-rounder, Hirst, who also seems to have been the most rounded human being: the most sane, the most balanced, the most content with his lot, the most uncomplaining, the most easy-going, the most persevering, the most generous to others. He had the humanity, as well as the modesty, of the great Edwardians.

The values he encapsulated are timeless, and without being jingoistic, quintessentially English. At the Royal Wedding in 2011, the nation roared itself hoarse as a modest, gentle, prematurely balding prince escorted his bride down the aisle. His younger brother looked as if he was the one brimming over with testosterone. But we didn't want Harry as our future King. We wanted William.

Two days later, the nation said goodbye to one of its favourite sporting sons, Henry Cooper. Our 'Enry had a fearsome left hook, splashed on the Brut like a teenage boy in love, but could not have given himself airs if he had lived till 150. Cooper's death marked the end of an era. 'His grandfather was a bare-knuckle fighter and even his grandmother was said to have boxed like a man,' according to one obituary, which conjured eye-watering images of family tiffs chez Cooper in late-Victorian London. But the huge affection in which he was held was revealing. Cooper's Hirst-like modesty was his trump card.

Some things never change. From boyhood onwards, the male of the species will always dream of being a hero, of scoring hat-tricks and centuries, of captaining the side, of getting to the top, of leapfrogging rivals, of scaling new peaks, of conquering undiscovered worlds, of achieving fame and fortune, of being adored by women and worshipped by children. If he is lucky, he may achieve some of those things.

But if he is a *real* man, without pomposity, without arrogance, he won't be afraid to get 'em in singles. Or even sequins.

APPENDIX

Few sports fans devour statistics as eagerly as cricket-lovers, and I am sadly conscious that my book has offered readers lean pickings in that respect. These random facts and figures from the fast-changing world of masculinity are intended to make good that deficit.

* A survey for British Social Attitudes in 1984 found that **43 per cent** of people agreed or strongly agreed that 'a husband's job is to earn the money; a wife's job is to look after the home and the family'. By 1990, the figure had fallen to **25 per cent**.

* In 2005, according to NHS data, **98 per cent of fathers** attended the birth of their children; **48 per cent** also attended antenatal and parenting classes. In 1965, a similar study had found that only **5 per cent** attended the births.

* A 2010 poll by Opinium Research found that **one in seven British men** used make-up products, ranging from face powder and fake tans to eyeliner. Of regular make-up wearers, **40 per cent** said their female partners sometimes helped them apply their make-up, while **25 per cent** said they would not be comfortable going to a pub without make-up.

* In 1999, according to a survey for the Office for National Statistics, the average age of men at the time of their first marriage **exceeded 30** for the first time – in the 1960s and early 1970s, it had been **below 25**.

* Contrary to the urban myth that men think about sex every seven seconds, the average man thinks about sex **13 times a day**, according to research published in the *Daily Telegraph* in 2010. No statistics are available for how often men think about cricket. The same research concluded that the average man had sex **twice a week** and that **nearly three quarters of men** were happy with the amount of sex they were having.

* Asked in a 1999 MORI poll which of their dreams they would like technology to help them achieve, **23 per cent of men** said 'a partner of their choice', while **36 per cent** said 'to play sport at the top level'.

* Market research published in 2000 revealed that the men's magazine market had increased by **1,000 per cent** since 1993. *Loaded*, *FHM*, *Maxim* and *Men's Health* were all launched in that period.

* In a 2010 online survey by barbecue specialists Broil King, **19 per cent of men** reckoned they were better at barbecuing than their friends, **20 per cent** said they would be undeterred from barbecuing by bad weather, **97 per cent** claimed to know when meat was cooked properly and **11 per cent** confessed that they felt connected with their inner caveman as they cooked meat over a fire.

* In a 2001 MORI poll, **25 per cent of men** said that the biggest drawback to Valentine's Day was not knowing what to buy their partner. In the same poll, **16 per cent of men** said that they worried about getting a Valentine's Day card from their mum or dad.

* In a 2005 edition of *New Scientist*, it was reported that fathers of children under five spent an average of **two hours a day** on child-related activities; the equivalent figure in the 1970s was **15 minutes**.

* According to a 2000 sociological study, men did an average of **50 minutes of housework a day**, compared with **90 minutes** for women in paid employment. The same figures for 1960 were **10 minutes** and **110 minutes**, respectively. Of the men surveyed, **60 per cent** claimed to do more housework than their fathers.

* In a UK-wide survey for National Hand Hygiene Awareness Week in October 2009, **40 per cent of Yorkshiremen** – the highest figure in the country – admitted to not cleaning their hands on a regular basis after going to the bathroom.

* A MORI poll conducted in 2000, after Prime Minister Tony Blair's son Leo was born, found that **81 per cent of men** approved of new laws entitling fathers to up to three months' unpaid paternity leave – although **26 per cent** believed that taking paternity leave would damage their career prospects.

* Between 2006 and 2008, according to market research by Key Note, the number of men regularly surfing the internet at home rose from **64.2 per cent** to **71.4 per cent**. Over the same period, the number of men regularly doing DIY fell from **54.6 per cent** to **40.9 per cent**, while the number of men participating in organised sport on a regular basis fell from **36 per cent** to **29.6 per cent**.

* A 2009 study for the German Society of Ophthalmology found that, on average, women cried **between 30 and 64 times a year** and men **between 6 and 17 times**. The average female crying session lasted for **six minutes**, the average male one for **between two and four minutes**. The same study showed that, up until the age of 13, there were no significant differences between boys and girls, either in the frequency or duration of crying episodes.

* In a joint 2010 survey by *Cosmopolitan* and the website Askmen. com, **5 per cent of men** said that real men never cried; **39 per cent** said that it was only appropriate to cry in response to tragedies, such as the death of a loved one; **27 per cent** said that crying was admissible at any time; and **29 per cent** said that it was all right to cry at any time, but not publicly.

* A survey in March 2011 by the Blue Ribbon Foundation found that only **65 per cent of men** said that they would go to a doctor if they were experiencing chest pains.

* A 1999 survey by Mills and Boon found that **37 per cent of British men** admitted they were bad kissers, **22 per cent** said they would die for their partner and **4 per cent** said they would send their partner a romantic email.

* In an opinion poll conducted before the Royal Wedding in April 2011, **49 per cent of men** agreed that the law should be amended so that, if Prince William's first child was a girl, she should succeed to the throne; **26 per cent** disagreed. The remaining **25 per cent** either did not understand the question or stayed schtum.

* In 2007, according to market research by Key Note, **19.9 per cent** of men bought a condom, as opposed to **43 per cent** who wore one.

* According to a 2011 survey of 3,000 Britons by Superdrug, men spent an average of **22 minutes a day** in the shower, compared with **23 minutes** for women. In the same survey, **two-thirds of men** said that they were proud of the fact that they took care of their appearance, while **34 per cent** said they did not see why they should not take as long as women to get ready for the day.

* In a survey conducted in 2009, **18.4 per cent of all men**, and **33.1 per cent of men aged between 20 and 24**, said they were 'cutting down on alcohol for health reasons'.

* Men still rely on women to choose **51 per cent** of the items in their wardrobe, according to a 2011 survey of 1,984 adults for the fashion brand Joe Brown's. The survey found that men spent an average of **50 minutes a month** clothes-shopping, compared with **two hours** for women, and that **68 per cent of men** admitted to wearing what the women in their lives wanted, just to keep them happy.

ACKNOWLEDGEMENTS AND BIBLIOGRAPHY

A particularly big thank you to Matthew Engel, my editor at Wisden Sports Writing, not just for commissioning such an eccentric-seeming book, but for providing unstinting encouragement and advice. I have had some fine editors over the years, starting with Nigella Lawson, no less, but none has come close to Matthew in terms of close textual criticism. The rigour with which he has vetted my manuscript for clichés, repetitions, unsupported generalisations and factual errors has been an education in itself. Any inaccuracies or stylistic inelegances which have slipped through the net are my responsibility alone.

It has been a great pleasure to collaborate with Charlotte Atyeo, Emily Sweet and Sarah Greeno at Bloomsbury. Their enthusiasm, professionalism and attention to detail have been exemplary.

Others to whom I am indebted for help and advice include Stephen Chalke, Derek Hodgson, Murray Hedgcock, Simon Briggs, Patrick Humphries, David Frith, Clive Ellis and Paul Cheall; Lindsay Watkins, who shared some fascinating memories of her grandfather George Hirst; Andre Gren, God's gift to Bradford; and David Natzler, who contributed the news item which lowers the tone in the Michael Vaughan chapter.

I am particularly grateful to Sir Michael Parkinson, who took time to share his memories of Yorkshire cricketers with me and entertained me to a stonkingly good lunch at his pub in Berkshire.

And thanks, as ever, to my partner Julia, a self-evidently fine judge of manliness, who has put up with my eccentric writer's hours and kept my spirits up at times when morale was flagging.

The main cricket books I have consulted in the course of researching this book are:

The Official History of Yorkshire County Cricket Club, Derek Hodgson (The Crowood Press)

Wisden on Yorkshire: An Anthology, Ed. Duncan Hamilton (John Wisden & Co.)

Magnificent Seven, Andrew Collomosse (Great Northern)

The Faber Book of Cricket, Ed. Michael Davie and Simon Davie (Faber and Faber)

Hirst and Rhodes, A. A. Thomson (The Pavilion Library)

A Summer of Plenty: George Herbert Hirst in 1906, Stephen Chalke (Fairfield Books)

Herbert Sutcliffe: Cricket Maestro, Alan Hill (Stadia)

Five Five Five: Holmes and Sutcliffe in 1932, Stephen Chalke (Fairfield Books)

Hedley Verity: Portrait of a Cricketer, Alan Hill (Mainstream Publishing)

Brian Close: Cricket's Lionheart, Alan Hill (Methuen)

No Coward Soul: The Remarkable Story of Bob Appleyard, Stephen Chalke and Derek Hodgson (Fairfield Books)

As It Was: The Memoirs of Fred Trueman (Pan Books)

Fred, John Arlott (Sports Pages)

Boycs, Leo McKinstry (Partridge)

Boycott: The Autobiography, Geoffrey Boycott (Pan Books)

Dazzler, Darren Gough (Michael Joseph)

Dazzler on the Dance Floor, Darren Gough (Hodder & Stoughton)

Time to Declare, Michael Vaughan (Hodder & Stoughton)

Of the non-cricketing books I have read, the following were particularly helpful:

Sporting Supermen: The True Stories of Our Childhood Comic Heroes, Brendan Gallagher (Aurum)

Yorkshire Greats, Bernard Ingham (Dalesman)

Untold Stories, Alan Bennett (Faber and Faber)

Plain Tales from Yorkshire, Roger Mason (Futura)

The Edwardians, Roy Hattersley (Little, Brown)

The Thirties: An Intimate History, Juliet Gardiner (Harper Press)

English Journey, J. B. Priestley (Penguin)

Fighting Through – From Dunkirk to Hamburg, Bill Cheall (Pen and Sword Books)

Sporting Lives, Michael Parkinson (Pavilion)

Parky: My Autobiography, Michael Parkinson (Hodder & Stoughton)

The Time of My Life, Denis Healey (Michael Joseph)

Never Again, Peter Hennessy (Jonathan Cape)

Family Britain: 1951 to 1957, David Kynaston (Bloomsbury)

Nobbut a Lad: A Yorkshire Childhood, Alan Titchmarsh (Hodder & Stoughton)

The Pendulum Years, Bernard Levin (Jonathan Cape)

State of Emergency: The Way We Were, Britain 1970–74, Dominic Sandbrook (Allen Lane)

A Tour in the Game, Irene Murrell (The Book Guild of Lewes)

Weekend in Dinlock, Clancy Sigal (Secker & Warburg)

Real Men Don't Eat Quiche, Bruce Feirstein (Pocket Books)

Iron John, Robert Bly (Rider)

Men Are from Mars, Women Are from Venus, John Gray (Element)

The Dangerous Book for Boys, Conn Iggulden and Hal Iggulden (Harper Collins)

For the Hedley Verity chapter, I have also drawn on the BBC's online archive *WW2 – People's War* (www.bbc.co.uk/ww2peopleswar)

INDEX